"Over the years, Booth would have a police record that stretched from the greater Los Angeles area up to Oakland, Berkeley, Stockton, and Portland, resulting in no less than five prison sentences, mostly served in either Folsom Prison or San Quentin. It was in the latter where Booth met Robert Tasker, who, at the time, was editing the prison's in-house literary magazine. Recognizing Booth's ability to spin tales of past exploits, Tasker urged his fellow prisoner to contribute to the magazine. Before long they were both sending pieces to H. L. Mencken's *American Mercury*. Mencken was more than receptive, having long harbored a fondness for stories by convicts, criminals, and low-lifes, with their no-nonsense, tough guy style of writing…

"Booth seemed a natural writer when it came to putting his stories on paper. Though the result can be uneven, at times overly wordy, at other times too pulp-oriented, his writing, at its best, shimmers in its matter-of-fact honesty."

—from the introduction by Woody Haut

STEALING THROUGH LIFE
by
Ernest Booth

**Introduction by
Woody Haut**

AN IMPRINT OF STARK HOUSE PRESS

STEALING THROUGH LIFE
Copyright 1927, 1929 by Alfred A. Knopf, Inc.

Published by Staccato Crime
An imprint of Stark House Press
1315 H Street
Eureka, CA 95501, USA
griffinskye3@sbcglobal.net
www.starkhousepress.com

"Ernest Booth: Thief, Writer, Recidivist" ©2023 by Woody Haut

All rights reserved under International and Pan-American Copyright Conventions.

ISBN: 979-8-88601-037-4
Staccato Crime: SC-008

All Staccato Crime titles are edited and produced
by David Rachels and Jeff Vorzimmer.
Book series design by ¡caliente!design, http://caliente.design, Austin, Texas

This is a work of fiction. Names, characters, places and incidents are either the products of the author's imagination or used fictionally and any resemblance to actual persons, living or dead, events or locales, is entirely coincidental.

Without limiting the rights under copyright reserved above, no part of this publication may be reproduced, stored, or introduced into a retrieval system or transmitted in any form or by any means (electronic, mechanical, photocopying, recording or otherwise) without the prior written permission of both the copyright owner and the above publisher of the book.

First Staccato Crime Edition: May 2023

New and Forthcoming Titles
From Staccato Crime

SC-001 *Bodies Are Dust* — P. J. Wolfson
SC-002 *I Was a Bandit* — Eddie Guerin
SC-003 *Round Trip/Criss-Cross* — Don Tracy
SC-004 *Grimhaven* — Robert Joyce Tasker
SC-005 *Fully Dressed and in His Right Mind* — Michael Fessier
SC-006 *How to Commit a Murder* — Danny Ahearn
SC-007 *Room Service* — Alan Williams

W. R. RIDDLE, Sheriff　　　　　　　　　　　　　　　　　　　　GEO. P. MORSE, Under Sheriff

OFFICE OF THE
SHERIFF OF BUTTE COUNTY
OROVILLE, CALIFORNIA

Card No. 62.　　　　　　　　　　　　　　　　　　　　　　　　September 28, 1917.

Arrest for Jail Break, Forgery

ERNEST G. BOOTH

ERNEST G. BOOTH, self-confessed and convicted forger, Preston School parole violator, escaped from Butte County Jail on the night of September 27, 1917. The above is a fine picture of Booth, who is the same man who escaped from Constable J. A. Peck of Chico, Cal., and for whom he offered a reward. (See Peck circular, August 3.)

DESCRIPTION

Aged 20 years; height, 5 feet, 10 inches; weight, 180 pounds. Well built, erect, military training; brown hair, grey eyes, fine teeth; very white, well formed hands; fine, healthy complexion; extremely genteel appearance.

Dressed when escaped: Light brown flannel military shirt; light brown khaki trousers; tan shoes; old soft hat. (May steal change.)

Booth gambles, but neither smokes nor drinks; great ladies' man and fine, smooth, convincing talker. Solicitor for enlarged-picture firms. Well educated and fine carriage and general appearance.

Police Record: Oakland, No. 4792; Berkeley, No. 497; Portland, No. 3192. Also Los Angeles and Tacoma, burglary and forgery. Very clever, dangerous man.

ARREST AND WIRE MY EXPENSE.

　　　　　　　　　　　　　　　　　　W. R. RIDDLE, Sheriff of Butte County,
　　　　　　　　　　　　　　　　　　　　Oroville, California.

An Arrest Flyer for Ernest Booth, 1917

Ernest Booth: Thief, Writer, Recidivist
by Woody Haut

The opening paragraph of Ernest Booth's extraordinary 1934 memoir *Stealing Through Life* could be thought of as the author attempting to explain his own particular criminal code. It begins: "There are those of us—thieves and poets—who are born complete. The stern realities of life are inverted and become only so many evidences of unreality. Within ourselves we have a complete world of our imagination." The paragraph ends with the author declaring: "We are the odd ones. The criminals, the geniuses, the builders of Utopias." For Booth, poets and thieves are synonymous. Not the white collar thief who, in Woody Guthrie's words, "will rob you with a fountain pen," but the sort who *steal through life* because it's an unequal world in which, as a Nobel Prize winner, once wrote, "to stand outside the law you must be honest." That's the theory, and it would be nice to think of Booth as some kind of *poéte maudit*, alongside the likes of Villon, Genet, or Mesrine, all of whom saw thievery as an anti-bourgeois, even artistic, statement. Certainly, a case could be made for Booth if only he'd been more successful as either a thief or as a writer.

Born in 1899, in Oakland, California, Booth's father, Stuart W. Booth, was a prominent East Bay journalist. Ernest Booth, a. k. a., Ernest G. Granville and Roy W. Reeves, began his criminal career early on. Not quite 14, he was arrested for burglary in 1912, found guilty and sentenced to two years in the Preston School of Industry reform school, in Ione, near Sacramento. He soon developed a reputation for his ability to escape from any institution that held him. It began in 1917 when, on a forgery charge, he scarpered while being transported from Wisconsin to California, then had the audacity to send a newspaper clipping about the escape to his Milwaukee jailer. At 18, he was arrested again, this time in Oroville for stealing a car. In 1920, he convinced his girlfriend to embezzle eight hundred dollars from her employer, who happened to be a superior court judge. Clearly, not a relationship that was going to last. Unlike his involvement with Valdera Millikan who he married in 1924. A few days later, perhaps needing money to fund his matrimonial pursuits, Booth robbed a bank in Oakland, deploying what the local press called an "ammonia bomb," which led to alliterative journalists tagging Booth as "the ammonia bank bandit."

A few days later the police caught up with Booth, but he managed to escape once again, this time from the Alameda County jail, only to be picked up a month later again while dining in a posh San Francisco restaurant. This time he was packed off to San Quentin. While in the prison hospital where he was said to have tuberculosis, Booth attempted another escape. While guards watched the prison variety show, Booth tied some of the hospital's sheets and blankets together and climbed down three stories to the ground. Unfortunately, the makeshift rope was cut by a fellow inmate out to curry favor with the warden, and Booth ended up back in the prison hospital, this time with two broken legs.

Over the years, Booth would have a police record that stretched from the greater Los Angeles area to Oakland, Berkeley, Stockton, and Portland, resulting in to no less than five prison sentences, mostly served in either Folsom Prison or San Quentin. It was in the latter where Booth met Robert Tasker, who, at the time, was editing the prison's in-house literary magazine. Recognizing Booth's ability to spin tales of past exploits, Tasker urged his fellow prisoner to contribute to the magazine. Before long they were both sending pieces to H. L. Mencken's *American Mercury*. Mencken was more than receptive, having long harbored a fondness for stories by convicts, criminals and low-lifes, with their no-nonsense, tough guy style of writing, and an implied politics capable of shocking the high-brow critics and stuffed-shirt dignitaries that Mencken so detested.

Booth and Tasker struck a deal: Tasker would write about prison life, and Booth, who was the more experienced crook, would write about the events that led him to prison. The result was Tasker's 1928 prison memoir *Grimhaven* followed, six years later, by Booth's *Stealing Through Life*, which mainly consisted of stories—"We Rob a Bank," "A Texas Chain Gang," "Ladies of the Mob," "Ladies in Durance Vile"—that had appeared in Mencken's magazine, along with some added material. Both books would be published by Knopf. The Oakland *Tribune* might have been talking about *Stealing Through Life* as a whole when they said of Booth's story "We Rob a Bank," "[It] has just enough fact in it to convince the police of its verity, and not enough detail to permit them to decide whether he is taking literary license, giving a composite picture of bank robberies, or actually thumbing his nose at the sleuths over his skill in perpetrating a robbery that was not accredited to him."

It's been said that the prison doctor smuggled Booth's work to Mencken, who handed it on to Knopf. However, in *Grimhaven*, Tasker claims he was the book's intermediary. Regardless, Booth, during those years behind bars was making an inordinate amount of money off the stories he'd written. Hollywood studios couldn't get enough of them. According to Philippe Garnier in his book *Spitballers and Scoundrels*, Booth made some $28,000—these days equal to about half a million dollars—during his stay in prison. No wonder inmates, hearing about Booth's success, thought they too might be able to cash in on their exploits. Suddenly everyone wanted to write for the prison magazine and attend the prison's writing group to the point that in a March 1928 article in the San Francisco *Examiner*, Judge C. E. McLaughlin, a member of California's State Board of Prison Directors said, "We're running prisons, not literary bureaus. The board has no time or disposition to read this material and see that it is in proper shape." At San Quentin, warden "Big Jim" Holohan maintained, somewhat resignedly, that a dozen convicts "were preparing material with an eye on the outside market" adding that between 1927 and 1929, "Tasker and Ernest Granville Booth had had such a grasp on the Hollywood market for crime stories that they'd had to split the pie between them." Likewise, Court Smith, Holohan's counterpart at Folsom Prison, had to grudgingly acknowledge that "[Three] motion picture concerns are now negotiating for film rights to Booth's *Mercury* article "We Rob a Bank."

During his incarceration, Booth contributed to "Ladies of the Big House" (1931), starring Sylvia Simms, and was said to have made $15,000 for his story "Ladies of the Mob," which would become, in Reuben Mamoulian's directorial hands, *City Streets* (1931). The latter carried with it Dashiell Hammett's first screen credit; thirty years later, it was a major influence on Jean-Pierre Melville's film *Les Doulos*. While *Pick-up*, the picture Paramount made in 1933 based on Booth's "Ladies in Stir," was such a success for director Marion Gering and star Sylvia Sidney that the pair went on to make three more movies together. Not to mention Metro's purchase of *Stealing Through Life*, which was destined for Rowland Brown, but, for some reason, was never made.

Recognizing the debt he owed to his fellow inmate, Booth dedicated *Stealing Through Life* "To Robert Joyce Tasker, who said, Jim Tully isn't the only Bum who can write—why don't you have it a try?" It's a tribute that shines a light on Tasker's role in encouraging Booth, while containing a shout-out to Jim Tully, a widely read writer who, while ensconced in Hollywood, was living off his past life as a hobo, boxer, circus performer, occasional jailbird, Chaplin publicist, and Hollywood reporter. It was Mencken who sent Tully, known to have the meanest mouth in Hollywood, to Folsom to interview Booth. For Mencken, Tully was yet another proletariat writer out to challenge the orthodoxy of bourgeois society. What's not known is whether the likes of Tully, Booth, and Tasker considered their literary and Hollywood careers as just another scam or as a legitimate pursuit. In any case, they were clearly more than willing to be co-opted so long as their pockets were being filled with money.

Booth seemed a natural writer when it came to putting his stories on paper. Though the result can be uneven, at times overly wordy, at other times too pulp-oriented, his writing, at its best, shimmers in its matter-of-fact honesty. It might have been his life in the demimonde, a place where Tasker was little more than a tourist, that made Booth's writing superior, or at any rate more colorful, than his prison pal's prose. According to novelist and noir expert Vince Keenan, Nancy Barr Mavity, once the literary editor of the Oakland *Tribune*, wrote a review of Booth's only other published book, the 1945 crime novel *With Sirens Screaming*, in which she said that Booth presents a more "complex and psychologically interesting problem" than Tasker as "he is a bona fide criminal who accidentally can write—not a writer who incidentally served time in prison." Yet his incarceration did little to alter Booth's proclivities or his barely stated politics that can be gleamed in Booth's citing his partner-in-crime Red, who tells him, "Poor people are the best friends a thief can have." On the other hand, Booth takes great delight in describing a criminal life lived in the moment:

> It seemed childish to scheme and talk. We knew what to do. There was a bank on the other side of the Bay that we could rob of perhaps a hundred thousand dollars. Should we rob it together? That was the extent of our reasoning. Nothing of right or wrong entered into our calculations. Any aversion I might have entertained, in

the dim, remote past, to such proceedings had been sublimated and found its outlet in past justifications of similar actions.

Though he lobbied for Booth's parole, Mencken had doubts about whether he was actually fit to be released. In a letter to John Fante, Mencken concluded that Booth was "probably an incurably dangerous man," and it might be a good idea for him to stay in prison. After interviewing Booth, Tully also concluded that Booth was too much a career criminal to be allowed to re-enter the general population. This just after Tully had stated in the press that Booth and Tasker were "the only really promising writers ever developed in American prisons. They are great artists, and I am hoping that after they have satisfied society they will be given a chance by the world to realize their genius." But after talking with prisoners, Tully even came to question Booth's honesty, believing he had taken the exploits of a fellow inmate and, in his so-called autobiographical "Texas Chain Gang," assigned them to himself. Meanwhile, Fante, living in nearby Roseville and acquainted with the prison doctor at Folsom, wrote to Mencken about another Booth scam: "It seems Booth has been trying to convince the medicos that he belongs to the TB ward. According to the doc, he went so far as to bring to the hospital the sputum of a bona fide sufferer, claiming it to be his own, but the deception was discovered. Now, ironically enough, Booth *has* got tuberculosis! The doc is not very sympathetic, feeling that, now that Booth is a sick man, the best place for him is Folsom."

But, then, Fante had little regard for Booth as a writer or, for that matter, as a criminal, though that did not stop him from thinking he'd been treated badly. Neither was Fante beyond poking holes in Tully's Booth interview, opining "that Tully's declaration that Tasker and Booth were members of the same gang of crooks, and were sent up on the same charge, [is] a patent lie to anyone who knows the facts." According to Fante, hardly known to be magnanimous towards fellow writers, Booth was a "phoney," and Tully's article was "so unfair and inaccurate" that from the date of its appearance the prison writers to a man have "hated Jim Tully's guts." Moreover, he maintained it was Tully's article that prompted Warden Court Smith to stop all interviews and barred prisoners from publishing in periodicals outside the prison walls.

Tasker was paroled in 1929, but Booth would languish in prison for another eight years. Despite his doubts, Mencken did his best not only to influence the parole board, but to convince Hollywood studios that Booth was the real deal. Naturally, Hollywood was more than willing to exploit Booth's knowledge of the criminal world, not to mention his ability to put an evocative sentence together, all to add a bit more realism to their gangster and prison movies. When Booth was finally paroled in 1937, the *Oakland Tribune* ran a caption with his photograph reading, "He'll Be Back"—meaning, of course, back behind bars. But at last, Booth, no longer in the best of health, was free to work in Hollywood, albeit with a parole restriction that he wasn't to write about anything to do with his criminal or prison activities. Instead of writing about what he knew best, Booth was reduced to spending time slaving over the likes *Fremont the Pathfinder* and *Penrod's Double Trouble,* as well as turning out treatments for $50 a film. It was only this parole came to an end in 1940 that he was finally able to spread his wings in films like *Women Without Names,* adapted from Booth's play, directed by Robert Florey in 1940 for Paramount, with a screenplay by pulpster Horace McCoy. Booth also worked as a screenwriter and technical advisor on *Men of San Quentin* (1942) which, ironically, features a prison variety show similar to that which Booth used as cover for his failed escape two decades earlier. Despite or because of his criminal and penal background, Booth was becoming something of a man about town, the subject of a feature in the *San Francisco Examiner* in which Booth, no longer living in Hollywood, was pictured with Valdera in Santa Cruz, along with the surprising claim that he was now writing love stories for women's magazines.

Booth had come a long way from making the kind of money he had amassed when he was serving time. Consequently, to supplement what was now, for him, a relatively modest income, he decided to go back to what he knew best, meaning the more lucrative business of armed robbery. This at a time when he had become the go-to guy for the police whenever they were in search of a suspect. A prime example of this, and the beginning of the end for Booth, was the 1941 murder of the wealthy dowager, Florence A. Stricker who had been robbed and bludgeoned to death in her Los Angeles home. The police brought Booth in for questioning, but, in the end, had to release him, though not before Booth had spent two days in jail on a weapons charge after guns were found in his home.

Probably with an ulterior motive, Booth took a job as a shipping clerk, but was soon fired on suspicion of stealing a thousand dollars' worth of women's slacks and selling them to other stores at a cut-rate price. Worse was to come when, in 1943, the police hauled him in for questioning regarding a burglary at the Portland Cement Company involving a quarter of a million dollars in securities. In the end, they had to let him go. Then, in 1947, radio calls went out for Booth as a suspect in an armed robbery. The police announced that said suspect was armed and dangerous, a suspected drug user with connections in Hollywood and downtown Los Angeles. A police description at the time provides a vivid picture of this would-be *poète maudit*: "48 years old, 5 foot 11, 160 lbs.—blue eyes, brown-gray hair, receding hairline, high forehead, slender build, hollow cheeks (TB), dimple in chin, turkey neck, slightly stooped, walks with slight limp. Usually wears blue pin-striped suits. When operating, talks with gruff voice. Has been employed by Warner Bros. studio and as camera repairman for Don Blitz Camera Shop in Hollywood. Has habit of flashing large bills." He was finally apprehended by the FBI at what was then, as now, one of L. A.'s favorite watering holes, the Musso & Frank Grill.

After questioning Booth, the police found he, in fact, had been involved in that Portland heist, as well as a series of west coast bank robberies stretching from Seattle to Pasadena. A judge set bail at $50,000. In the summer of 1947, he was found guilty and sentenced to twenty years. That Oakland newspaper had been right. Booth was back. Transferred to McNeil Island Penitentiary in the state of Washington, he would never complete his sentence. He died in prison of tuberculosis in 1959. As the *New York Mirror* reported, "E. G. Booth always had difficulty deciding whether to write about crime or go out and commit one. He tried both, and both occupations paid him well." As Booth once said, "[One] does not go back. One progresses— either to chaos or to understanding." A precursor to the likes of Chester Himes, Larry Bunker, Albert Nussbaum and Malcolm Braly, Booth's *Stealing Through Life*, along with his more pulpish *With Sirens Screaming* (1945), testify as much to Booth's ability as a writer as to his criminal tendencies. Yet in spite of *Stealing Through Life's* opening paragraph, Booth was neither a genius, nor builder of utopias, nor all that innocent. He was one of the odd ones, a success at being a failure, and, by stealing through life, able to live deep within his imagination.

London
February 2023

Sources:

Philippe Garnier, *Scoundrels & Spitballers: Writers in Hollywood in the 1930s* (Black Pool Productions, 2020).

Vince Keenan, "Golden Age Hollywood Was Full of Ex-Cons," *Crime Reads* 16 January 2020 (https://crimereads.com/golden-age-hollywood-was-full-of-ex-cons/).

To
ROBERT JOYCE TASKER,
who said,
"Jim Tully isn't the only Bum
who can write—
why don't you give it a try?"

And to
WILLIAM MACKELLIP,
who said,
"Sure! Do so and I'll type it for you."

This Book
is
fraternally dedicated.

PREFACE

This book was written with the idea of showing several years of a so-called hardened criminal's life. I have tried not to play favorites in presenting any characters. If some names be obviously changed, or localities left vague, the change does not detract from the scene and they are better thus. However, many portions of it could and do fit one section of the country as readily as another—like the parts in which they are laid. If the book scorches a few official whiskers, it also strips from various thieves the romantic glamor which fiction has glossed over them.

I have sought to present no glibly connected story, for the obvious reason that such a story must contain many elements that are lacking in life, as it is lived. Certain people who appear for a brief space and then are dropped from the further progress of the action, have been dropped because they had contributed their portions—they had been exhausted. And in the same manner some actions do not seem complete—because actions are like that. If the book starts on a plane rather different from the usual "prison" story and then descends to a lower, less pleasant plane, I attempt no excuse other than, that it is so written because it was so lived. The usual manner of presenting this class of material is to end the book with its author embracing a ready-made salvation, or protesting that he has been reformed! I maintain that any young man or young woman living through such experiences most certainly is reformed—*almost with each passing moment.*

In all the prison fiction I've read, the author seeks to impress upon the reader how terribly he has suffered and that from that misery has risen a glorified "repentance," a sort of throw-back to some childish state wherein are contained all those fleeting joys which are promised to the righteous. But it seems to me that one does not go back. One progresses—either to chaos or to understanding. And when a man reaches that state of appreciation which enables him to see objectively the things which formerly were subjectively a part of him, then he has in truth been re-formed. But not into a model, nor into a representative of a group.

The pages which follow constitute an effort to work out the fundamental causes which brought me to prison. I do not want to appear in the light of attempting to justify my present position. But if the so-called "crime-wave" is due to such criminals as I have met, both official and in the "underworld," then to calm that wave and give to it the tranquility the reformers moan for is but a matter of intelligent application of simple changes which, I believe, are all too obvious.

Stealing through Life

CHAPTER 1

[I]

There are those of us—thieves and poets—who are born intact. Complete. The stern realities of life are inverted and become only so many evidences of unreality. Within ourselves we have a complete world of our imagination. This has been with us as far back as our conscious mind can take us. Within this realm of our own possession we retreat when confronted with things that do not fit into our preconceived scheme of things-as-they-should-be. And to us, those things that annoy and vex: being "normal," doing as "other boys and girls do," acting and conforming to others' conception of what we should be—all these have no place in our life. We are the odd ones. The criminals, the geniuses, the builders of Utopias.

I was about ten years old and had been arrested while a playmate, Buddy and I were "trying to see the world." Our plan had been rather hazy. We knew there were trains leaving the Sixteenth Street depot and I had read a book written by "A-No. 1," which told of his experiences as *King of the Tramps*. At the time of reading, it held all of romance and enticement. Years later I met this King of the Tramps! Hugo was right: "Apotheoses are ever doomed to melancholy endings!" But the fact that trains went from that station was sufficient. We would climb on one, mount the top—and in glorious independence ride to our fame and fortune. I liked that "fame and fortune" stuff then. Horatio Alger's moral cardboard capsules had assured me that everything would come out right if only I met enough trouble to combat. I should return rich; I should be home again in the nick of time to save the family's cottage from the clutch of the heartless mortgage-holder and "all would be well in the end."

The fact that I had no troubles bothered me. I was next to the youngest of a family of four boys; I had the most adorable mother that ever lived and my father was comfortably situated, financially. There was, apparently, no reason for my leaving a pleasant home and the love and attention of parents who sought only to educate me, willingly to clothe and feed me and to prepare me adequately for the time when I should have to win my own food and clothes.

I recall now the manner in which I would listen to a discussion of my elders. Watch their actions. Memorize their words. Then, when I was alone, I would bring these actions, words and subjects out for review. Saying the words with as nearly the same intonation as that with which they were originally uttered, mimicking the gestures, I would watch for the effect upon myself. In this way I learned early to understand the thoughts that prompted such utterances. That I found many of them hollow and even foolish, did not deter me. These revelations, instead of instilling a distrust, created a sympathetic attitude within me—gave me a sense of superiority. And I took great delight in knowing how others felt when they said: "We've had a lovely time; enjoyed ourselves ever so much."

Is it a matter for wonder that, with this faculty early aroused and quickly developed, I became impervious to the efforts to fit me into the mold that was set for me—along with hundreds of others? I experienced a restless, growing dissatisfaction with the world in which I was living. People said things. The words told one story, the thoughts underlying them told another—vastly different. I disliked this pretense, this evasion of the true idea their minds held. Not prudish, or precocious, but—at that time—a sincerely honest craving for expression of real thoughts.

Voicing this desire as correctly as I could assemble it in speaking to my father one day, I received the illuminating answer: "If visitors at our house really told your mother how they felt after a few hours of scandalizing the absent friends— you'd be an orphan. No, Ernest, it is best that we all keep up this pretense of liking others even when they annoy us. But aren't you getting into rather deep waters for a youngster?"

Deep waters for a youngster! Why, I'd always thought about these problems. He thought I was a child! And he had said "it is best that we keep up this pretense of liking others. . . ." Why? Why was it best? Who said what was best and who said what was not best? The idea of pretending to like someone—utter rot! I would never pretend to like someone and if it was only pretense that brought us together—I would not be with that person.

I sought answers to other questions that presented themselves and received like replies. I dove into books. They too presented people who were not perfect. But the author explained the reasons for their movements and helped me over some spots that threatened to mire me down. I wonder if Dickens imagined, as he wrote *Oliver Twist,* a chunky, somber-faced lad poring over the pages of that novel, visualizing the most minute details of Oliver's life and longing to know the griefs and miseries that befell Fagin's pupil? I actually ached to feel some misery. So completely had I exchanged places with Oliver that I keenly regretted the absence of snow and sleet from the climate in which we lived. Often I would go out into the foot-hills east of Oakland and read portions of that book. Then, relaxing, I would stare over the Bay and into the great beyond and by continual suggestion of this sort developed a mild hypnosis which transported me away from the sordid world where "it was best to pretend" and into the world of stern hardships and great emotions. You see, I had reversed the usual order of existence. The only reality was the world of my imagination. . . .

Inevitably Buddy and I came together. He was a quiet, mild-tempered, blond lad, slender of build, hesitant of action, yet possessed of the same type of dreamer's mind. He was about two years my senior, but smaller in size than I and, as his folks were seldom sober long enough to know if he was attending school, he had not yet learned to read. Hours we spent together in the hills, in the attic of my home, in the loft of what had been a stable and coach barn, or on the rear portion of my home lot. Hours during which I read to him. Stumbling through the words that proved too long, changing others when the sentences stretched out too far; then discussing the story and its characters for days after, when we could not sneak up to one of our retreats. It was necessary to sneak up to them because of the disfavor in which Buddy was held by my parents. His family were from the wrong part of Ireland. And though Buddy was born in Oakland, just a few streets from where I had been born, it didn't alter matters he was *persona non grata.* That our common interest was welded by this opposition is indisputable. Our meetings took on the added zest of something accomplished despite opposition. The time together was doubly cherished because of this unexplained hostility towards him. If I had been given any reason as to why he and I should not associate, I should probably have considered it and debated with my parents, succeeding in winning them over in the end to liking Buddy.

But I was told not to play with "that boy." When I asked for reasons, I was informed that I had "been told"—did I have to be "told again"? Still—had I been told one hundred times, it would not have mattered; Buddy was my pal.

From speculating on adventures, we moved logically into putting into action what we had learned from our reading and discussions. *The King of the Tramps* finally showed how it was done. Presto! We donned overalls and sweaters over our suits; and though it was not considered good manners by the King to carry food, we decided that the mere fact that other tramps begged their food was sufficient justification for us to carry ours along with us. If *they* depended on haphazard supplies, *we* would be different and know an independence that they could not attain. Then, too, I was not so sure that we could get far enough into the country on the first "ramble" to take us beyond the houses that held the city-folk. Hence our flour-sack and the supply of groceries.

I had obtained them at a grocery where my family had a charge account. My indiscriminate selection of food-stuffs probably aroused the clerk's suspicion, for he telephoned my home and, luckily for me, my older brother answered. He told the clerk that my mother had no doubt sent me down and that it was all right. A bit nervously I received the package and Buddy and I departed. . . .

Five o'clock that evening found us near the train tracks of the station. We were tired and footsore. We had trekked from East Oakland, half-way around Lake Merritt, through a part of Piedmont—pausing frequently in vacant lots to fortify ourselves from the sack—and arrived at the Bay shore just as lights were beginning to wink on in houses and stores.

The sharp fire of our enthusiasm had dwindled to a small, flickering flame. But this was in keeping with the misery that was to be ours, the misery and grief I had wanted to know. Buddy "guessed it was going to be cold." I wondered how it would feel to be riding the top of a passenger train while the cold crept into my bones to chill and numb me so severely that I could just manage to hold on until the train reached a warm, well-lighted station. That I should be able to retain my hold until the warm station was reached I had no doubts. It had to be that way because I saw it thus.

Several trains passed by as we huddled in the gathering night. Their rumble and roar, the shrill whistle of wind and the fleeting glimpse of passengers comfortably seated at the windows, all took on a peculiar significance. They suddenly became strange. They were different from the illustrations and descriptions in the book. On the trains we saw were no "blinds," no "trucks," no steps by which we could climb to the car tops. And even if we could have seen them, the speed of the cars prevented any attempt to catch them. No—it was different—very, very different from the scene I had visualized. . . .

For an hour we had been watching and eating. Then we compromised our intentions; we would go nearer the station and if no train stopped within the next half-hour, we would postpone our trip until the next day and hunt shelter for the night. Carrying the sack, I led the way past the piles of ties and darkly gleaming rails. Repair-workers had erected a sort of lean-to shack from some of the ties, that they might eat their dinners without interruption by blowing sand from the great dunes near by. Remains of their small fire lay at the edge of the semicircular enclosure. This was similar to pictures of tramps' abodes that we had seen in illustrations; but being found so near a large city discredited it. It didn't have tone enough. I recall sniffing contemptuously as we paused to inspect the arrangement.

A hundred yards from the station we halted and had waited but a moment when a train came slowly past us. Calling to Buddy, I grabbed the hand-guide above the steps and slung the sack over the rung, holding it firm with my knees. The cars were barely moving as we tried to wedge ourselves between the raising-platform and the steps. It was a close fit and not an extremely comfortable one, but there we were—started at last on our great adventure!

The movement of the train decreased until we were at a complete stop. A few moments we remained quiet. Then with a jerk the cars started—backwards! A whistle, an answering toot and the cars were jerked to a halt less than fifty yards from where we had boarded them. Not a very auspicious beginning.

It was easier to sit in that space than to risk looking out and being caught. I had read somewhere of a chap who had looked from a moving train and had had his head cut off by some obstruction or other. I decided to take no chances. Again the train moved forward, for a short interval, then halted. Twice this was repeated. Each time we moved about a car-length, then abruptly stopped. We stood at a standstill for a full thirty minutes, waiting for the train to resume progress. Becoming restless by the frequent passage of other trains, I ventured to look outside, then called to Buddy.

We alighted and I pointed out to him the dark windows of our cars and the track they were on; a siding and the train "parked" for the night. It must have been a "local" that operated only during the rush hours of the evening, when the ferries disgorged their hordes of workers returning from the day's labor in San Francisco.

We walked back towards the station. It was ablaze with light and we could plainly see the uniformed officers and attendants. For some reason those blue uniforms of the policemen there repelled me. Probably because they were symbolic of the orderly world I was trying to leave behind. I immediately associated them with the forces that were conspiring to prevent me from attaining the happiness I was positive would await me at the end of the tracks—that is, it would be there for me after I had suffered enough to make everything come out all right in the end.

Again we were at the leaning ties of the track-workers' emergency lunch-room. I surveyed it less disdainfully. As we stood within its shelter, the wind from the Bay was warded off and I felt a warmth that made me feel kindly disposed towards this grotesque haven. . . . Buddy and I seated ourselves for another discussion. But the darkness, the cold, the recent disappointment on the train, combined to thwart our formulation of a plan for journeying to our goal.

Time passed and we ceased to talk. A few scraps of sacking and a tattered coat afforded poor covering, but we wrapped them about our legs. I opened another can of sardines, but fish had become an unpalatable offering. I munched on a cookie. Buddy dropped off to sleep. I wondered: whether or not we could get a train early the next morning; had my people missed me; did the clerk in the grocery know that I had not been sent to get the provisions; was it possible for me to get to sleep. . . .

Hours later when I awoke, Buddy was crying softly. He had been sitting up most of the night, he told me and he was "co-o-o-ld." I took the articles from the flour-sack and deposited them where they would not get soiled, then wrapped the thin cloth about Buddy's shoulders. We stretched out prone on the ground and snuggled close together. When we next awoke, the stars were beginning to fade in the east. A thin sickle of yellow moon hung as if suspended over the dark mountains of the Marin County shore.

My side and back ached. A small piece of wood, which had served as a common pillow for us, had imprinted its grain on Buddy's cheek. Rubbing the side of my face confirmed my suspicion that I, too, had received my first marks of "the road."

We started a small fire with the charred remains of the trackworkers' wood and attempted to toast some bread. The resultant blackened and burned bread was eaten, but I was keenly aware of the difference between it and the crisp, browned toast that would be served at home for breakfast.

With the warmth of the fire something of the thrill of achievement was mine. I had lived away from home a whole night! I had actually passed fourteen hours "on my own." And I was alive and independent! That our faces and hands were grimy, that our eyes were sticky with heavy, unrestful sleep, that our clothing was soiled and that our food-supply was meager—all this seemed not to matter in comparison with the fact that I had lived away from home one night. Really lived that time—not just imagined doing it. . . . Often I had visualized such adventure, but it was composed of intangible stuffs, filmy, gauzy—scenes wherein I moved, clean, perfectly dressed and impervious to the assaults of hunger. . . .

We washed our faces and hands in the salt water of the Bay. There was a considerable amount of foam clinging about the rocks from which we dipped the oil-scummed water and, being white, it suggested a better dissolvent of the dirt. We applied this foam generously. It was thick, scummy stuff and had the same cleansing qualities as thin glue. But it did loosen some of the dust and smudges and a vigorous rubbing with the lower part of our sweaters produced—for us at least—a satisfying result.

That day was passed in wandering about West Oakland—the Little Africa of the West. Negroes of all shades and shapes passed in review before us. Several of them held our interest long enough for us to follow them, because of the gaudy clothes in which they disported themselves.

I recall one huge, long-armed black who would doubtless have interested anthropologists. His head sat abruptly on incredibly wide shoulders. His legs were short and bowed, ending in a pail of enormous yellow shoes. His suit was of a blatantly loud, striped material and the derby, perched at a rakish angle on his head, was banded with a wide, aggressive yellow ribbon. We first observed him in profile and the glitter of his raiment dazzled us. I laughed—the Negro frowned. We followed him. I wanted to see his face and decide for myself how closely he resembled the apes in the circuses.

Evidently annoyed at being trailed by two small "'no 'count white trash," he quickened his gait and we did likewise. For probably three blocks we stayed fifty feet behind him. He would pause, to turn and look sullenly in our direction and we would affect an interest in the store windows. Several times this was repeated.

He stopped. We did the same. He looked at us a full minute, then retraced his steps towards us. I was looking at his face and was so occupied in my study that I felt stricken with a sudden, nameless fear when Buddy grasped my arm and said: "We ought to beat it."

The Negro was perhaps fifteen feet from us and advancing slowly, portentously. Then, as he came closer, I saw that the balls of his eyes were not the clear white of the usual gentleman of color, but instead a mattered yellow. Abruptly the fear left me. I had heard my father tell of the South African blacks, whose eyes, when yellow, denoted the coward. One could dominate them by the power of the eye. I stood firm and returned his stare as ferociously as he gave it. He came close. Buddy, loyally, stood beside me.

"What yo' all lookin' at?"

"You!" I replied. "Now leave us alone."

There were a few pedestrians and those were Negroes. "Yo' all bettah stop followin' me!" He was towering almost over us.

I yet held my eyes to the swimming yellow ones. I felt that he should soon weaken under my direct gaze, but a small doubt was filtering into my mind as to the efficacy of this treatment. The doubt became a certainty in the failure of the theory, as the Negro swung one arm out with the intention of slapping my face.

Buddy kicked at him. I was angry and frightened; I dodged the blow and ran. Buddy and I gained the center of the street and paused a moment to calculate our chances of picking up a rock or two and offering him our regards with them, but he had started in pursuit of us, so we scampered to the other side of the street and down a side alley. Blacks with yellow eyes may be dominated by white men's eyes in Africa, but the principle doesn't work in West Oakland, California.

In the alley, at the farther end, we roundly cursed the Negro. Our profanity was excellent, diversified and rather comprehensive for two so young. Buddy had brought the most choice gems of our swear words from home. I rather envied him this advantage and felt that, despite the other qualities my home afforded, it was not quite so complete as it should have been.

Though I could never imagine my father letting loose with any of the phrases that rolled so easily, for my edification, from Buddy's tongue.

Our curiosity had led us into a near disaster. But we rebuilt the affair to suit ourselves. Buddy's kick had so crippled the Negro that he had known a terrible suffering. This had been the reason he had not pursued us farther. Then, too, so we said to ourselves in the seclusion of our alley retreat, the big brute had not dared to follow us when he saw us pause at the curbing as though to fortify ourselves with rocks. No—he was afraid. He would have done many cruel things to us, but our ready nerve and determined attitude had saved us from harm. On the whole we had acquitted ourselves creditably. . . . Having thus satisfactorily disposed of the incident, we investigated the floursack, which I had retained throughout the impending disaster and brought out sufficient food to take the edge off our appetites.

[II]

An alley cat strayed into view. We had attracted him by the smell of sardines from the opened cans before us. He greeted us with purrs and soon I was feeding him a fish at a time. Other cats materialized. The final can was opened and we alternately fed and petted the assortment of cats. Aristocratic cats with markings of distant royal lineage; scrawny cats with brown and gray stripes; black-and-white cats with green eyes. To me—crediting them with various qualities—they afforded an interesting hour. I named one particular cat Gentleman Jim. He had an easy and effective left hook that carried him into the midst of the scramble for a portion of the fish and enabled him to emerge victorious. By dint of much coaxing I succeeded in enticing him to within reach of my hand. He had a rather disdainful mien that was appropriate to his name and I directed Buddy's attention to this characteristic. There was even a tuft of fur rising from between his ears, which coincided with the famous "pomp" of the ex-heavy-weight champ.

"Watch him now, when I give him this piece of tail," I said to Buddy. "He takes it as though he were doing us a favor. He must be a sort of mayor, or senator, or maybe a king of the cats." I proffered the bit of fish. Jim accepted it, then turned and stalked off, head high, tail switching, his head warily shifting from side to side.

Jim had consumed the fish and was washing himself!

"Gentleman Jim—hell!" observed Buddy. "He ain't that kind of a cat. He's a she—look!" The proof was indisputable.

The sardines distributed, the cats lost interest in us. A few prowled about the alley, speculatively eyeing our flour-sack. I rolled a ball of bread and soaked it with fish oil. The result was a tantalizing, bounding sphere that smelled of fish, but proved to be something unpalatable when nibbled. The remaining cats evinced their dislike of this after a few disappointing chases of bread-balls and left us.

A gate in the fence at our side was pushed open and a tall, thin lady of almost olive complexion appeared. "What's youse boys doin' heah? Bettah you be gittin' 'long to school—truant officer gwine to git you, if you doan't!" She emptied into a can the pan of garbage she carried and then inspected us more closely.

I returned her look, preparing to spring up and away at the first hostile move from her. Rows of clean, startlingly white teeth glistened as she smiled upon us, then chuckled. "Why, strike me dead! You 'uns is shore 'nuff white chillen!"

Quick to resent the implied insult, I stood erect. My cap had slid down over one ear and my hair was not visible. I pulled the cap from my head. "Of course I'm white!" I asserted stoutly.

She laughed. The rising crescendo of the musical southern Negro in her voice seemed to give the notes form. I imagined I could see them dancing on the air.

"'Course you is, honey," she spoke through her mirth. "'Course you is. But a pusson'd haf to look mighty clost to be suah!" Again the dancing laughter.

"Why?" Buddy, beside me, asked.

"Jus' you look in a mirrah. Lawd! Yore 'bout the two dahkest white chillen I ever see!" Then her face sobered and she said: "Wheah yore folks is at?"

I didn't take kindly to this questioning and would have terminated it, but something of the woman's happy nature had entered into me and I was not disposed to end the talk. My fertile imagination came into play and improvised an orphanage from which we had run away. Buddy flashed appreciation and commendation of this tale. And the woman evidently believed it, for she was immediately sympathetic and inquired as to how they had treated us and how long we had been away and where we were intending to go. I recalled some of the experiences of Oliver Twist and gave them a modern setting. Following my recitation, she insisted that we come in to her "place" to wash up and have breakfast. Not without some misgivings, we accepted.

Through a small, congested yard and into a two-storied building she led us. The kitchen was clean and seemed unusually well stocked with food and utensils. I had visited frequently with the various cooks that prepared the meals at my home and was capable of differentiating between kitchens.

Under her direction we washed ourselves, even discarding our sweaters and submitting to having our necks scrubbed. The water in the basin gave mute evidence of the justice of her mistake in judging us to be of dusky parentage.

While she busied herself with preparing a meal, I walked about the room and even ventured down the hallway past closed doors until I reached a large front room, which seemed filled to overflowing with gilt chairs, a few lounges and several pictures. A peculiar, though not wholly unpleasant, odor hung heavily within the room.

The chairs were of a type new to me and the bumpy padding of the lounges bespoke hard and frequent usage; but it was the pictures that captivated my attention. Nude women, in poses devised to best display their charms, showed from within the gilded frames. In the half-light of the room I felt a creepy sensation, as though I had walked into another world.

Somewhere down the hallway a door creaked and footsteps sounded softly and ominously as they approached. Panic-stricken that anyone should find me in the same room with the pictures, I dropped to the floor and wriggled under one of the lounges. The sound I made attracted the attention of the person, who came directly to my place of concealment. Fearfully, I peered from under the edge of the lounge and saw two bare, brown legs rising from a pair of pink knitted slippers. Perspiration stood out on my forehead. Flashing across my mind were pictures of horrible tortures inflicted on white boys who ventured into the clutches of Negroes. Some atavistic impulse rendered me prey to the superstitions of my primitive forbears and I experienced a quick agony. Damocles, dining with the sword hair-suspended above his head, knew not a more poignant suspense than I as I observe those two not badly shaped legs.

"What's youse hidin' under dere fur?" The tone was apprehensive and in that note of uncertainty I felt as a condemned man does when informed of a reprieve. But I remained silent. I was not certain I *could* speak—and I was not curious to experiment.

"Cum out from dere." The wavering note remained, but the brown legs stirred and a pink kimono came into view as the owner squatted to look under the lounge. I could not see the features of the dark, frizzy-edged blur that appealed to be a head, but after a glance, white teeth flashed—just as with the tall woman—and again a laugh greeted me when I had expected a growl. Assured by the mellifluous tone that the possessor meant no harm, I crawled from my refuge.

She was a splendid type of Amazon. For so large a woman her movements were surprisingly quick. She drew the folds of her thin kimono carelessly together as she smiled at my evident discomfiture. Inclining slightly towards me, that she might better observe my face, I was made aware of an increase in the peculiar odor that had seemed to hang, suspended, in the air of the room. I felt a prickly sensation along my spinal column, which traveled upwards until it reached my scalp. I have since then encountered odors and smells that have given rise to every reaction of which the human body is capable, but never have I experienced the weird and incomprehensible agitation that first whiff of an animal woman aroused. And, curiously, it attracted by its very strangeness. One speck of my mind told me I should be horrified—the other speck (I've since been convinced that I've only two specks), the more powerful, answered the stimulus in kind. I did not resent her arm about my shoulders as she guided me back to the kitchen.

Buddy was seated at a table. Our eyes met and suddenly I knew that I had been removed from him by the recent incident. The gulf of an exotic experience lay between us. It was as though I saw him at an immeasurable distance. True, nothing had happened that could be explained in mere words, but I was painfully aware of having made a tremendous advancement into a sphere that previously I had entered hesitantly and then only in my imagination. I felt that I had received a special dispensation of the gods in thus being initiated into the heretofore esoteric world of women. A slight wave of pity swept over me at sight of Buddy. His light-blue eyes, under almost colorless brows, gave him an innocent, infantile appearance. He knew so little of life! While I could already picture the change in my countenance. My hand rubbed my chin, duplicating the gesture I had seen an uncle employ when deciding if he should shave that day or let the beard grow a trifle longer.

"Look heah, Lulu! Look who all I jus' got in the pahlah." The scantily clad girl—for she was not more than twenty—indicated me.

"Now, Miss Julie, you g'wan an' get some clo's on yore-self, an' leave 'at child wif me. Dey's two orphans—an' I is gwine to feed dem," Lulu asserted, with an authority I thought strangely placed in a mere cook. I know now that she combined the occupation of "morning cook" and "madame of the house."

After favoring Buddy with a sympathetic glance Julia obediently withdrew.

"Jes' you draw up a cheer, an' eat yoreself some breakfus, jes' lak yore friend is," Lulu said.

She heaped before us a quantity of pancakes and syrup and filled two large glasses with milk. Industriously we did justice to her offerings, pausing only after the plates were wiped clean.

In response to her inquiry as to our names, I chose Jack and labelled Buddy "Bill."

"What wuz you doin' in 'at pahlah, Mister Jack?" she asked.

"Just looking around—I never saw a place like that before," I explained.

"Bes' you doan't never see no mo' lak it, either," she remarked, shaking her head. "Dat's for older men, not chillen. An' even when you is older, you bettah stay 'way from dem Pahlahs."

Buddy evinced a curiosity to know what sort of parlor it was "best to stay 'way from." While Lulu was busy for a moment with the stove, I whispered that I would tell him "all" when we were alone. . . . With our stomachs replete, we were ready to start traveling again.

Thanking Lulu for her kindness, we made as if to leave.

She would not listen to my protestations and insisted that we remain for a while until she had served the "girls" their breakfast and then she would help us figure out what we had best do. I was becoming drowsy and was nothing loath to rest awhile and Buddy evidently did not want to leave until he had had at least one glimpse of the "pahlah." Shortly we dozed off to sleep and although I had a faint recollection of being carried somewhere, I was not certain until I awoke in a strange room, with Buddy, fully clothed, on the bed at my side.

[III]

The room was close and though the curtain moved faintly in its opening, there was not sufficient air within the place to prevent its seeming hot. Faint noises from the street reached me and upon going to the window I was surprised to find the shadows lengthening from the west. Almost evening—our entire day gone!

Rousing Buddy, we stole down the stairs and entered the long hall about midway between the kitchen and parlor. There was considerable activity about the rooms on either side and a door opening near us disclosed Miss Julia and some gentleman of color preparing to rejoin the group in the parlor. She smiled delightedly as she saw us. "Dis is dem I tole you 'bout," she said to her escort.

He inspected us uninterestedly. "What you aimin' to do?" he asked.

I wanted to tell him that that was our business, but Julia caught my eye and in the message she flashed I read that an agreeable answer was expected.

"We are going up into the country," I informed him. "We are going to beat a train from the Sixteenth Street station tonight." There was a satisfaction in repeating the words I had read—they gave us a sort of standing. We ceased to be orphans—we became Knights of the Road.

His mouth widened into a grin. He looked at Julia and together they laughed the full, hearty, joyous laughter peculiar to their race.

"Boy," he said, "you talks lak a sure-'nuff rambler, but you sure is young for dis beatin' business." He leaned over and turned Buddy's face, the better to inspect it in the light from a gas-jet on one wall. "—And dis heah boy is a tramp, too?"

"We both are," I said, with a rising note of resentment. "What's so funny about that? Do you think we're babies? Bill's fifteen and I'm almost sixteen." I boosted our ages to a height I believed would seem probable.

"Ain't they darbs?" queried Julia. "Look at 'em, Alec jus' as 'pendent an' suah of demselfs! Bettah you is givin' 'em some help—dey runned 'way from some place 'at dey is whipped—Lulu tole me."

He help us! How could he do anything for us? I would not accept money from a Negro and began to say as much when he asked: "Where 'bouts up in the country is you aimin' to go?"

I wasn't certain where we would go, exactly—the King had not written anything about a definite objective. He just took a train and held it as far as he could, then took another train and—suddenly I thought of Chicago. I had relatives there. It would be a lark to surprise them. I pictured their concern and our nonchalance, as we casually explained that we had crossed half of the continent to say hello to them.

"Well, we are going to Chicago—first. Then to New York, I guess."

"Lord! You sure got 'nuff territory laid out for yoreselfs!" He seemed impressed by our sincerity, though surprised by the assurance with which we spoke of traveling three thousand miles. "An' how is you goin' to get dere?"

"Mount the top—on the—that is, underneath, or ride the trucks. We aren't particular. It's all the same, just so we get there." I was thinking rapidly, to recall other ways of riding trains without paying fare and wishing I had brought the book with me. A fellow gets rusty so quickly in his profession if he doesn't keep up his studies . . .

Alec scratched his head. Several other girls besides Julia had joined the group. She motioned them away, then led us to the kitchen.

"Lulu, we is gwine to fix dese boys so's dey can get to Chicago." Julia and Alec stood before the tall woman. "We is gwine to have Alec hide 'em away in a linen-closet on de train, ain't we, Alec?"

Alec was not very enthusiastic. He allowed that a porter's job was not so easy to get and he didn't want to lose it and that sometimes the conductor inspected the closets. But Julia had ideas of how best to attain her ends.

"For yore baby, honey, you is gwine to do it, jes' this oncet." The words were coaxing and Julia put her face close to his cheek. "Ef you loves yore baby lak she loves her man, you is gwine to do it, ain'tcha?"

Alec wavered. Lulu added her support to the cause. "If dey ketches dese chillen, dey's bound to whip 'em awful; I know how dey does in one of dem places. An' a big, fine, smaht man lak you ain't gwine to let no ole conductor-man ketch him, is he? Bettah you help, Alec."

It was finally agreed that Alec would stow us away in a closet and do his best to ensure our safe arrival in Chicago. But we were made to promise, under dire penalties, that, no matter how uncomfortable we were, we would not make any noise and that we would never tell a soul who had hidden us, were we discovered. We assented readily, even volunteering to say that we had evaded the porter and had hidden ourselves. We were to be at the station exactly at midnight and remain on the Bay side of the tracks. At a certain car we would find the floor-door open and after coming through it we were to enter the closet he indicated to us and remain there. With these details smoothed out, Julia departed with Alec, presumably to show him "how much his baby loved her man." ... Lulu set more food before us.

Pleasant and solicitous for our comfort, she inspected our clothing and assured herself that it was not in need of repair, the while advising us how to conduct ourselves after we reached Chicago. Work was the main theme of her talk—honest work. Learning some trade—stealing nothing—and avoiding "pahlah houses" were the things she tried to impress upon our minds. She spoke to us as if we had been ten years older and made us promise repeatedly to write to her and if we ever got into trouble to get a lawyer immediately and have him telegraph to her.

"Dey's only one way to live dis life, an' you boys done got a pore start. But doan't never steal nuffin'. Never steal! Lots of folks doan't think dat dis"—indicating the house—"is much of a bisness, but I always runs it hones'. Nobody was ever robbed in my house—an' nobody never will be, either. 'Cause I'm black doan't mean I doan't feel an' think lak any body else." ...

Honest Lulu. Engaged in the oldest of the world's professions, yet dignifying it with your conception of honesty. Helping two youngsters to escape from the law you believed was seeking to hold us in bondage, yet you were sufficiently concerned with our future to lecture us on the essential need of attaining an honest view-point. Knowing, from the fullness of your experience, how destructive the intended protective force of the law can be, you sought to shield us from tangible forces and prepare us to combat the intangible temptations that you knew were awaiting us. In your blood flowed a passion for fair and square treatment and you said you were black, yet showed a soul clean and white. Gifted with an appreciation and tolerance worthy of the greatest of your sex—what Fate made possible the Gargantuan jest that place you in the position of "madame" in that house? Was this the reward of your passion for honesty—or did you acquire those qualities only through the position assigned you? . . . Years later I listened while the little blond lad you lectured so earnestly that evening was condemned by "virtuous," Christian, female jurors, who were *not* black of skin, to be hanged by the neck until he was dead; and I've wondered. . . . Yes, honest, black Lulu, I've wondered often who distributes those attributes of divine origin. . . .

[IV]

"Guests" were arriving for the evening's entertainment. Lulu was relieved from her kitchen duties by a large fat woman who waddled grotesquely about the room, filling trays with glasses of liquor and preparing sandwiches. We were unmolested and received only an occasional nod from Julie as she entered or left the kitchen. Other girls and men appeared momentarily in the hall, silhouetted against the parlor lights, to disappear into the side rooms.

Somewhere out in front of the house a girl raised a plaintive voice in a blues-song. Then nearer to us another started the wailing lament of "that bad, bad Stackalee. . . ." We listened, spellbound by the quality of the voice—so new, so weird, yet so hauntingly familiar. Then the singer drifted, with only slight change of *tempo,* into the seemingly endless verses of the adventures of John Henry.

"John Henry" came in a sad, slow moan, dirge-like in its low, primitive prolongation:

"John Henry tole his cap'en one day:
 'A man ain't nuffin' but a man,
  But 'fore ah'd let yo' hit me on the ——— wid dat
   strap,
    Ah'd die wif dis hammer in mah han'. . . .'
     Hey . . . hey . . . hey. . . .

"John Henry said:
 'Look yondah what ah see!
  De steam-drill's broked,
   An' de watah's done choked.

> *But she'll nevah go down on me....'*
> *Hey ... hey ... hey....*

> *"John Henry had a little son*
> *An' put him in his han';*
> *De fust words little Henry spoke was:*
> *'Ah wants t' be a ste-e-el-drivin' man!'*
> *Hey ... hey ... hey ..."*

The last "Hey, hey, hey" dwindled away and a masculine baritone boomed out, rich and sonorous:

> *"Fair Brownie, Fair Brownie,*
> *Who can-n-n yore rag-ler be-e-e?*
> *If yo' ain't got no rag-ler.*
> *What fau-u-lt yo' ft-i-ind in me-e-e?*

> *"Fair Brownie, Fair Brownie,*
> *Where di-d-d yo' hi-i-ide las' nhite-e?*
> *Yore shoo-o-rd ain't buttoned,*
> *An' yor-r-e hair ain't ri-hite."*

Assuming a dominating tone, he continued:

> *"Fair Brownie, Fair Brownie,*
> *Cum heah an' get down aw-o-on yore knees...."*

And the girl, replying in the same chant, but with mock supplication:

> *"Sweet papa, yo' too dawggone hahd to*
> *ple-e-ease...."*

The barbaric rhythm from the piano drowned out the remainder of the duet and through the open doorway I glimpsed a black girl in the throes of a Black Bottom dance. Then the door closed and a decade passed before I witnessed that dance again and when I saw it, it was performed by a white woman—the wife of a state senator....

[V]

Bunny glanced at the rear door and I nodded assent to his unspoken question. Together we gained the yard and halted a moment to accustom our eyes to the gloom. Here the air was sharp and overhead a few stars were winking out of the inverted purple bowl of heaven.

Above the alley a window opened, a woman spoke softly and again a mournful voice rose and fell in the mystical wavering of a blues:

> *"Ah wan' a ridah—I wan' a ridah*
> *Jus' lak o-o-ole Jesse James—*
> *One'll shoot out mah lights,*
> *Lawd, An' kick out the window-panes."*

And as though crooning in her ear came her companion's answer:

> *"When go' see me comin'.*
> *Get out yore fryin'-pan.*
> *Cook cawn-bre'd fo' yore husban'—*
> *Poke-chops fo' yore ma-a-an. . . ."*

This was a rare stratum into which we had been projected, but with the coolness of the evening, lowering the temperature of our blood, came the urge to move. We decided to walk about the block and then return. There was ample time—it was about eight o'clock.

Once on Seventh Street, we loitered in front of shop-windows and saloons and presently arrived at a poolroom. In large letters over the door the proprietor informed the world in general and boys under eighteen in particular, that minors were not allowed within. Immediately we desired to go inside. There was nothing inside that we could not see through the large front windows, but that there was a prohibition against our entering made the interior the most enticing of all places. Several colored men adorned the sides of the entrance. Mindful of the dire consequences possible if we paid too close attention to them, we gave them but a casual glance and walked by the doorway. A few feet beyond we paused.

"We must go in there," I said. "We just have to see that place from inside."

Buddy agreed and it became at once essential to our education that we inspect the pool-players at close range. Mentally bracing myself, I took a firm grip on Buddy's sweater-sleeve and together we breasted the door. I rather expected to find some sort of invisible barrier that would bring us to an abrupt halt. It was with a sense of conquest hardly attained that we traversed the narrow room.

A group of Negroes was standing and sitting about one table and their absorbing interest in the player tensed to make a shot enabled us to approach without attracting attention. An elongated black, whose white shirt lay open at the throat, leaned over the table, preparing to drive the cue ball, just as we arrived at the opposite side. The low, hanging lamp cast a yellow cone of light on his perspiring forehead and made black patches of his eyes. The lower part of his face seemed to catch and hold the reflected green light from the cloth on the table's top; a sinister composition.

Deliberately he centered his cue, paused, then straightened up and reached for a small cube of blue chalk resting on one rail. Frowning fiercely, he studied the lay of the balls, the while applying chalk to the end of his cue. Minutely he inspected the cue tip. Several Negroes stirred and I witnessed a quick exchange of glances between the player and a stout, hook-nosed half-breed who stood near by, holding a cue in his hand like an Assyrian lancer at rest.

The player bent over the table and after a moment's hesitation jabbed with his stick at the ball, which went off at a tangent! Chagrin, bewilderment and then anger flooded over his face. The fat Negro laughed, harshly, tantalizingly. "Hot damn!" said the thin one.

What happened immediately following his exclamation I can only indicate. He swung the cue viciously and crashed it on on the fat man's head. A score of spectators started up and away. Buddy and I were knocked down in the stampede.

Regaining my feet, I grabbed Buddy and ran a few steps, then stumbled and fell. Several men walked over or on me, during my effort to rise. In my panic I had become confused as to direction and ran back towards the table. The fat man was bleeding freely from a cut over his eyes and while he wiped away the purple stream with one hand, he brandished a huge, shining blade of steel. Razor or knife—it was a wicked weapon. The tall man was fumbling in his pocket and as I stood frozen, too fascinated to move, I saw the steel cleave a flashing circle through the air and disappear in his up-thrown arm, to reappear an instant later. To my startled gaze it seemed to have passed through the arm and I wondered why the severed member did not fall. A widening stain of red slid down his white shirt-sleeve. With a bellow of animal rage he retreated and with his uninjured arm whipped from his pocket a duplicate knife or razor.

For a moment they faced each other. . . . Two quick feints with the deadly blades, then they closed in, slashing and hacking furiously. I turned and ran, scampering through the rapidly thinning crowd at the doorway and rejoining Buddy on the sidewalk. We raced across the street and found refuge in the first darkened alley that presented itself.

Several police whistles were blowing. Their shrill, mounting calls impressed me as being an appropriate expression of the elemental passions I had just seen rampant. The reverberations of a night-stick pounded on the pavement brought answering aid—and together we shivered as the quiet of our retreat became vibrant with the disturbance created by the increasing crowds in the street.

I had read of combats, but witnessing this murderous fight had dwarfed the bloodiest descriptions of them. This had been real—and yet its very vividness had made it seem unreal. The details, when recalled, presented themselves in different guise from that in which I had seen them. I reconstructed the affair for Buddy and I am positive I supplied much that I could not have seen. . . . And since then I have listened to witnesses swear to the details of a robbery that I *knew* did not occur. Curious— how the mind, when emotionally heightened, photographs an event in conformity with the manner in which one wants to have it occur.

And so I credited many slashes and skillful feints to those two Negroes that could not have been made in so brief an onslaught. As I finished talking, I felt the impression of reliving that moment and yet it seemed to have happened years before.

Thoughts for our own safety impelled us to leave the alley— at the opposite end—and return to Lulu's.

The kitchen was deserted for the moment. Suddenly the thought came to me that we should have a long, hungry trip to Chicago unless we provided food for ourselves. I was not certain that Alec's helping us included the furnishing of meals and I expressed this to Buddy; we decided to forestall possible famine. Retrieving the flour-sack, we left the kitchen and slunk down the alley to emerge on Sixth Street.

It was probably ten o'clock then and the grocery-stores were closed. We walked several blocks in the vain hope that we should find one open. Though we had no money, I held some idea that I could convince the clerk that he would be taking no risks in "charging" any purchases we made. Another stoic had done so—why not the one we sought, also

"I think we're out o' luck," Buddy observed as we stood before the darkened windows of a store that displayed various food-stuffs.

"Looks that way," I admitted, "but we just got to have something—something more than what we have now. This wouldn't hardly take us to—to—" I sought some intermediate point and floundered on—"Denver and that's only a little ways."

"Yeah that's so," Buddy said helpfully.

"Well, we got to have some," I reiterated, wishing for Aladdin's lamp. "Here's plenty in this window- and there's nobody on the street watching us . . . an' this glass wouldn't be hard to break—we could send the man the money for it after we get to Chicago."

"Do you think they'd catch us?" Buddy looked cautiously about the place.

I had never been caught before, so it was logical that I should not be fearful of consequences this time. True, I had never "purchased" groceries in the contemplated manner.

"No, I'm sure they won't," I asserted. "We can—well, break the glass easy and then grab what we want and run to Lulu's."

"But she don't want us to steal anything," protested Buddy.

I weighed this. The thought of possible hunger was heavier. "—And we could leave the sack out in the yard, so she wouldn't see it."

After some scouting I located a stone and while Buddy watched the cross-streets to warn me of anyone's approach, I assailed the window. The first time, I started the stone in a swing from behind me, intending to hold it in my hand and shatter the glass; but just before it met the glass, I jerked violently at some inward revolt and the glass remained intact. Twice more I attempted to hit the window. Each time something restrained me. I had read of "Daring Thief Crashes Rock through Window and Makes Escape with Loot!"—but I was not a daring thief and

I wonder how many burglaries reported as being perpetrated by such have been preceded by similar hesitation.

Rejoining Buddy for a moment, I made the excuse that I thought I heard someone coming. His "It's all right" gave me the impetus I needed and returning, I walked quickly up to the window and hurled the stone against the glass. A report, thunder-like in its suddenness, rent the air about my ears. I stepped closer to the building and saw a jagged hole about six inches in diameter where the missile had entered. It lay within, amid a pile of tumbled cardboard containers. Strive as I might, I could not reach up to the hole and then down to the floor of the display. I strained and shivered, imagining that the next second would mark the opening of the door and the materializing of the shop-owner. For what seemed an hour—and was probably less than half a minute—I sought to widen the hole. Suddenly one large piece of glass slid from the shattered pane and crashed to the pavement. The tinkling, silvery sounds brought Buddy to my aid. Through the now enlarged hole we could reach the "loot." Rapidly we transferred the objects we grabbed to our sack. It was filled to overflowing. I tried to swing it over my shoulder, failed, then started dragging it behind me. Buddy trotted at my side, his arms hugging additional provisions to his breast.

We reached the corner and turned down Seventh Street. Glancing back, I saw light fill the windows over the store. In a near panic we ran as fast as our impedimenta would permit us. The stolen goods were growing heavier the farther I dragged them. Buddy stuffed what articles he could into his shirt, that he might lend me assistance in pulling our load. Before the block was traversed, that weight behind us had slowed us to a fast walk. An epitome of a thief's life: the drag and hindrance of his stolen plunder. The greater the amount of loot, the greater the hindrance!

We had just arrived at the next street when a scurrying of feet assailed our ears. Before we could dodge, or run and hide, two policemen turned the corner and were full upon us. Their speed carried them a few feet past us, then one halted and looked quickly at us. They had responded to a telephone call to arrest—and probably fight—"daring burglars," and they had almost run over the objects of their call: two badly frightened kids. Checkmate!

The one who had stopped called to the other: *"I think it's these damn brats, but take a look and be sure."* Then turning to us, he reached an enormous but efficient hand under the collar of my sweater and pulled me over to where Buddy stood wide-eyed and open-mouthed. As the officer reached for him, Buddy cringed, then sprang away and ran like a mad dog down the center of the street. Instantly I sought to hamper the officer by attempting to twist away from him. He cuffed me—not too severely—and growled that he would "paddle my if I didn't stand still." Buddy disappeared between two houses and, even through the cold fear of my predicament, I felt a glad relief that he had escaped.

The other officer, returned from the point where he had given over his pursuit of Buddy, proved to be a surly sort. "You damn kids are always raising hell—bet you're the same two who's been breaking all these windows down in this part of town. White kid, too. What you doing in nigger town? Where do you live?"

To tell him the story of the orphanage would not avail me anything. Unable to manufacture any explanation—other than that I didn't have any home—I decided to say what I have frequently said in unpleasant situations since then—nothing. On that evening it served me excellently.

"He's too scared to talk," suggested the first officer.

"Let's see what damage is done, then ring for the wagon and take a look around for that other kid."

Returning to the scene of my recent depredation, we were met by an excited colored man who explained how he had heard the burglars and immediately phoned the police. He expended a sad glance on the broken window and informed me that my "pappy" would have to pay for it.

I remained quiet, hoping the officer would release his hold upon me, but he failed to do so. . . . Buddy would go direct to Lulu's, I reasoned and if the police did take me to jail, she would do whatever was necessary to get me out. The thought of how horrified my parents would be should they learn of my arrest and deed made me weak to the point of fainting. Mother would cry and hold me to her. Father—well, I didn't think he'd cry, but I was sure he'd hold me, though differently from Mother. . . .

With a great clattering of hoofs the "wagon" arrived. Groceries, sack, the Negro and I were set inside, then one officer stood on the rear steps. The other returned to his regular beat.

There were fresh, dark stains on the floor of the wagon. I gazed upon them in the dim light from the lamps on the corners we passed. Noting my evident interest, the officer enlightened me: "That's the same sort of a card you'll be leaving if you don't stop stealing."

I was trying to unravel this twisted remark when the driver shouted over his shoulder: "Didn't get time to clean it out—it's from them dinges, Jim."

"Think they'll die?" Jim asked.

"Sure. The fat one was dead before we got him to the hospital."

"The fat one!" I exclaimed involuntarily.

Jim looked quickly at me. "What do *you* know about it?"

I intended to say that I had seen the fight, but something cautioned me. The tone of his voice implied that he would be interested if I knew about the fight—and I couldn't imagine any good coming from anything he had an interest in so I again said nothing.

We soon reached the station. The desk-sergeant said. "You're young as hell to be out stealing, kid." . . .

They searched me, but there was nothing to indicate my name or home address. I told them I was Jack Brown. And after a half-hour of futile questioning, during which I maintained a stubborn silence, they escorted me into the jail proper and locked me in a cell. It was a portion of the Old City Prison, which was contained within that old eyesore the City Hall, before the present one was built. Though isolated from the other prisoners, I could hear their drunken cries and obscene shouts.

I had sought misery; I wanted trouble; the desire for grief and hardship had torn me from a clean home—and I had found all I sought. A man usually does find what he seeks. And yet—

Alone in the chill darkness, I found it increasingly hard to retreat from the intrusive reality of the ill-odored bunk and the sickening stench of mingled disinfectant and human filth. The cold bars of the cell front, when I grasped one in my hand, dispelled—for what remained of that night at least—all possibility of retreating into the world of imagination and inverting or denying their reality.

I pulled a greasy blanket over me and the warmth of my body soon brought into action hundreds of bedbugs. I fought a losing fight and I was forced to drop on the bunk by the insistent bludgeoning of Somnus. . . . I wondered whether Lulu knew of my whereabouts; how long I should be able to withstand the stinging bites of the bugs; what the morning would bring. Could I possibly awake again after sleeping in such a foul atmosphere?

I was aware that I was striving desperately to discard the immediate discomforts and find release in "my dream world." Then dejection settled over me, to be succeeded by despair and a dull, aching lonesomeness. I missed Buddy—if I were with him, I should not care so much. But I had run the gauntlet of human emotions that day and wanted help in understanding their relation to me. . . . Lower and lower into the morass of my thoughts I sank. The last waking memory I had was of some inebriate with a sentimental mood singing in a distant voice:

*"When you co-o-me to the e-e-nd of a perfect
    day-y-y. . . ."*

CHAPTER 2

[I]

Struggling up through layers of sleep, I was jerked from beneath the dirty blankets by a jailer. Out into the corridor he pulled me and in the gray light (which I have later learned is peculiar to jails) I was confronted with the form of my father. I was wide awake in the instant.

"Is this him?" queried the jailer, turning me about, that my face might be visible.

"Yes." In a tone that conjured in my mind pictures painful to behold. "Yes, that's him. Will you bring him along with you?"

The jailer would—and did. We arrived after my father in the office of the chief of police.

His face almost hidden behind an enormous walrus moustache, the chief addressed me. His voice had the roll of thunder in it. His eyes, glaring from between narrowed slits, darted punctuations to his continual roaring. Dirty and disheveled, my cap in one hand, my eyes centered on his, I stood but a few feet from where he and my father were seated. The volume of his voice would have sufficed to carry his tirade twenty times the actual distance between us. He was rough, abrupt, immoderate, almost ferocious. He stormed and raved at me. The space between us seemed to increase until I felt as though I were in a remote desert. He was the great censurer—a modern Isaiah.

He upbraided me for the anxiety and worry I had caused my parents; condemned me for my act on the night previous; enounced me for a worthless, unappreciative son; labelled me a liar because I had not given my right name the night before; branded me a traitor to society because I had refused to divulge the name of my companion; and finally consigned me to a terrible lifetime of shame and dishonor. In this prophecy he was not sparing of details. I would grow up to be a thief. I would steal trivial things for a while and then, becoming more reckless, I would commit robbery and eventually murder someone and be hanged for it.

He mapped out my future with an eloquent fervency that precluded any doubt of his visualizing it other than as it would be. So complete was his delineation that I mused on the attractiveness of having my life already prepared, shaped, colored and presented to me. It was the first program of the "dim, distant future" that had been given me. I wondered how he knew so much.

But throughout it all I maintained my stare at him and though he seemed to dissolve into an enormous head, the mouth of which spouted torrents of abuse through its coarse, stained-gray covering, my eyes remained in direct line with his. Frequently a hand would flash up and into view, like a bloated gob of pasty dough, distorted and out of focus.

My father kept silent. I believe that scene was a part of a pre-arranged plan to scare me and bludgeon my nature into a fear of ever committing a like act again. They succeeded in arousing my curiosity—and disgust. If they sought to "teach me a lesson," they failed, woefully. Instead, they awoke a lively inquisitiveness. There I was—a confirmed criminal and not yet eleven years of age. I became impressed with a sense of inward betrayal; there was some portion of me which others could see—some characteristic aggressively criminal—and I had lived all those years in total ignorance of my possession of it! What treason was this I must become more introspective—I must become better acquainted with this trait. It is not good that a man live in ignorance of himself. "Know thyself," our preacher had admonished at one sermon I had been forced to remain awake and hear....

The chief's day having been started in a manner to his complete satisfaction, he turned off the verbal pyrotechnics. Not abruptly, but spasmodically. A roll and rising crescendo ending in a flare, then a few lingering sparks. Like a geyser that had attained the zenith of its eruption and died away in decreasingly tempestuous gushes, so his voice quieted.

Then I learned from my father that I was to return home with him; that they had been searching the city during my absence and that I could not have left town because the police had been informed and were watching all the stations and street cars. I wondered why I had not been recognized the night before. His preposterous statement rang false to me, for I knew that I *could* have left the city—would have left it but for the arrest. That ubiquitous *"but"*! . . . His absonant assertion held a challenge to me—and I accepted it, for future settlement.

Father took me back to the store in West Oakland, paid the owner for the damage, almost succeeded in forcing an apology from me, then brought me home. After a conference with my mother they decided that it would be best to send me up into Mendocino County to live with my uncle's family, while I completed the two remaining years of grade school.

Buddy was lost to me for the next four years. I didn't even get a chance to talk to him, although I did see his sister, Pearl, for a moment as I was being escorted to the street car on the morning I left for the ranch. She informed me that Buddy was home....

[II]

Life on my uncle's ranch was, at first, a very dull existence. It was located in a remote valley, reached only by stage; the solitude and endless sameness held little of attraction for me. But soon I was looking inward for diversion. I was developing rapidly—physically. When I left there, I was of the stature and weight of the average man. And in the interval I had learned to provide for my own amusements. Reading constituted the greater portion of my pastime. Although I learned to handle guns and became an expert shot with both pistol and rifle, there were many days in the woods when I would lie for hours with a gun beside me, while I absorbed ideas and experienced adventures from printed pages.

At home there had been considerable musical talent in the family. My father was a pianist of rather unusual ability; my mother sang, splendidly and often; a girl cousin frequently played violin accompaniments to Father's music. It was natural that I should miss these things on the ranch. My aunt's efforts to force from a creaking old Sears and Roebuck organ the semblance of "Go Tell Aunt Sally" usually started me on a search through the hills for "Sally." Should I have encountered her, instead of telling her that "the old gray goose is dead," as one is admonished by the song, I should have entreated her to return with me and assuage my aunt's desire to see her—and so perform an act of charity and graciousness, by accepting the fifteen or twenty messages contained in the verses direct, once and for all time, from my aunt seated at the organ. Two years ago, when thousands were asking, in the words of a popular song: "I Wonder What's Become of Sally?" I could have enlightened them. She died the day I poured a kettleful of boiling water into the bellows of that organ....

By dint of much coaxing I persuaded my father to send me a phonograph. He included a generous assortment of records. From those two winters I passed with that music has resulted an appreciation of music which has carried me through many periods of stress. Discriminately selected pieces he sent to me. Pieces that I never tired of playing. Even now, as the phonograph at my side plays some selection containing a refrain from one of those old favorites, the memory of that ranch-house living-room returns with startling vividness. The green paint on the wall before me seems to dissolve and again I am before the huge open fireplace of my uncle's home. The warmth and glow of burning logs, the dancing flames and miniature sky-rocketing sparks, the creeping red designs that constantly change against their background of velvet-black soot, the fragrant incense of blended pine and oak—I can almost hear the whirling of that cylinder machine as it pours its melody into the room. . . . But my cell-mate coughs, a bedbug scampers across the wall; I must bestir myself—the picture is shattered!

Uncle didn't take kindly to the "music box" when first I received it and it was necessary to carry it out of the house when the desire for harmony became insistent. Later he tolerated "that infernal racket" and I believe he was not really displeased when I presented the phonograph to him at the time I returned to Oakland.

[III]

From the ranch the hills swelled rapidly upward until they reached the dignity of mountains, about two miles from the house. On the ridge of a range above our place was a small clearing, within which a modern bungalow, built under the direction of the owner, was surrounded by a small orchard of fruit-trees. Stately redwoods towered back of this cultivated area and wild animals paid frequent visits to the hen-house and vegetable patch. A person of mystery—Mr. Bruce lived up there, ministered to by an old Indian woman. The natives of the country spoke of Bruce in the tone reserved for great scandals, probably because he had come into their country without introduction, paid cash for his land and labor and preferred the solitude of his retreat to the garrulous gatherings about the general store. Conflicting conjectures as to who he was ranged from the guess that he was an absconding bank-cashier to the idea that he was a crazy inventor, or a man who had been disappointed in love.

I climbed the mountain several times and watched him as he sat on his porch reading or staring into space. He impressed me as being one whom I should like to know. One day, late in the afternoon, as I passed by his place on the descending trail to my uncle's house, I met him. He made as if to step aside, to allow me room to pass him on the narrow trail, when he noticed a book I held in my hand. His glance traveled from the book to the rifle in my other hand and then to my face.

His face was pale and his eyes were black. The contrast startled me. Taller than I by an inch or two, he had the forward-inclining shoulders of the advanced consumptive. But his voice, when he spoke, held a quality strangely misplaced in that frail body. The words were vibrant—I actually felt them enter my consciousness, as though they had form.

"Rather unusual book." He had read the upturned title. "Cervantes is not the usual author people read hereabouts." There was a trace of irony in his emphasis of the "hereabouts." His eyes lighted and the shadow of a smile played across his thin lips.

"He's rather good, though," I conceded, as if to justify bringing him "hereabouts."

"Yes, rather." His smile widened. "Have you read the other volumes?"

I had not completed the first one and was delighted when he offered to lend the other three to me.

With no questioning as to my parentage or place of residence, he led me to the house and I talked there with him for an hour. There was a calm acceptance of me as an individual worthy of attention that flattered me immensely. He told me of Cervantes's life in prison, of his escapes, of his loss of an arm and gave me a book of Hugo's essays on great men, which enhanced the value of the adventures of the Don a hundredfold.

While I walked down the mountain I pondered over this strange character. Intelligent, keen-minded, tolerant of my inquisitiveness, he maintained a dignity which I instantly respected and later learned to admire. But I did not tell my uncle of the meeting.

I had many talks with Bruce. Soon I had placed a confidence in his omniscience which enabled me to inquire into many phases of life that heretofore had been closed to me. With him for a guide I delved into subjects that I should have hesitated to mention even to my father. And always he answered me sincerely, sympathetically; and on the infrequent occasion when I probed too deeply in my search for hidden information, he would send me into his library for some book or encyclopedia and together we would find an explanation that I could comprehend. Often he smiled kindly at my questions and conclusions; a wan sort of smile, as though he had long ago traveled over the road I was walking along and knew the futility of the journey, yet was willing to aid me in the hope that I might find the goal life had hidden from him.

My adventure in West Oakland, my home life, my peculiar conception of the world I saw—and the world of my imagination—the prophecy of the chief of police—all these and more I told him about. He listened and commented upon them always, with an understanding that caused me almost to worship him. . . . The incident in the parlor with Miss Julia led him to enlighten me on the nature of a boy's development through the most trying period of his life.

"That first brief contact with a strange woman impressed you only because you had not been prepared for it," he said. "There is nothing weird or mysterious connected With it. Being a healthy young animal, you answered her emotionally. You could not have divorced your intellect from your body at that time and hence your response to the stimulus was that of a pagan. It is only by dint of severe self-discipline that one acquires control over natural desires. If one docs not exercise discipline, one is soon emotionally exhausted and is forced to turn to mental interests. Religion has been invented to promise all that society deprives one of here. But you will be far superior to that emotion if you understand it. Then and then only, can you enjoy it when you will and store it away when it would distract or harm you. . . But don't strive to enter into that relationship—allow it to assume only the minor part in your life to which it is entitled."

This was the prelude to other, more intimate lectures. Later he told me something that seared itself into my memory as with a white-hot stylus. I can even recall the age-old look of his eyes as he said: "Live clean! Nature has given you an exceptionally healthy body—don't soil it."

On another occasion we were seated on a log near an opening in the forest, the valley stretching out before us, the smoke from two tiny houses far below rising like thin, pale-blue ribbons into the evening air and Bruce commented on the chief's tirade against me.

"Crass ignorance. No mortal with a grain of intelligence would have directed your mind in such a channel. But," and again the slow smile, "you're not impelled to justify his word-pictures, are you?"

Often he ended statements with a question that required an expression of opinion from me. And he gauged his progress with the subject under way by the answer I gave.

There were days, particularly during the winter, when I would arrive at his home only to be met by the Indian woman and told I could not visit with Bruce. On those times I felt a keen sense of loss. He never referred to his illnesses, but each succeeding relapse was longer and when he had recovered sufficiently to permit his sitting out on the porch, I noted silently, but with inward pity, that his cheeks were more sunken, his lips tighter and his form more slender. Though always his eyes remained aglow, as though lighted from within by a dark light which had burned for centuries.

Death was so remote, so impossible of being conceived as having any relation to me, that I thought of it only for other people, persons whom I did not know; and so Bruce was "going to get better and be able to go fishing with me." So firmly was this fixed in my mind that I bluntly asked him his views on death. It was following a time when I had not been able to see him for almost two weeks.

"Death?" Bruce seemed to attach no special significance to the question. "Death—well—it is the opposite of birth. One is born, lives a few years and dies. It is a natural and inevitable experience."

"But after—?"

"After? That is debatable. It is an individual proposition. If you believe in an 'after,' then you can take that consolation for the happiness and joys you miss here. If you do not believe in an 'after,' then you may be agreeably surprised if there is one. The greatest artifice of the ecclesiastic imagination was the crediting of the soul with immortality. It was a necessary invention, for without it people would have learned to live naturally and the priests and popes and kings would not have been able to hold them in subjection. Once they had impregnated human thought with the belief in an immortal soul, it became an easy matter to control and direct; for if one questioned the truthfulness of that belief, one was an unbeliever and was put to death to convince him of his error. The lessons thus taught—and their numbers are legion—were effective because no one has ever returned to dispute them. But death itself is not to be feared. One religion, that of the Assassins, is predicated upon one's dying a violent death that one may the sooner enter the glorious voluptuousness of the promised 'after.' A greater mind than mine pondered over the question you have asked and his results have been translated into English by Fitzgerald. Read and re-read Omar's *Rubaiyat* and then ask yourself the question you've presented to me."

Dutifully I wrote down the title. "But doesn't the Bible explain about death and life hereafter?" A note of awe had crept into my voice. "There is so terribly much of it."

"The Bible, Ernest, in the version we have now, is the most beautifully written of books. But it is, at the best, but the compilations of centuries of rewritings and revisions and was first prepared from the fables and myths of the preceding centuries. Buddhism, the tales of the ancient Greeks, Romans, the Assyrians, Jews—all have been plagiarized and woven into the Christian Bible. The loveliest of Jewish women is favored by a white dove—the passionate Leda is visited by a swan. Centuries intervene, but how do they differ in essential significance? No—don't attempt to answer—later you will understand. I don't know how much Biblical reading you have accomplished, but when you again turn its pages, do so with a view to learning excellence of composition. For between the Canticle of Canticles and the Apocalypse there lies the range of human emotions. The first is the verbal portrayal of the heights of ecstasy—the other the darkness of horror and bottomless despair. Between, you will flounder in much that is to be treated as one always treats poetry. But I fear I confuse you. Accept those parts that your reason will permit and when a blind, unquestioning belief is required—well, be ever wary of anything or anyone who presents you with any formula which guarantees to cure all your ills or solve all your problems. A ready-made garment to protect you through life has never been made . . ."

A few minutes later I sensed that he desired to be alone and upon my rising to take leave he proffered his hand. I grasped it, though we had never shaken hands before and he looked deeply into my eyes. Returning my firm pressure, he spoke and there was an ominous note of finality in his words:

"You're going to make a mark in this world—great achievement or great tragedy. Watch yourself—you're growing up fast! . . . Good-bye." . . .

[IV]

Jake rode to the ranch late one afternoon. A fine figure, magnificently proportioned, his sleeves rolled almost to his shoulders, his hat hung on the saddle-horn, hair tousled and dark. About twenty years old—yet with a face scarred and lined as though from forty years of dissipation. There was considerable of the brute about his rough voice and powerful movements. I knew him only as the reckless son of Old Jake, the owner of a small homestead not far removed from my uncle's place. I walked over to where he and my uncle stood, engaged in conversation.

"Might as well start tonight," Uncle was saying.

"Yep. Can't get there too soon to suit me. How about the brat—is he going?" Jake indicated me and I flushed with resentment at the name.

"How about it—want to go out after deer with us?" Uncle asked.

"Deer! Why, I thought you said the season was closed."

Jake laughed and my dislike for him increased.

"Well—" my uncle paused. "Yes, it is—sorta. But it's like this. Those laws were made for city people—to keep 'em from coming up here and killing off all our game. With us it's different—we only kill to get meat to eat."

My uncle was known, in the parlance of the valley, as "an honest, upright, God-fearin' man," and I was surprised at his interpretation of the law. So there were two laws; one for "city people" and one for "us." That was my first real encounter with the fine distinctions of law-abiding citizens when some statute stood between them and their desires.

Of course I accompanied them on the hunt. Out from the thinned timber we followed into the virgin forest a trail which guided us to a small camping-place high in the mountains, about five miles distant from the ranch. The horses were tied to saplings. Night crept out from the roots of the trees and rose about us. Jake kindled a fire. The contrast of rosy light on dark bark and low-hanging redwood branches caught my fancy.

Jake and my uncle, working in quick, efficient manner, soon had coffee boiling over the fire and then drew scattered limbs and broken bits of trees to form a circle around us. I watched them and thrilled in a mild sense of adventure. This was the camp of brigands; we had eluded the authorities; we were safe in the fastness of the mountains; our plunder was safe in the bags and sacks that held food, pots and pans. The heightened interest this imaginary significance of sleeping in the open gave to the night was too much to contain. I wanted to share it. I voiced it to my uncle, within Jake's hearing.

"Brigands! What in the name of Nick has got into you? Do you mean that we're thieves? I'll tan you good if you say anything more like that." Uncle was not in sympathy with my little flight.

Jake grinned and entered the circle of light with heavy horse-play. Grabbing his gun, he struck a pose and shouted: "I'll not surrender unless you kill me. I'm king of the bad men. Gr-r-r! Is that the way they do it, brat?"

"You stop using that name!" I wanted to fight him, but at my approach he cuffed me aside. . . .

"Leave him alone, Jake," my uncle said.

I scarce heard the words. With the slap on the side of my head he had awakened a sudden, blinding madness. Unusually sensitive and even more so since my acquaintanceship with Bruce, this crass repulsion brought a flashing, insane desire to kill Jake. I was amazed at the force unleashed by this aroused temper, but within the instant I had snatched a rifle from its leaning position against a tree, drawn back the hammer, levelled the gun at his heart and pulled the trigger-release. . . . My back was to the light, while he stood in the flare from the fire. The movements with my hands were mechanical, my eyes were watching him; he still held his rifle in one enormous paw and convulsively jerked it backwards as the flame spurted from the end of my gun. The jar from the recoil of the thirty-two forty knocked the madness from me. I saw Jake half turn and loose his hold upon his rifle. Then he settled slowly to the ground and reclined on one elbow while he inspected the reddening fingers of his hand.

It happened so quickly that my uncle's shout of warning penetrated to my consciousness only after Jake was on the ground. Then realization of the tragedy and stark horror gripped me. I experienced a violent trembling, though still continuing to observe Jake as though I saw him enact the scene on a stage. It seemed to bear no relation to me. Coldblooded? Not that—but a curious detachment. One part of me was holding that rifle and shaking as in the grip of a tremendous ague; the other part of me—the part that had stood aside and watched this drama—was viewing the scene with unalterable gaze. Though I wished to do something, the desire was impotent to move me. I watched as my uncle sprang to his aid, inspected his side and rose with a sigh of relief at learning that the bullet had struck the stock of the rifle and had been deflected from entering Jake's body. Two fingers were torn and his hand and arm to the elbow were numb from the force of the impact.

I expected some punishment, but Jake interceded. Looking curiously at me, he announced: "He's got the temper of a wildcat."

Jake sterilized his fingers in a salt solution, then wrapped them in strips of torn shirting. My uncle lectured me on the use of guns; they were for one purpose only—to kill! I've never forgotten that. But I've also learned that a gun as an auxiliary to a simulated rage or temper seemingly about to be satisfied by the use of that gun will attain results with no necessity for killing.

I was sorry that Jake had been injured, ashamed of my act and soundly berated myself for it. He watched me closely during the following day—and let me severely alone. Although it had approached dangerously near to a fatal lesson, I had learned that respect and independence could be attained if I asserted myself. So, though I knew a great sympathy for him in my heart, I maintained a quiet reserve in my outward conduct, which must have spoiled what little pleasure remained for him in our hunting.

In speaking to my uncle he said: "It was my own fault. I called him 'brat' when I knew he didn't like it. I'm lucky he didn't plug me."

To my impressionable mind came: "Ah! If I don't want to get plugged, I must not annoy anyone!" I filed that thought in a cross-index mental file, so I could find it through either reference. . . .

Under cover of darkness we returned to the ranch. While Jake assisted my uncle in quartering and skinning the four deer we had killed, I got another glimpse of the mental operation of grown men in the matter of the applicability of the law. They were discussing a woman, the valley's "bad woman," who lived in a small cabin with her daughter, whose father was unknown.

"We ought to run her out of the country," Jake said. "She's an awful slut. Brown's boys is goin' down there pretty often. An' there's others, too. It's against the law in this country for a woman to act the way she does. Someone oughta do something about it."

My uncle agreed with Jake. "The way she dresses and cuts up is a caution. I hate to go near the store for mail when she's there."

I had seen Jane and her spindly daughter. Jane, so far as I was able to judge, dressed neatly, was always clean and carried herself with a pride that I had seen in few of the respectable women of the valley. Her coming to the General-Store-Post-Office-and-Stage-Stop was always an occasion for lowered voices, turned heads and covert glances. Through it all she moved with complete unconcern.

Her cabin was about a mile from the store and probably two hundred yards from the main road through the valley. It was considered an owlish bit of repartee when one of the natives would remark that he saw "so-and-so's rig down the road about a mile." That rigs stopped there during the evening was common knowledge. And since the population of the various ranches and farms and homesteads scattered over the valley would not exceed five hundred, she seemed, to me at least, to occupy a necessary position in the life of the country, though not a very enviable one.

[V]

A few days later I was at the store. I had ridden horseback to school and then stopped for some minor purchase on my return home. The afternoon was mild, but the day had been hot. While I sat on the porch, listening to the store-owner and an old, rawboned mountaineer debate the reasons for the sinking of the *Titanic,* Jane entered the store. The store-keeper continued his talk, although I was positive he had seen her. A few moments passed and yet he paid no attention. Drawn into the store by I knew not what force, I found her seated on a chair near the big, swollen stove.

"Hello, youngster," she said in an even voice. "Are you working here now?"

"No, I'm not—Jane." I was surprised at the ease with which her name fell from my lips. "But if there's anything I can get you, I'd be glad to." This was common practice. Often when the owner was not in the store, customers would help themselves and leave behind a note or the cash-payment on the counter.

"Thank you. That old fossil would let me sit here for an hour before he'd come in." Her face was half concealed by the large straw hat she wore, but her mouth was smiling. I noted with a curious thrill the tiny lines at the corners of her lips. What stories had written in those marks?

Her purchases were few and easy to get. She doubtless made them conform to the articles in sight, that I might not be confused in obtaining them. It was an adventure for me. It impressed me as making some sort of a gesture at the narrowness of the other inhabitants' prejudice against her. I was aware that the store-owner and his crony had stopped talking and were listening to what conversation passed between us. And I knew that a full and none too accurate account of it would be rendered to my uncle.

"You going to live here all the time, now?" She was adjusting the packages in her arms and I wondered at the smoothness of the white roundness above her elbows.

"No. Only for a while. How did you know I wasn't born here?" I asked, wanting to help her with the load she was piling up.

She lifted her head so that I could see her eyes and regarded me intently. In the sudden glance I found an answering response to the thought in my mind; we were only talking that we might longer remain there. But she prolonged the fencing with words.

"Oh, I knew you ever since you came here, almost two years ago. I know everybody here." She smiled with her eyes and I felt again that she had told me more than her words contained. "I know all about you shooting Jake. And I'm glad you did—he's a beast!" She had lowered her voice and finished in a whisper, which gave me a delightful feeling of intimacy. Her eyes had flashed a quick anger, but the return smile in them made me wonder if I had imagined the flash.

She knew of our hunting-trip! Uncle, Jake and I alone knew about that! Who had told her? I made a quick elimination and my inference rested upon Jake. But I wanted to be sure. Then the thought: he wanted her driven from the country! I experienced a mild disgust at his subterfuge: saying *that* to cover up his real actions and desires. I glanced away from Jane lest she read the emotion on my face and misinterpret it.

Adroit woman that she was, she turned from the counter as though to leave the store. Suddenly I did not want her to go. I wanted to talk to her, question her, ask her many things about the—yes, I was playing with the thought that I was old enough to be favored by her.

"You have a long walk home," I said hurriedly. "Can't I—that is, I mean—would you let me carry those things? I have a horse here—"

"Say, your uncle would have a fit!" She stood in the strong light from the door and her thin dress was almost transparent.

"Let him," I replied, not yet looking to her face. "What do I care?"

"All right," she said and raised her voice, "if you insist, you can carry these groceries for me."

We walked side by side and I touched her arm in helping her down the steps at the end of the porch. I could feel the gimletlike eyes of the two men on the bench boring in my back as we crossed to the shade of a few trees where the horse was tied. I unslung a small sack from the saddle and deposited her packages on the few I had already placed there.

"Get up and ride on ahead," she said. "I'll follow and it will be less dusty walking for me."

That was not in keeping with my plan. But I knew I was doing something that would create a mild sensation and I was rather confused. I hardly saw her as I swung into the saddle and trotted up the road to where it curved and was hidden from the store by a clump of high brush and small trees. There I waited until she arrived. In the free-swinging stride of an active woman she covered the distance from the curve to where I had dismounted beside the horse.

"I thought you'd wait. They're an awful pair of rubbernecks down at the store." She was close enough for me to discern tiny bits of moisture on either side of her nose. The rather too dark circles under her eyes contrasted sharply with the rouge of her cheeks. In the bright light of day the skin of her face showed coarse and a suggestion of a moustache tinged her upper lip. The lower lip drooped slightly, exposing small, even teeth. As I was studying her, she bit her upper lip and then moistened it with her tongue. A hundred conflicting thoughts clamored for expression, but I stood mute, hating myself for not being able to say anything—even the most commonplace banality.

"Let's get going," she offered, evidently sensing something of the situation I was fighting against.

I started to lead the horse, that I might walk at her side.

"Get up and ride, youngster. I don't mind walking."

"Would you rather ride?"

"How?—cross-saddle?" She smiled as at a secret amusement.

"I could sling that sack so you wouldn't have to." I was annoyed with these details of procedure. I wanted to discard them and get to the thought uppermost in my mind. A mere decision as to how to ride was of no importance.

Jane looked to see if anyone was in sight, then grabbed the reins and swung herself into the saddle. "Now come up and sit behind me—if you want to," she invited.

I did. To steady myself it was necessary that I hold on to her. Her warm, soft flesh beneath the thin covering of waist was agreeable to my fingers. I was thrilling in the wildness of our adventure—and hoping that we should meet no one on the road. Her stocking-encased legs were exposed above the knees and the two vividly red garters added the needed touch to my anticipation. I was not clearly settled upon what I was anticipating—but those two crimson elastics seemed the tongues of something fascinatingly evil.

Jane was enjoying herself. I believe that she took a delight in doing things that would cause her to be talked about. But that she was impervious to what was said was evinced by her bearing when facing a crowded porch of scandalmongers.

She chatted and leaned against me, once turned her head abruptly and inadvertently scraped my face with the rough edge of her hat brim.

"Oh, that's too bad!" She offered ready sympathy. "I'll tend to that—is it bleeding much?"

It was a mere reddening of the skin, but I wanted to enjoy the full flavor of her sympathy and I pressed a handkerchief to my face without answering her question.

Before passing through the gate that let into her place, it was necessary for me to dismount. Still holding the kerchief to my cheek, I swung open the battered rails, then followed her slowly to the cabin. Here we were met by the daughter. A girl of about ten, small and bearing no resemblance to her robust, buxom mother.

"Hazel, you get some sacks and get some pine-cones. I want about fifty of them," Jane directed. "Hurry up and get started—we haven't any wood in the house."

Hazel never gave a sign that she had heard, but vanished silently in the direction of the forest.

Together we entered the larger of the two rooms the cabin afforded. Jane went to the kitchen in search of water. I inspected the room and was impressed with the orderliness of the place. A large, double bed occupied one corner, a huge fireplace half filled one wall, the carpet on the floor was freshly brushed and the table offered a neat glass of flowers on a white center-piece. My uncle's living-room suffered in comparison. I hesitated to clutter this neat arrangement with the packages and continued to hold the sack in my hand. There was a freshness and fragrance about the room that heightened my already active sense of imminent adventure.

Jane appeared, hat discarded to reveal heavy, coiled, yellow hair. She carried a basin half-filled with water.

"Let me see where I burned you, youngster." She inspected the cheek and the touch of her fingers was as ice against my skin. I became suddenly aware that I was standing off at one side and watching this woman and a strange boy. The boy's face was flushed and his eyes avoided a clash with hers.

I wanted that boy to continue to follow out the urge which had brought him into that room with the woman. As I gazed at them, he took the basin from her hand and set it upon the table. He edged closer to her and slowly his left arm stole upward until it encircled her shoulders. She placed her hands gently on his cheeks, staring deeply into his eyes—eyes which were opened wide. She moved closer to him—so close that I could no longer see the light from the doorway between them. Then she laughed softly and kissed him full on the mouth. The boy's arm encompassed her waist and strained her to him. A long moment they stood thus. Gently she withdrew her lips and spoke softly:

"Why, youngster, I'm old enough to be your mother."

"No, no," he breathed, "no—you're not."

Hungrily he followed her mouth, but she restrained him by cupping his chin with her hand. With one eyelid half drawn down she regarded him quizzically.

"I like you for saying that," she said, "and I guess you're right. You're not so young as I thought at first. You look to be about—well—eighteen."

I was glad for the boy, because he was four years younger.

The woman continued to speak as she held his chin and stroked his hair. But she was not talking to him; she detailed his features as though she were thinking aloud and seeing him for the first time in the illumination of the moment.

"Taller than I am; dark hair and fair forehead; and his eyes—oh, he's been through this before.—But no, I guess not—still, he has old, old eyes! They don't belong in a round, ruddy face like his." Her voice quavered and she spoke directly to him: "You're Irish and Spanish—odd mixture, but I like you because you said what you did. And now—?" There was a faint note of challenge in the uncompleted words.

She released his chin, extended her arms and folded him to her breast. And I watched the episode with pleasure, for in her movement was the gesture of one who welcomes with the heart. It was like the embrace of some great divinity; I understood how she could welcome and embrace him in particular, yet seem to include scores of others at the same time. The boy raised his head, retained his hold about her waist; but I imagined he was about to release her. I strove to make him discard that notion. I was alive with curiosity and a recurrence of the strange, tingling sensation Julia had aroused in me. I wanted that boy to satisfy his curiosity, too. Through a new, weird-colored light I watched them. . . . The boy hadn't answered her—he seemed unable to draw her to him or yet relinquish his hold of her. He was wavering on the edge of a portentous decision and, summoning all the mental force I could command—I pushed him over the precipice. . . .

It was all so logical that he should know that swift descent and swifter rise. It was an experience that was eminently proper under the circumstances. Everything combined to make it a perfect transition. The fitting woman, the isolated cabin, the definite and final renunciation of his youth.

Seemingly hours later I joined that boy as he walked through the door. His eyes were filled with gratitude and wonder. Whatever mysterious accomplishment had been wrought was irrevocably his; I did not seek to inquire of him then and now I am unable to explain it. In silence we mounted the horse and in perfect understanding we rode slowly through the soft evening. . . . He had made an advancement, attained to a dazzling height he could never again surmount and was moody and silent as he tried to adjust this new factor into his scheme of things-as-they-should-have-been.

[VI]

Local option as to sale of liquor had made the valley technically "dry." Wine and "squirrel whisky" were plentiful and anyone who desired a drink—or a gallon—of an intoxicating concoction could have it with no great trouble. Against the law to own, possess, or transport liquor—yet passing friends would stop and openly offer or accept it.

"Dad" Dutro, a great, hairy-chested, bushy-mustached blacksmith, introduced me to the nectar of the gods. I met Bacchus in a pint tin cup. The day was swelteringly hot. The interior of the blacksmith's barn was cool. "Dad" was about to throw an old coot over the wicker-covered demijohn when I entered.

"Just in time, lad. White wine you seldom get. Bring the cup from atop that pail." He accepted me as a brother reveler with a hearty smile that did much to break down my uncertainty. I had never tasted wine, nor any other alcoholic drink. But it was another new experience.

The wine was acrid and seemed rough to my palate. It was as though I had attempted to wipe the interior of my throat with a coarse cloth. After draining the cup I thanked him and seated myself to listen to his scoffing at the people who attempted to "keep a man from enjoying himself." Sure, some old fogies had voted the country dry, but that didn't count when a fellow wanted a drink. It was natural for a man to do what he wanted—just so he didn't bother other folks. And what harm in drinking? How did it hurt? "Dad" was intolerant of "people as meddle in other folks' business."

A farmer came with work to be done. "Dad" busied himself. I was feeling contented and at peace with the world. The up-ended keg supporting me was comfortable and the day just pleasantly warm—then. The tiny red flames from the forge danced in the rising current of air from the bellows; one of them left the bed of coals and rose speedily to the roof. It was attached to no inflammable material—it just rose and hit the roof. Then it spread out and broke into small, crimson stars which drifted back to join the dancing circle of flame at the forge. Again a tongue of fire broke from the others and shattered against the roof. Again it descended in an umbrella-like shower of sparks. I thought of sky-rockets bursting and showering their explosions on the earth. Then faster and faster flames broke from the forge. I gazed at them—fascinated. "Dad" and the farmer continued to talk, but their voices were indistinct. Several times I started to call to them that they might be warned of the danger in which they stood. Each time I made the attempt, they appeared less in need of warning. Their unconcern irritated me. Couldn't they see the risk they were taking by standing in those descending sparks? Then, following the upheaval of an especially large and vivid flame, I shouted and pointed. They looked up quickly. "Dad" approached me and peered over his glasses at me. Suddenly he burst out laughing. In the face of horrible danger he laughed! I had saved him from certain burning and permanent disfigurement—and he roared his mirth. To laugh at horror is one way of disposing of it, but to me, at that time, it was distinctly unappreciative of my efforts.

He returned to the forge and I was aware that the farmer, too, was enjoying himself by looking at me and finding something unaccountably funny. "Ingratitude is the reward of the world," was the thought that impelled me to rise and walk from the shop. I could hear their harsh laughter following me as I turned from the door and continued down the road.

For some reason the sun had become aggressively hot during the half-hour I had spent in the smithy. The road shimmered with heat and tiny, snake-like spirals darted from the dust before me. I tried to avoid stepping on them and discovered myself walking near the fence on one side of the road. I crossed over, in a zigzag course and experienced a greater difficulty in not squashing them. For fifteen minutes I walked on, gingerly, as though treading between eggs.

Then a team caught up with me. The driver reined his horses to a stop and invited me to ride with him to the gate that marked the entrance to my uncle's home. I accepted his kindness, but gained the high seat only with great difficulty. Leaving it rather too precipitately when I parted with him, I landed on my side in the shade of a tree. First assuring himself that I was uninjured, he, too, laughed and drove on.

That shady spot was the place I had sought without knowing it. The stubby grass was an agreeable cushion. The spirals continued to dart from the dust, out in the sun, but they could not whirl in the shadow's. I conceived the brilliant idea of outwitting them and also avoiding the smashing of them, by remaining there until evening. I probably dozed—though I am certain I was not sleepy—and was wakened by the rumble and clatter of the four-horse stage as it passed me.

Returning to the blacksmith-shop, I found it closed and so I went over to the store to get the mail for my uncle. I recalled some of the incidents of the afternoon and wondered at the heat's affecting me so oddly. Musing over the affair, I decided that "Dad" had been over-generous to me—but a small doubt remained. I was unwilling to admit that a mere cup of wine could make me act so ridiculously. Curious to satisfy myself on the matter, I returned and drank another large cupful the following day.

I watched myself closer than on the preceding day—yet the flames did weird dances over the forge, the road was filled with heat-spirals and the fences moved in towards each other until the passage left was alarmingly narrow.

I consoled myself the following morning, while my uncle upbraided me for "coming home in that condition," by thinking that I had to come home some time and that after all it was an experience which had taught me the foolishness of giving my intelligence over to the irresponsible whims of wine. I was satisfied.

CHAPTER 3

[I]

The change from the environment of the ranch to the activity, bustle and increased interests of the city marked the beginning of a new phase of life for me. My family had separated. It was one of those too common tragedies that pass through courts under the guise of incompatibility. Dad was living in the business district; Mother had closed our home and was "keeping house" for myself and three brothers in a flat. Dad provided for the expenses and I was to continue at school. There was no explanation offered to me. Some strain of puritanism prohibited any of the relatives from mentioning the disruption of our home. And in response to queries, I received a mild admonition of "not to think about it." The most powerful single event that I'd ever known, the one factor that should have been explained to me, was sealed. My mind was too tender to understand. I was not old enough to be told why the adorable little woman who had brought me into being was forced to take her sons and set up a separate home. The evasions of my inquiries irritated me, but a vast sympathy for my smiling and quietly efficient mother prevented me from breaking through the barrier of her brave appearance. I could not ask her, though I framed long questions and held long conversations with myself; it was impossible to start even the first query from my lips.

My father was obviously glad to see me when I'd call at his office. He was then located in a long, narrow store on Telegraph Avenue. A real-estate office ostensibly, but it was sub-let or desk room until it held an assortment of enterprises ranging from an express office to the editorial room of a weekly political paper. Into this maelstrom I was projected. Often I sat listening to the discussions of small realty agents, salesmen for some patented device, political hangers-on, women who cleaned and prepared houses that had been rented, stenographers and nondescripts who appeared to exist on the small "loans" they were able to extract from whoever would trust them. Customers and clients were escorted to the various desks ranged along the walls with an elaborate ceremony. It amused me to see an agent discard his sloppy attitude and speech, to assume the worried air of a harassed executive, when he would sight the approach of a client.

Insurance agents were plentiful and the notary-public signs were thick as circus posters on a billboard. Everyone seemed to have a big deal pending. They all lied to each other about the business they were conducting and the tremendous volume of business they had to attend to, yet they seemed to have time to talk for an hour or two or the whole day, if listeners remained.

There was one large, impressive gentleman who came often to that office. Frequently my father was away, occupied with his affairs and I cultivated this man. Within the first ten minutes of the initial conversation I held with him he told me that he had been mayor of the city some fourteen years before. My respect increased, though I sensed a false note in his telling me of his former position. It seemed too much like a kid who had knocked a home-run at some time in the past and was fearful that full credit would not be given to him. This ex-mayor was to me the great attraction of the office. He gave it a much-needed tone. I often watched him dispose of the city's problems with a wave of his fat hand. Then he would stroke his vast, rat-tailed moustache and proceed to explain how he would force the street-car company to do this or that.

Frequently I found *Saturday Evening Posts* on the desks. It gave a tremendous amount of paper for the expenditure of a nickel and reading it was considered a mark of culture. I often looked through it. Buried between pages of advertisements I once found a story that dealt with a certain Get-Rich-Quick Wallingford. The first illustration caught my eye—it was my ex-mayor! Even to the red carnation on the lapel of his too well-brushed coat.

Then I built about him and credited to him, schemes similar to those of Wallingford. I even regretted that I was too young to grow a full, dark moustache and play opposite him as Blackie Daw. I would observe his actions, mentally comparing them with those of the fictional character. He did not suffer by the comparison—rather, his manners impressed me as being more suave—and when he elected to grow ponderous in his talk—which was often—I could almost see him in the role of the master "bringer of cheer" to the benighted back-country people.

It afforded me no small thrill to know a mayor. Even an ex-mayor was better than no mayor at all. The man who had held the highest office the city could bestow sat and talked with me or allowed me to drink from the fountain of his wisdom. I wished that his coat were not so shiny at the elbows and that at least once he would wax generous and invite the whole hungry crew that sat about him to dinner, or that he would bring a box of cigars and genially invite everyone present to help himself. Instead he continued to wear the same coat and at times his trousers were not so sharply creased as they should have been. He was ever ready to accept an invitation to luncheon, or even to drink at the saloon on the corner, where he would nibble at free lunch. And he seldom left the office unless he paid a visit to my father's desk and extracted a pocketful of cigars from a certain drawer that appeared to hold them for his exclusive benefit.

Yet he was pleasant and condescending and I learned from him how little the ordinances and city laws really amounted to when they were contrary to the desires of "one of the crowd." He told me of how certain judges would readily dismiss minor cases against some of his friends, by his merely speaking to them about it. The next day he delivered an involved discussion on the inviolability of the law. It strengthened the impression my uncle's hunting deer illegally had made and the conclusion I formed was that laws were necessary only to curb some collection of people, as yet undefined, when they wanted to do something contrary to the wishes of "the crowd." Borne in upon me was the conviction that I should be superior to laws if I "belonged." To further that end and as a sort of initiation, I invited my mayor to luncheon one day. My father was generous in his allowance and I had about fifteen dollars in my pocket. I reasoned that a man the size of the mayor—I was then addressing him as "Your Honor"—would eat a great quantity and I wanted to make sure I could pay the bill. I suggested the finest restaurant in the city, knowing that the owner was a friend of my father's and that if my cash would not cover the cost of the entertainment, I could explain to him and be saved the embarrassment of requesting His Honor to make up the difference.

He accepted my invitation with a regal condescension. I sensed that I was being Honored. I regretted that I had not an automobile to convey us over the intervening five blocks to the restaurant. But when I suggested a street car, he said he would rather walk—it would serve to sharpen his appetite. I fingered the crumpled bills in my pocket and sighed. But the fleeting apprehension was lost in the pleasure I derived from walking with so great a personage. He nodded and spoke to numerous people in passing, once pausing long enough to shake the hand of a city employee, to whom he introduced me.

I was nervous, but tried to cover my feelings by assuming a careless attitude as we were led to a table which the mayor indicated. The waiter was not so obsequious as I would have had him be towards my guest, but I told myself that this was only because he was in ignorance of the personage's identity. . . . During the meal His Honor turned frequently, caught the eyes of various diners and smiled or nodded to them. I was enjoying myself immensely and was loath to leave when the repast was completed. It was with relief that I learned my "initiation" would cost me less than six dollars. As we drank our final coffee, he pointed out to me the guests of importance. There was a judge of the Superior Court. Next to him, with the large diamond stud and iron-gray hair, was the editor of the city's leading daily paper. And the woman half-turned from us—the one with the large picture-hat and rather too tightly fitting dress—had recently been involved in a divorce scandal. He presumed I had heard of it and I nodded agreement, though I had not the least idea of who she might be. A man and woman stopped by our table as they were leaving the place. Immediately the mayor and I rose. He introduced them and I was greatly flattered.

Leisurely we strolled from the restaurant and a feeling of being "one of the crowd" was mine. . . .

Again in the office, His Honor accepted a seat among his usual friends and I went to my father and told him of the privilege I had known.

"Took the old mayor to dinner, did you?" He turned to his stenographer and smiled. "Well, well, where did you go?"

I named the restaurant and added that he should have the owner speak to the waiter, who had seemed to lack respect for my guest.

My father laughed. "You've a lot to learn. That waiter probably knows more about the old windbag than you'll ever know. But at least His Excellency had a full meal for once. That's splendid, though." And again he laughed. I was uncomfortable under his conflicting statements.

"Didn't you know that His Eminence sells hams and bacons to the restaurants about town? That is, he does when he can spur himself to walk as far as their kitchens. Why, the old fraud hasn't done a thing since he has been out of office except sponge off his Republican friends. And he's living out at the Y.M.C.A.

now—and you've dined him in a manner fit lor a king. What are you trying to do—get him to help you steal some franchise from the city? He couldn't get a dog out of the pound now."

I was hurt—tricked. Another idol crashed and lay in ruins to mingle its dust with that of the King of Tramps.

My father disillusioned me further and then said, as though it was of no consequence: "We'll probably run him for mayor again this coming election. That's why we're taking care of him now. And he'll probably be elected, too. We can beat the present incumbent with a goat. The people are tired of his name and your Wallingford mayor will come in on a vote that'll be cast for him—not because of any merits *he* possesses, but because it will represent a protest against the mayor now in office."

That my father's prophecy was fulfilled did nothing to restore my faith in mayors. I discarded respect for all forms of authority after that and when anyone spoke of Civic Duty, or High Purpose of Public Office, or the Sterling Qualities of some Candidate for Office, I was suspicious of his sincerity.

I missed the tranquility of the country. There was nothing of its freshness and fragrance in the city streets. I missed the long talks with Bruce. The increased *tempo* of the city excited a craving which had but awaited this time to flare forth with undeniable demand for action. This combined with the excess of animal spirit generated by my healthy body. Soon I was seeking an outlet for this excess energy, this surcharge of exuberance. With a mind so keenly alive to all impulses and so ready to respond to any whim or fancy.—without the restraint of any moral conviction and devoid of any sense of obligation or responsibility—I embraced the many opportunities my freedom offered. Embraced them, but in the manner of an inquiring student rather than haphazardly.

School-studies occupied a meagre portion of my time. I was free most of the afternoons and evenings. Though my mother remonstrated with me about remaining downtown until late in the night, the fascination of watching people in crowds, attending shows and learning to play pool and billiards prevailed.

The girls at the school and even the boys in my classes, seemed unforgivably juvenile. I sought companions among the chaps several years my senior. I had not been able to locate Buddy. I had tried to trace him, but his family had moved. I tried to interest myself in athletics and found that only football would hold me. The mad, insane joy of crashing against another boy, or fighting through a broken field to gain an additional yard, supplied a thrill somewhat beyond words to describe. The sense of success hardly secured, the utter exhaustion that followed victory, or the unaccountable depression following on the heels of defeat—all were precious to me. But football season filled only the fall months.

My experience with Jane had satisfied my curiosity—for the time being. I divided girls and women sharply into two classes. If a girl was respectable and conducted herself according to the prescribed standards, she was worthy of respect and she was "square." Otherwise she was "kinky." I've forgotten where I first acquired those definitions, but they have remained with me for years. Experience and a broader understanding have enabled me to transcend those limitations. But, at that time, according to my classification, girls were either "square," or "kinky."

[II]

Red and I gravitated naturally to each other. He was then a few years older than I, but I knew myself to be his mental superior. He was an inch or two taller than I, but of a more slender build. Of Irish parentage, he had the high color of his race, a fine, firm chin and straight, thin-lipped mouth. One eye was disfigured by a cast and when he grew angry, this eye seemed to grow abnormally large. Confident in manner and slow of speech, he possessed the ability of indicating his thoughts with a minimum of action and words.

Standing on the curb opposite the entrance of a poolroom on Broadway was a favorite pastime. Commenting on the passing individuals. "Snide" remarks and obscene conclusions were exchanged between Red and me.

"She looks like a woman I knew up-country," I offered, desirous of showing my worldliness.

"Sloppy—too fat an' old." Red dismissed her.

"But how about this girl with the furs coming now?" I asked.

"Works at the dago shooting-gallery—chippy." Red spat as though to rid his mouth of a bad taste.

"Look, here's that little blonde again. She went up the street less than five minutes ago." I indicated a neatly dressed girl about eighteen years old.

"Yeah, she's by here lots. Works in the candy-store. Gives you a smile when you buy something, but won't give you a tumble on the street."

The driver of a "For Rent" car, parked near us, strolled over. A shifty, squinty pair of eyes, separated by a prominent, sharp nose, showed from beneath the visor of his cap. Round-shouldered and stooping in his walk, he looked like a pallid bird of prey.

"How's it? Got a snipe?" His voice was disagreeably oily. Red gave him a cigarette.

"Trying to pick up some broads?" He leered at me.

"What's it to you?" I resented his intrusion.

"Nothin'—only I could square it for you. Keen skirt, too." He observed us closely. This was the first time he had spoken to us, though he must have seen us several times on this same street. "I can run you down to her hotel in a minute—wanna go?"

I could visualize no "broad" who would have this person pimping for her other than a scrawny duplicate of him. The picture was not attractive. While I mused over the situation and debated the advisability of again entering into a relationship that Bruce had told me not to hurry into, Red made the decision for us.

"What do you think we are—a couple of chumps? We should be giving you dough for what we can get ourselves. Mope! Screw! G'wan—I'll bust you in the mouth!" Red turned his bad eye upon the chauffeur and raised a hand as though to put the threat into action. The driver retreated.

"He's an awful harmless ding," Red said. "He can't steal because he ain't got the guts and he just gets by with that car and his bum broad."

I had been studying Red's actions and words. I was interested in his certain and positive knowledge. There was nothing that I had mentioned but what he had immediately classified and then seemingly applied some formula to, which gave him a satisfactory result. Dago shooting-gallery girl, chippy! Shifty taxi-driver, ding! They fell into their respective classes, fell hard and irrevocably. I wanted to acquire that trait and really studied Red's manners, tone of voice, expressions and tried to make one of my eyes open with the same formidable glare as his. It gave me the feeling of being a different person when I partly succeeded.

The street at this hour was vibrant with the first evening theatre-crowd. The color of conflicting shades blended in the soft, yellow light from the store windows. Clanging cars dinned raucously behind us, or screamed to a stop at the corner. From a movie palace came tortured snatches of the *"Merry Widow* Waltz." I drank in everything. It seemed that I thirsted for this pageantry of color and answered the call of the city with some part of me which had not yet been fully aroused. Still I remained standing on the curb, an observing and critically inquiring spectator. I was glad to be there—but I felt removed from the crowd. Red suggested that we go upstairs to the poolroom and "shoot a few games."

There I met other boys and young men and was accepted as one of the regular habitués. No one indicated that he did not believe me to be the necessary eighteen years of age to remain in the place. The attempts they made to amuse themselves impressed me so being unnecessarily serious. Small-ambitioned thieves and petty sharks abounded. Red steered me clear of most of them and I was grateful to him; and yet I could not work up the interest that he and others displayed over the games. It was the characteristics of the players that I wished to observe. I credited many attributes to those fellows that they could never have possessed. I suffered constantly from disillusionments. I picked out—for observation—a chunky man of perhaps twenty-five. His face was bovine and his brow swelled forward over his eyes. On one cheek was a livid and ugly scar, extending from his ear to the edge of his mouth. Probably a thief of importance—at least a "yeggman." I noticed that most of the other fellows avoided him. He walked with a swinging of his shoulders that seemed to denote tremendous strength. Having made the circle of the room, he stood near where we were playing. Little bulges of muscle rose and fell beneath the skin at the angle of his jawbone and I held the fantastic notion that he sought someone—with no good purpose in mind should he meet that person.

Red stood back from the table, awaiting his turn to play. My "yegg" approached and spoke quietly to him. Turning slowly about, Red faced him and stared disgustedly from the bovine face to the heavy shoes and back to the face.

"No—I don't care if you didn't eat for a week."

I was closer when the panhandler replied: "Aw, please. Jus' a thin dime or two. Christ! I'm hungry enough to scoff the layout."

Glancing quickly about to see if any of the attendants were looking his way, Red jabbed the "yegg" swiftly and effectively on the jaw. He staggered back, rubbing the injured spot and whining: "Aw, don't—lemme alone." Then he hurried to the stairs and went out.

"Them damn hypos give me a pain," Red commented and resumed the game.

Later I questioned him about "hypos." I learned that, contrary to my belief, the men addicted to morphine are not always thin and pale. That a great many of them are healthy in appearance and continue so until many years of jail confinement and under-nourishment have lessened their resistance to the inroads of the drugs, is a fact well established. I hold no brief for the use of drugs—but it does help a man to "do his bit" in prison and lessen the length of his journey to oblivion.

Other players were also exposed, proving to be far different individuals from what I had pictured them. I learned that I should not judge a man until after I had heard him speak and in this I found some strange contradictions. A boy who seemed not more than fifteen and whom I had pictured as being able to come into the poolroom because of the attendant's laxity, proved, upon acquaintance, to be a man almost twenty-five and with a record in police circles that included one reform-school term and a year in San Quentin. Fred, this boy, was slight of build and innocent in guise. He dressed neatly and expensively and on later occasions I would often fail to notice his presence in the poolroom, so unobtrusive was his manner of walking and conducting himself.

This Fred, Red and I soon formed a trio. Fred was surprisingly well-informed on the activities of thieves. He held forth on the various trials and convictions of men and escapes from jails and prisons, with a keen appreciation of what the men had to contend with. If a certain burglar, whom he named, had only engaged the attorney Fred suggested, that burglar would not have been convicted and Fred would not have had to carry hacksaw-blades to the county jail to aid the former's escape. And Fred was rather disgusted that the burglar had not met him, according to their agreement before the escape. He was an instructive chap and although he always understood Red when the latter spoke in slang, Fred elected to use good English—as he knew it.

"One of the worst marks a fellow can have on him is a lot of slang terms," he explained to me a few days after our initial meeting. "You have to watch yourself all the time. Suppose that you are being questioned by some smart detective and make one slip. Instead of using the best language you can, you complete your denial of being guilty and knowing anything of the crime by adding: 'It's a bum rap.' Then you might as well begin phoning for a lawyer, because you're going to stand trial for that charge. Watch yourself. It's all right to understand a lot of the guff that passes for conversation—but don't make a practice of speaking in those terms. Sometimes, though, when you're with some thieves—good ambitious men, too—you have to use their language so they won't think you're trying to high-tone them. I met some men while I was across the Bay, who knew that I was born a hoodlum and yet they looked at me with suspicion when I spoke good English to them."

Another time he told me: "Never make a flashy appearance. A lot of these men here will steal enough to buy a silk shirt and a gold watch and chain and right away they want to get a big, yellow, twenty-dollar gold piece and suspend it from the chain. No one but a cheap gambler or a 'mack' does that. But you don't have to worry. You don't look like a thief—and you know how to dress, but you should tell Red not to do so much posing with you in front of this place. The city detectives are always walking by and they become familiar with your face. Then something happens and they get a scrambled description and immediately try to fit it to you. I wouldn't come up here as often as I do except that I'm trying to find a friend of mine who just came out to the Coast."

His calm acceptance of me as a thief, his suggestion that I prompt Red on his conduct and his advice on dress were all interesting to me. They opened a door to a strange world wherein moved strange and attractive characters. Under his guidance I learned to recognize the undercurrent that flowed beneath the surface of the poolroom. I had sensed it before, read of it, but had never been able to plumb it.

[III]

One evening soon after, the three of us were walking along Seventh Street towards Washington Street. Opposite the entrance of a pawnshop Fred paused. Red and I hesitated and then followed his gaze into the window. A great display of tools, guns, clothing, violins, trinkets, trays of watches and other evidences of individual hard luck rewarded our inspection. But it was towards the guns that Fred directed our attention.

"We should get a couple of them," he said. "If we're going to get started, we might as well prepare ourselves. Look at that large, nickeled six-shooter with the staple driven into the butt. Some wild man owned that at some time—you can see cowboy written all over it. A vicious-looking gun like that will help a lot. Shall we get it?"

Recalling my experience with Jake and my uncle's definition of a gun, I temporized. "How much will it cost?"

"We'll find out." Fred preceded us into the shop. The gun was laid upon the counter for our inspection. Uncle Ben explained at great length on the merit of the weapon, even offered to supply us with a load of cartridges. There was not one question about what we intended to use it for. Several more revolvers were exhibited and I was attracted to a smaller but equally efficient gun. Testing the spring by snapping the trigger gave me a sense of mastery and superiority. I also felt a restraint tugging at my desire to own it, but I compromised by telling myself that the gun would come in handy if I should go to the country again.

We bought three revolvers, accepted the Jew's cartridges and gained the street just as a local train stopped to disgorge its passengers from San Francisco. "Let's go to Fruitvale on this train and try these out," I suggested.

Swinging aboard, we traveled in separate seats to our destination. By walking a few blocks we were in the foot-hills and soon we exhausted our supply of ammunition. It was the work of only a few minutes to repair to a hardware-store and buy fresh cartridges.

Things were moving too rapidly to suit me. I would not withdraw from the others, but I was aware that before the night was over, we should have committed some crime. I was not sure that I wanted to start that night. While I had thrilled to the various accounts of crimes I had heard recounted, or read about, it was a different thing when I faced the immediate prospect of being an active party to the offence. I do not think that there was anything of fear entering into my hesitancy. It was just the same, curious twisting of realities into dream-stuffs. I could visualize a robbery or burglary, but only when some other persons consummated it. I could not see myself actually engaged in it.

Then an odd—and to me strangely opportune—incident occurred. As we stood grouped on a street corner, a man and woman drove up in a high, swaybacked automobile. They left the machine and entered a drug-store near by. Through a window we could see them seated at a counter while the clerk prepared drinks for them.

"Let's borrow that car," I suggested. "I can operate it—the old man's got one just like it. Let's take it for a while." I did not consider borrowing a car as anything more than a lark. And it would serve to prevent any action that night; also, it would allow me time to decide to what extent I would permit myself to progress.

"Suits me—if you can get it started, we'll climb in," Red said.

A self-starter was a luxury then unknown to car-owners. I set the spark and throttle levers and in my haste I advanced them too far. The second twirl of the crank awoke the engine to life with a roar that should have aroused the neighborhood. Scrambling hastily over the side and into the driver's seat, I had just started the car from the curb when its owner rushed frantically from the store. Fred and Red produced their guns and threatened him with death if he did not stop. He did. And with the engine racing madly, we careened down the street at the terrific speed of thirty miles an hour.

We laughed and joked as I guided the machine through East Oakland and around the head of Lake Merritt. There was a picnic joviality about the three of us. It was a great lark! The chagrin and amazement of the owner was portrayed for me and with each telling it grew more humorous—to us. We had no definite destination, but I continued to drive out towards Berkeley, weaving our course so as best to avoid cross-streets.

Some of our high spirits had left us when we reached the edge of the campus at the University. The gates were open and on to the grounds we drove. Lights showed in some of the buildings—others were dark. There were lights on the roads of the premises only at irregular distances. At intervals couples walked about. Several times we passed other cars.

Suddenly Fred spoke. "Let's stop and hold up someone here!"

I slowed to a stop, but allowed the engine to idle.

Red was agreeable. Any dissension on my part was not anticipated and quickly the simple parts we were to play were assigned. Fred directed it, after remarking that this would be a better way than being afoot: we should be more sure of getting away.

"You stay with the car, ready to drive when we finish. Red and I will get out and stop the next man that comes along. Soon as we get what he's got, we'll jump in the car—and you can drive like hell away." Fred had lowered his voice and in the darkness of the road the proposed plan assumed the proportion of a gigantic feat.

We waited several minutes. Since our lark had turned into the more serious business of highway robbery, I felt a hundred noises creep out of the night. Over the engine's rumbling I could distinctly hear the footsteps of some approaching couple. My head was whirling—I gripped the steering-wheel and clenched my teeth. I tried to see the faces of Red and Fred and though they were but dim white blurs, I could sense that they too were not so nonchalant as they would have liked me to believe. If an honest opinion had been expressed by us at that moment, I am sure we should have declared ourselves in favor of renouncing the plan and continuing our ride. It was the ancient herd-instinct that buoyed us up; forced us to continue although we separately did not wish to. Fear of criticism from each other, rather than daring or willingness, held us to the declared intention of committing robbery.

The two approaching proved to be young men—students, no doubt. Red opened the side door and stepped out to meet them with a request for a match. As one of them reached into his pocket to oblige, I heard Fred's voice and strangely pitched it came to my car.

"Hold up your hands—we're going to rob you."

One of the intended victims laughed. The other snickered.

"Tomorrow night is initiation, fellows. Starting rather soon, aren't you?" They advanced a step towards Red.

"Do as you're told—or you'll get killed," snarled Fred. And his anger at the trick his voice had played him was apparent in the words.

The two victims must have complied. I was moistening my lips and trying to keep my eyes from blinking rapidly—and I could follow no more details of the robbery. There were a few telltale sounds: rustling papers, muttered protests, feet scraping on the pavement—and then Fred shouted in my ear: "Get started!" I did—and the most fervent Christian never fled from the path of the devil with more speed than that which I forced out of that car.

Keyed to a high pitch, I was unable to fall asleep for hours after we divided the loot, abandoned the car and separated with promises to meet on the next afternoon. I had expended one-third of my share of the loot in street-car fare and received the biggest thrill of my life!

CHAPTER 4

[I]

Reading of the robbery the next afternoon, I seemed not to be concerned in it. In cold, black news-print there was nothing of the thrill it had afforded me while actually participating. Written in the approved style, the account depicted the robbers as experienced men. That an automobile had been used called for additional comment. That robbery on the campus was probably the first time a machine had been used in Oakland for that purpose. Soon after that there was a deluge of "jitney-bus bandits" in operation.

One of the students was a scion of a wealthy family and I wondered why one whose parents possessed so much money should yield up less than fifty cents. . . . But I knew the thrill of robbery. And having experienced it, I was not anxious to repeat it. That we got so little money did not matter—to me, at least. I had become an accepted thief and the feeling of *camaraderie* it gave was agreeable.

But Red and Fred deplored our "hard luck." They were anxious to go out on another expedition. I can understand their point of view now. Then it impressed me as being hoggish. I saw the affair in the colored light of the emotion it aroused in me; they saw it in the gray light of necessity. They had room-rent to pay and food and clothes to buy; I had not considered those things of any consequence. My room at home was ready to receive me when I chose to go to it; that I did so only after I had no other place to go to was of no importance—the room was still there. Food was always ready and awaiting me at the regular hours, or I could dine with my father, downtown. And clothing—well, clothing was obtained by going to a certain store and picking out a suit and whatever other things I wanted and then signing a sales-slip that debited the total to my father's account. That my room would ever be closed to me, or that food would not be ready, or that clothing would be refused upon my request never entered my calculations. Those things had always been—why should they change? Particularly, why should they change when they fitted into my conception of how things should be?

[II]

Within a few months the tinsel had worn off the attractions offered by the poolroom. I saw it for the shoddy place it was. I could and did, sharply differentiate between players and "hypos" and petty thieves. At greater intervals some flashy thief would appear and be talked about for several days, only to fade into the unknown whence he had come. Red, Fred and I were together often, but I was not included in any of their burglaries or robberies. Frequently I visited with them in their rooms and discussed places to steal from, but they were an efficient pair and a third—particularly one who did not care about the amount obtained—was rather a hindrance.

I sought to calm the growing restlessness within me by reading and remaining home for a few evenings. But while my eyes followed the lines of a page, my mind would be toying with some fantastic adventure. All too regularly I read whole chapters and could not recall even the general theme of the story.

By chance I glanced over a book containing the deeds of Raffles. Here was a gentleman-burglar who combined faultless dress and polished manners with an amazing degree of cleverness. He would visit a house, strip it of its valuables and if interrupted, politely but effectively subdue the intruder—and leave with a pleasant comment on the excellence of the evening. Splendid!

With Red informed of my desire to accompany him on a burglary, he welcomed my company soon after that. We walked down to the shore of Lake Merritt and followed its edge until we were almost into Piedmont. The houses in that district were large and usually had ample grounds about them. Flower-beds and shrubbery offered plenty of protection to cover our approach. Together we crawled into one yard and crouched near a lighted window. We could see the family seated about a dining-table and a serving-maid moving from place to place.

"We'll try to make it in through one of the windows on the other side," Red explained. "Usually when they are eating, there is no one upstairs. But if you'd rather, we'll try a sneak through the front door."

I had ideas of how I wanted to enter. Second-story work and active climbing about ledges was the scene that I held. To walk in the front door was taking a too mean advantage. The damp grass had wet my hands as we approached and I clenched them tightly—I can't explain why, but it seemed to slow down some generative force within me.

"Suppose the door is locked?" I asked.

"Probably won't be—they usually leave them open," Red softly answered, "and if it ain't, we can go upstairs and prowl through every room."

"And if someone comes—?"

"That's what we got our guns for. Let's give it a try."

We did and the door yielded easily. Stepping into the lighted hall and feeling the warm air on my cheek gave me a mild shock. Odd—how stories had never described this and the queer feeling that coursed through me. Movement in the direction of the dining-room, farther along the hall, reached us; first in a low, cadenced murmur, then as a faint tinkle, as of glasses and plates. A door creaked lightly. I was keenly alive to every movement and even registered Red's breathing as we crossed on tiptoes to the staircase.

Catching a passing glimpse of myself in the round mirror of the hall rack, I started up and squared myself to fight—only to realize my mistake. Red grinned. We walked near the edge of the stairs and to this day I can recall the huge, turned balusters that flanked that ascent. There was a faint layer of dust on the uppermost rung of their bulging sides. I rubbed a finger on one of them and it left a long streak.

An electric globe lighted the hall of the second floor. One door was open and the carpet in the room extended out to join the strip on which we were walking. Posting me at the doorway, Red entered and I could hear him pulling drawers from dressers and bureaus. I was acutely attuned to the faint noises emanating from the floor below—heard Red's movements—and yet caught the sound of a passing machine in the street. I felt as though I were an unusually sensitive magnet and all disturbances were drawn to me. The most minute sounds magnified themselves and reached me with a force that caused me to sway from side to side like a reed blown in conflicting winds.

Something clattered to the floor within the room. Red cursed and rejoined me at the door. "Watch the stairs—see if they heard it," he whispered.

The noise, in the anguished stillness, had sounded like the collapse of one of the four walls. A door opened and someone walked rapidly to the front of the house. She paused at the base of the staircase, then started up with quick, light steps. I caught a flash of white dress and dark head before Red pulled me into the room.

The girl's ascent of those steps seemed terrifyingly long. In my imagination I could see them stretching down an incredible distance from where I had stood—then dropping away into a deep gorge—and as she climbed, they lengthened as though they were part of an escalator. She was walking up them, but seemed never to come nearer; marking time, as it were, with the movement of the steps on the endless belt. I was gripping Red's arm with one hand. I wanted to remove the hand, but it remained of its own volition and despite my desire to pull it away. As the sound of her footsteps grew louder with her approach, Red whispered: "Hold your breath till she goes by." We were concealed behind the door, Red may have held his breath—I swallowed mine.

She proceeded down the hall and entered a room, busied herself for a few moments and emerged presently, carrying a coat and humming softly—the *"Merry Widow* Waltz"! Passing within a few feet of us, I peered through the crack between the door and the hinge-post and caught sight of her face for a fleeting instant as she paused before descending the stairs. Occupied with her thoughts and unaware of the scrutiny to which she was subjected, there was a placid wistfulness in her expression that brought me a quick flush of shame. Some mysterious force passed between us and she abruptly stopped humming, glanced from large, startled eyes over her shoulder and then with a toss of her head to dispel the momentary alarm turned to the stairs. A trace of a smile appeared for an instant and she vanished from my sight.

"Let's get this over, Red." A distaste for continuing further with the burglary of this particular home filled me. Red misunderstood me and thought my desire for haste was prompted by a loss of nerve.

"Take that room and I'll skin through the next one. Leave the door open, but work fast! Look in the drawers and under the lid of anything setting on the tops. Hurry"

The room I was to investigate was the one from which the girl had come. Her face haunted me—stood before me as I crossed the threshold—and I should have felt no amazement had she materialized in the instant I stood there, so vividly had her features registered in my mind. Faint, elusive, tantalizing, her presence remained. I have never forgotten the peculiar scent that struck my nostrils. A perfume I cannot name. But once years later I encountered it and in a flash I was transported to that room, where I stood in a whirlwind of indecision. To touch anything belonging to the girl would have been a sacrilege. It was one thing mentally to prowl through a house and steal from phantoms who inhabited the various rooms, but to see the owner of the jewelry or cash I was wanting to take—that was another matter, I waited a few moments, then left the room and entered another, larger bedroom. There the strong, acrid odor of tobacco fumes bespoke masculine occupancy and offset—for the nonce—the indecision and as if to make up for my negligence or impotence in the girl's room, I tore open all the drawers and rifled them without a qualm. There was no money, but I found a watch and a broken signet-ring. Hastily I searched through the pockets of the clothing in the closet and discovered a few pieces of silver.

Red rejoined me and I displayed my loot. "One more room," he decided. "We'll make it together."

With a speed I had not suspected him of possessing he had soon worked his way through possible hiding-places. There was little of value. He took a manicure set and a few other trinkets of feminine adornment. I was amused, for I knew that they would bring but a few cents when he offered them for sale. I did not know, then, that Red made presents of those things to the "girls" in Sixth Street houses in exchange for their favors.

There was no unusual activity on the main floor to disturb our descent, but as we reached the foot of the stairs, a door opened and there was a burst of voices. The family had come from the dining-room and as they saw us, a sudden hush fell upon them. Red bounded to the front door, flung it violently open and leaped across the porch. I followed close behind, almost landing upon him after vaulting the railing. The clamor of the hue and cry rent the wake of our retreat. Gaining the street, I glanced back and saw figures moving excitedly on the porch. Then a shrill, wavering blast from a police whistle sounded. In the darkness it impressed me as being uncomfortably near.

Sprinting, I caught up with Red at the intersection; together we made the turn and continued at top speed in the next block. I had prided myself on my ability to run and I was surprised that Red could sustain the speed with which we were traveling. He was breathing easily and after a few blocks we slowed to a trot and upon reaching a lighted avenue assumed a natural gait. We boarded a street car and were soon in his room in a cheap hotel. There he explained some of his beliefs about "keeping fit."

"You have to keep your wind in this racket. Now if we was a couple of hypos, we'd a dropped dead before we went a block. Smokin' and hittin' the booze cuts your wind to nothing. About the only protection a guy's got is to keep himself in condition. You don't smoke, do you, Ernie?"

"I have been trying it—lately," I admitted. I was again engaged in one of my curiosity experiments.

"Well, you know your own business. I'm no preacher but use your own judgment."

I did. And I didn't smoke again for several years.

I received about ten dollars for my share of that burglary—although it was reported as having cost the residents of that house several hundreds. Reading of it, I was affected by the loss someone suffered. Red and I divided twenty dollars after everything except the trinkets he had gathered had been sold. The pawnshop-owner would be forced to surrender the watches and rings as soon as the police check-up would identify them and the Jew would be reimbursed by the owner. But the actual difference between the value of the articles and what we received was too great to countenance any other explanation than that burglary was a poorly paying profession—for a thief. I've thought on that often.

[III]

Fred was duly informed of our narrow escape and it seemed to me that there was more pleasure in retelling it than there had been in experiencing it. In the recitation I could see the whole picture, imagining that it embodied completely the same charm as one of Raffles's episodes. But I refrained from mentioning my curious thoughts when I saw that girl. Red and Fred would have scoffed and undoubtedly laughed—and rightly, too—for I suspected that they, also, held some such thoughts at one time or another and made light of them only to cover their real emotion. Perhaps I am wrong in flunking so. But at that time I did not know how vastly different their conception of such things was. I believed that most young men of my age had about the same reactions as myself and to understand that some of them were absolutely devoid of imagination was impossible.

One evening Fred and I were together in a stolen machine. We had no particular object in mind; we were just cruising about, enjoying the drive and exchanging places at the wheel every half-hour or so.

"That night-time prowling, as Red calls it, is not so good. I knew a chap who followed it for years. All over the country he traveled and he was considered good, too. Then he got the notion of settling down. He married some little waitress, bought a house out in that district where you and Red were the other night and continued to pay night calls—but always over in San Francisco, or down the Peninsula. One night he was going in a window of a house that's all dark and someone cut loose with a shotgun. Christ! What a mess! He's doing ten years now—and you should see him dragging what's left of his body around the prison yard. One side paralyzed, one arm blown off and he looks sixty years old instead of thirty."

"That's terrible. Can't we do something for him?" I couldn't say more just then, but the words came from my heart.

"There isn't anything to do. His wife was about to have a kid and when she read of it in the papers, she went crazy—and he's about half insane, too. He don't care whether he ever leaves prison—there's nothing for him to come out to, now. . . . So, you see, that night-time work is not so good." Fred shifted over and I took the wheel, but I had no interest in the car at that moment.

"The best way," Fred continued, "is to make those places in the daytime."

I didn't quite follow the logic of his reasoning, but listened as he detailed the "best way."

"We can take a machine and drive around about one o'clock in the afternoon, right after lunch. People have a habit of going to town about then and when we see a woman with maybe a kid or two leave some house, we can be sure there's no one else at that place. Then, too, we can ring the bell and make certain. We can go in with a pass-key through the kitchen door, or if the windows open on a porch that's screened, we can enter that way. But Red's wrong about night work. It's three times higher in penalty if you get caught—and even if the worst comes in the daytime, you can usually give some money to a lawyer to arrange for a county-jail jolt."

Red was wrong! How was this that Red and Fred did not agree? Dissension among partners? A lack of complete harmony?

That had no place in the life of a thief—at least I could not place it there. I was yet to learn the disillusioning truth; thieves are ever arguing and disagreeing and fighting among themselves. But Fred's foresight in anticipating the penalty one risked started me thinking in a new direction. I didn't believe I'd ever again see the inside of a jail. The single night I had stayed in the City Jail seemed ages past, yet I could recall it and I had no wish to duplicate the experience.

I saw no reason why I should duplicate it. Along with other events of my life up to then it had occupied but one place and not a very large one either. I knew what jail was like—that settled it. My curiosity on that point was surfeited.

Daytime burglary occupied my thoughts for a day or two and then, cutting my school classes at noon, I joined Fred and together we went to Berkeley. There was a special significance in walking along a street when I was engaged in watching for people to leave their homes, that I might enter and steal from them. On any other occasion those homes and gardens would have been mere houses—but with each house a prospective mountain wherein we might strike gold, their very staid and reserved appearances added zest to my walk. I saw them in a new light. They were treasure coves in which lay concealed riches. It was not impossible, I told myself, that we should find a house used as a cache by some super-burglar and have the fabulous wealth of his efforts at our disposal. The thought pleased me and I wondered how I would word the note we would leave behind—for it never occurred to me to plunder one of the profession. Mentally inditing various phrases to express our regret at having discovered his hiding-place, I played with the picture his face would present when he should read our apology.

A machine stopped before a large, imposing house. Presently a woman and a child left the house and were driven away in the car.

"That's a gift," Fred said as we strolled past the house. "We'll be certain, however. You ring the door-bell and if no one answers, I'll go around back and let myself in and then come through and open the front door for you."

In response to my repeated summons a maid appeared. I was disconcerted. But using the first name that came to mind, I asked her: "Does Mr. Curtis live here?"

"Yes," she replied with a tone which indicated that I was stupid if I did not know that Mr. Curtis *did* live there. I was nonplussed. Why in the world did he? Of all the names possible to select I had picked at random the very name of the actual resident.

"Mr. James Lawrence Curtis?" I amplified the name that I might have excuse for taking leave.

"No-o-o," she said slowly, but more attentively. "I believe that is the name of one of his brothers. Will you step in a moment? I'll make sure—I've only been with them a few weeks and I'm not positive."

I stepped in, not daring to risk suspicion by refusal. Then, as I sat in the library, alone, the explanation for the odd choice of name struck me. There was a Mr. Curtis, a friend of our family, who lived in Berkeley and unconsciously I had allowed my feet to follow that portion of the town streets with which I was familiar and his name had suggested itself through association. I had been tricked by my subconscious mind! Some time in the past I had recorded that name and it had lain dormant until an emergency had called it to life. I marked that trait and resolved to inspect any impulses that sought to make me speak during moments of stress thereafter.

The maid returned to express her regret that she could be of no help to me—there was no one connected With the family of her employer by that name.

Explaining the incident to Fred, after we had chosen another neighborhood in which to continue our work, I observed a slightly cynical and unbelieving light in his eyes. For a moment I wanted to tell him that if he didn't believe me he could—what? Well, nothing could be done about it—and how was I to be sure that I had correctly interpreted his thoughts? To convince him that I had spoken truthfully, I was anxious to enter a house and complete what the maid's presence had prevented in the other one. I assumed an aggressive leadership—and felt his resentment. But I was determined to reverse his opinion. Of such queer desires are monstrous deeds spawned.

It was a waste of time to walk and wait for ever for people leaving to indicate an unoccupied house. I rang the bell of a likely-looking place. No one answered. I rang again—no answer. Fred waited a hundred feet distant. Again I rang—long, insistently. Positive that the house was for the time untenanted, I followed the cement walk to the rear entrance. The screen door was locked. I shook it vigorously. I was about to open my pocket knife to sever the thin wire screening so that I could raise the catch when a florid, bulky woman appeared. Evidently I had aroused her from a nap, for she frowned upon me, saying: "What in the name of heaven are you trying to do—break the door down"

"Oh, I beg your pardon. I'm taking subscriptions for the University paper" (I couldn't recall the name of it), "and I wonder if you would like to subscribe?" Fred bad suggested that excuse.

"You're wondering, are you? Well, take yourself off and do your wondering some place else. You college kids are always selling something. And I don't want to be subscribing—so get along with you."

I did and felt a passing sympathy for the "college kids" who would canvass that house with the prospect of selling something. On my way around the house I quoted, more or less correctly: "On the dead efforts of past failures you shall raise yourself to success."

Fred had disappeared. For several minutes I looked about for him, then became alarmed. Perhaps he had been caught at something! The police knew him as a burglar. But perhaps he had grown tired of waiting, I reasoned, the memory of his suspicious look returning to me. Torn between these conflicting thoughts, I was in a quandary about what to do. If he had been arrested, I should return to Oakland, tell Red and try to influence my father to help him. If he had deserted me—I shook off the thought as being unworthy and concluded that he had entered some house and would shortly reappear.

If *he* could display such initiative, *I* could—and did! Quickly I rang several door-bells. If they were answered, I excused myself. At about the fifth attempt I was on a porch that extended the width of the house. The vines, trellised up to the porch roof, afforded a natural screen for me. There was no response to my ringing and I tried a window. It opened. Mindful of the experience of Fred's prison acquaintance, I poked my head inside and called softly. No response.

I observed that the room contained no sign of late occupancy. Stepping over the window-sill was an achievement. It marked the definite act of burglary committed by myself.

Rooms have personalities. That first one, though not vastly different from the great parlor in my own home, where we lived before the family separation, assumed the strangeness of a foreign castle. The hangings, the rugs, the period furniture, the table with its leather-fringed covering, even the smoking-set and its several, differently shaped pipes, bespoke a discrimination on the part of the owner. The silence within was alive with noise. Little ringing sounds played about my ears. Large-eyed and motionless, I glanced about and listened. Even the noise of my swallowing sounded in my throat as though that channel were a megaphone amplifying the gurgling. I moved a step forward and awoke a multitude of infinitesimal sounds: the tiny squeak of sole-leather, the faint brushing together of clothing, the chafing of flesh against my stiff collar. Placing a hand on the back of a chair to avoid my threatened loss of balance, my finger-nails clicked sharply against the wood, like the metallic tapping of a telegraph key. I took a firm grasp on the flat back and to me came the memory of a performance I had once witnessed. A hypnotist was standing behind a "subject," making long, downward passes with his extended hands. With each pass the subject swayed forward, then backward—drawn, apparently, by a force emanating from the rigid fingers as they swept down behind him. The swaying increased until the subject fell back like a tree cut at its base and the hypnotist reached outward, catching and lowering the man to the floor. I knew the sensation of that subject and wondered who was exercising this current upon me. I turned suddenly about and the movement freed me of the illusion. I smiled at my foolish fancy, then set my teeth and lowered my head with the same aggressive spirit I had used in bucking into a line of football-players. It required considerable determination to breast and pass through the invisible hindrances and on to the hallway outside the room. I was not aware that I was fighting myself, but when I reached the stairway, I realized that I had been straining and struggling like a swimmer in a surf.

Rooms *do* have personalities. The four or five I entered that afternoon were as distinctly different, one from the other, as are the races of the earth. I could almost create the occupants from the indications of their traits and personal likes. The location of a table near the bed and the interesting conveniences revealed when the drawer was opened; the meticulous care displayed in disposing articles upon the dressing-stand; the indifferent arrangement of clothing—dresses, shoes—not the negligence of a maid, but the careful placing in just that careless order—the position of twin beds—the sag in the long-made-up cover of one of them—all these evidenced the characteristics of the rightful tenants. And in glimpsing them I knew a sense of stolen intimacy that fascinated. I was so occupied with conjecture that, although I looked into many probable hiding-places, I had not taken a single article. Having enjoyed fully an hour, interspersed with moments of exquisite nervous tension in the inspection of the upper-floor rooms—opening letters to read parts of them, disturbing dresses hanging in closets for the mingled scents they exuded—I decided to purloin some mementoes of my visit. It would be necessary to convince Fred, when I joined him, that I had actually consummated a burglary unaided.

A few dollars and one five-dollar gold piece; a breast-pin, set with questionable stones; a heavy watch and broken chain; some beads, partly unstrung—they were a brilliant green and I credited them with being emeralds. Then I discovered a large suit-case—this suggested the silver plates and forks, knives, spoons. I returned to the lower floor, where I soon located a great quantity of silverware. Some of it was wrapped in soft, thick, cloth packets. I recognized them as containing "company silver"—hence more valuable. Carrying the loaded suitcase, I paused to inspect the table drawers in the library, then went out through the open window.

A passing vehicle seemed unduly noisy after the stillness of the house. I stood with my load hold in one hand and recalled the heaviness of the sack of groceries when Buddy and I had essayed an escape, after the alarm of our first burglary. Regardless of the worth of my burden, I would discard it if necessary, *this* time, I promised myself. Twice I started to leave the protection of the vine-enclosed porch and each time I drew back to allow some pedestrian to pass. What if he were to turn in here? Suppose the owner returned? The suspense of waiting was great—I wondered if I had better leave by the back yard. Dismissing the idea, I forced myself to walk to the steps and down the sidewalk. I had the sensation of walking in a dream. In the sunlight I imagined that I stood revealed as though in a glaring white spotlight upon a stage. Residents of the other houses, seeing me, must know that I had just burglarized a house. My appearance, as I viewed myself from one side, seemed to cry aloud of my deed. A man walked from the corner and started directly towards me. There was something terrifying in the measured, regular stride. What if he lived in that house? Suppose he were to recognize this suitcase? I felt faint and my insides seemed to collapse as the distance between us lessened. I wanted to cross the street, but could not force my feet from the direction that was bringing us face to face. I wished mightily for the power to stretch the street to infinite length, having him—a small, dark dot on the opposite end, going in the opposite direction.

Perhaps ten feet intervened when he suddenly raised his eyes and for a moment they held mine. Blop! I heard the drop of some ghastly weight within me. My load had grown increasingly heavy and with this additional weight I veered to one side—away from him. Just as he was about to collide with me, he turned slightly and with the movement I tensed myself, prepared to receive a tremendous shock. . . . He passed on his way. The relief of his passing was like the sudden calming of a terrific wind I had been ploughing into. I nearly fell forward upon my face. . . .

The reaction, after I was safely settled on an Oakland-bound car, was normal. I felt as though I had been drained of every ounce of blood in my body and continued to sit upright only because the cold rush of wind, as the car sped along, had frozen me in that position. When I left the cur, I walked stiffly, like a rheumatic old man who has remained too long in a cramped pose. The joints of my frame actually creaked.

When I took the stuff to Fred's room, I was surprised to find him there and upon my questioning his movements after he had left me I received no reply. He dismissed my queries by waxing enthusiastic over my deed, complimenting me on the completeness of my "haul" and estimating the probable amount by which *we* should benefit from the loot. But his words were hollow—they had no force after the emotional orgy of the afternoon.

[IV]

I left everything with him except the money, which we divided. I wanted Red to share in the proceeds. When I broached the matter to Fred, he objected strongly, as though I had suggested a monstrous thing. I was taken aback, for I had considered the three of us as partners, to share alike. But Fred insisted that he and I were entitled to this—if Red wanted anything, he would have to get it. I was disgusted with his attitude and although I did not press him for an explanation of his sudden disappearance, the thought left a distrust I did not wish to hold.

Where I had given my confidence, I had given completely, without reserve. There had never been any calculation of degrees of trust; either to the utmost or not at all.

Then, while he was inspecting the silver, I saw him in a new light. I was—for that moment—divorced of my rose-colored emotional glasses through which I had heretofore seen him and in the cold white light of reason he suddenly appeared selfish and avaricious. There was about that simulated innocence of his face the built-up guise of a mouth of one who has had his teeth extracted. The formation of the outside of the mouth appears shrunken and when a false set of teeth is inserted, the lack of real, honest foundation is all too evident. Even the counterfeit attempt to regain the original appearance betrays itself. And that was Fred. Surface. And a bolstered surface—no foundation. The realization increased my disgust. I left him abruptly.

The following day we met by accident. He told me he had arranged to sell the silver and that he wanted me to accompany him to see exactly how much we got. He thought the amount would be a couple of hundred. And he wanted me with him. I did not greatly mind if I never saw the stuff again. The disillusionment had almost effaced Fred from my mind and the disappointment I had suffered upon learning his shallowness had left me cold, indifferent.

I went with him, however and learned the reason for the shrinkage on the value of stolen stuffs. A thief who must dispose of his goods through a "fence" is nothing other than a plain damn fool. That silverware was worth at least twelve hundred. I compared a similar set in a jewelry store and priced it, later. After much haggling and browbeating, which at times virtually amounted to threats to call the police, Fred and I each received fifteen dollars.

Since that experience I have never had the desire to steal silverware or cheap jewelry. The owner lost so much and the thief got so little—it looked like a contemptible act to give another's possessions into the hands of an unprincipled Shylock, who would not hesitate to report to the police all information in his knowledge if it would save him a day in jail.

[V]

The rupture with Fred served to bring Red and me closer together. There was little said of Fred; we mutually sensed each other's dislike of him and ceased to meet or discuss him. With Fred discarded, the portrayal of the risks involved in nighttime burglary seemed not to have the restraining effect the first telling had invoked. That one man had been shot and crippled was unfortunate. But I had never been shot—why should I ever be? Such is the supreme egotism of youth.

Although I did accompany Red several times during the next few months, when we burglarized various houses, after the first three or four I lost interest. There was no great attraction in continuing with endless repetitions of an experience with which I was all too familiar. But I did derive a tremendous, never-failing excitement in paying informal visits to residences during the daytime. Frequently I stole nothing, contenting myself with exploring desks and nibbling dainties from the pantries. The theft of an automobile became a commonplace.

School ceased to hold out any interest for me. Probably this was because of the prosaic manner in which lessons were given. There were thirty to fifty in a class and all of them were to learn the *same* explanations of involved problems, commit to memory certain rules enabling us to find the contents of a cone or the amount of air contained within a given space. What a bore! After the excitement of robbery, grand larceny and burglary—to sit at a desk and ponder over such trifles!

There were two boys in my class with the same initials as mine: Barry and Borne—"the three B's." Our teacher, a Miss Maxwell, was a small, bright-eyed woman with quick, birdlike movements and I often likened her to a watchful mother-hen. To some extent I found companion spirits in Borne and Barry. Borne was a mild-appearing sorrel-top with prominent teeth and possessed an unusually active mind. Barry was cross-eyed, wore heavy-lensed glasses and had a snubby red bulb for a nose. One time, attempting to make use of his father's razor and finding no beard to work on, he shaved off his eyebrows. The result was a premature Ben Turpin. The classroom was in an uproar within a minute after he entered, purposely late. Miss Maxwell fluttered about, trying to stem the tide of mirth and then burst out laughing herself. Barry was dismissed for the day and in loyalty to him and because it would afford us a chance to cut classes, Borne and I joined him. Three abreast, we marched from the room, vowing never to return until "those children" had "learned some manners."

[VI]

Our reckless and irresponsible thievery culminated in our arrest when I was a trifle over fifteen years of age. We had entered a prominent clothing-store in Berkeley and removed a great quantity of suits, shirts, shoes and other things. Piling them into the machine, we had driven to Oakland, unloaded them and returned for a second load. In the interval the burglary had been detected. The police system of Berkeley was just being founded on a more or less scientific basis and instead of assigning four or five burly blue-coats to guard the store after the discovery, one man was sent to watch it and the skylight whereby we had gained entrance was left untouched. After a cursory glance about the street I had climbed to the roof and lowered myself inside and passed more goods through to Red by means of a barred, rear window, which let out on an alley adjoining the building. We were permitted to work uninterrupted until the machine had been filled. Red advised me to come out and join him. When I walked up the alley, he had been arrested and I was promptly and effectively subdued before I could use my revolver. I was rather stunned at the quiet efficiency of the arresting officers. In their actions there was nothing of the manner of the chief I had met. Instead, they carefully searched us and led the way to the station—probably eight or ten blocks away. They left one man to watch for any of our "friends."

There had been none of the brutal treatment I had been told to expect and I reasoned that this was because they did not want our outcries to be heard by passing pedestrians. Once we were in the jail, I believed, they would make up for it.

Instead, we were separated and two officers tried to question me about the location of the remainder of our loot. I stubbornly refused to answer the questions. I carried nothing that would indicate where I lived or who I was and they were baffled, for the evening, in gaining information. I kept repeating to myself the admonition Red had frequently given me: "Don't say anything. Nothing. Just get a lawyer and let him do your talking. Don't try to explain anything—you don't have to. They can't make you do it. Don't say anything. They may beat you up, but *don't say anything!*"

While the coaxing and patient questioning proceeded, I compressed my lips and was thoroughly uncomfortable. I rather believed they would exhaust their patience and resort to sterner measures; and I wondered how long I could fight the two. Not long, I concluded—they were two husky ex-college men. But I would not talk—even should they beat me. So firmly had I fixed that in mind that when one of them asked if I should like something to eat before being locked up, I couldn't answer him. They seemed amused at my stubbornness and locked me in a cell for the night.

I saw Red the following morning as we were being taken to a restaurant for breakfast. August Vollmer, the chief of police, had been unable to secure a decent place to have food prepared for prisoners and had elected to feed them at a place about a block from the jail. The street and bustle of early morning life impressed me as being very desirable after the hard boards of the cell-bench. I tried to speak to Red, but I was handcuffed to a frowsy bum and could not come near enough to Red to talk without being overheard. I was not unduly worried. I was too interested in the working-out of some explanation to give my father. There was nothing within the realm of reason that I could say, so I decided that the sooner I got in touch with him, the sooner I should know how long I had to remain in jail. My greatest worry was that I had been so foolish as to be caught. I could see, all too plainly, how senseless our second trip to the store had been. But I was interested, from one minute to the next, in watching the routine of the police as they put us through the usual measuring, finger-printing, photographing and questioning. That I would not talk was treated as a joke. To me it was serious. I wanted to talk—to my father. Or, if not to him, at least to Red. But since I refused to talk to the officers, I was not permitted to see anyone.

Taken into the office of the chief, I experienced a mild shock. I had expected to find a counterpart of the brutal and burly Oakland chief. Instead, I was conducted to a chair at a desk on the opposite side of which sat a mild-looking man with hair just graying at the temples. His manner was friendly, but with a hint of directness in his voice that warned me that I had met an intelligence far surpassing any I had yet encountered.

"Well, Ernest, you are in a rather bad hole, aren't you? He smiled, as though in sympathy for my predicament.

He knew my name! Quickly I traced the events of the evening and night in the cell and tried to recall anything that could have given him this information. Could Red have—no, I was certain of Red. But who? Where? I was baffled. For a fleeting instant a passage returned from some book I had read of thought-transmission. The fantastic notion loitered although I tried to elude it. I was amazed and little short of astounded when he detailed our movements of previous thieving, commented on the amount of goods stolen and named Red's room as the place wherein they had been recovered.

While he continued to tell me what I had done, Red was brought in and seated beside me. I glanced at him and his appearance strengthened the belief that he had not previously spoken to the chief or any of the officers. I was alive with curiosity and almost bursting to ask Vollmer how he knew so much of our movements, but he relieved me of the desire.

"Nice friend of yours—that chap Fred," he was saying to Red.

Fred! Fred again—but how?

Then gradually it was all made clear. Fred had read of our arrest in the early morning papers and had gone directly to Red's room. At first I credited him with the intention of removing any evidence that might remain in the room against Red, but subsequent developments impelled me to dismiss that notion. Fred had gone there and taken only what he could readily appropriate and in coming downstairs just at daybreak, he had encountered a wary landlord on the alert for roomers who might be departing without the formality of paying their rent. In the ensuing argument Fred had produced a gun and threatened the man and then escaped to the street. A policeman had summoned aid and Fred was arrested about three hours before the chief questioned us. The intervening time he had spent in recounting the various burglaries Red or I had committed. I think he credited us with some he had engineered. But to make certain, he gave the names of the pawnshops and second-hand-stores where we had disposed of the things.

[VII]

My father seemed more concerned with minimizing the affair in the newspapers than with upbraiding me. Red and I stoutly denied any knowledge of the other burglaries. That Fred had indicted us with so much was the fatal error. The police, while anxious to clear up the many crimes attributed to us, were inclined to believe that Fred had drawn heavily upon his imagination. The following day my father arranged for Red's release on a sort of "personal bond," guaranteeing to have him in court and the same afternoon he took me back to Oakland. He evinced a disgust for my allowing myself "to get mixed up until such men," as he put it. I knew he meant Fred.

Several weeks later I went to court with my father. The case had been transferred to the jurisdiction of the juvenile authorities. There were a few minutes of conversation between my father, the judge, the probation officer, Red and me. Then we were informed that we would have to report every week at the probation office. So far as I was concerned, that ended the affair. My father commented on the willingness of his friends to take care of his boy when in trouble;

"His Honor owes me this much, anyway. You should remember that you have a friend in him. I managed his last campaign and when he runs again I want you and some of your boy friends to post a lot of election cards for him and get your school friends to carry home his cards—in general, show you are appreciative of what he has done for you."

Red decided to move to San Francisco. And, because of the talk rife at the school over my arrest, I ceased to attend. Mother was terribly shocked and pleaded with me "not to continue with those boys," but to come to church and meet some real, worthwhile young men. Partly to please her and partly because I was disgusted with Fred's actions and betrayal I went to Sunday-school classes.

I'll draw a merciful curtain of charity over the disillusionment I suffered there. I should much rather meet and live with the most vicious and heartless thief that ever entered a penitentiary, if he be honest in his expressions and opinions, than dwell among the group of "nice boys" constituting that class. They professed an intention of living according to some divine plan of life and yet were talking scandal of each other constantly; or agreeing to some strict pledge of non-smoking and then immediately going to the basement of the church and lighting up their cigarettes. They sang the praises of feminine virtue and looked askance at the least suggestive remark, but as soon as possible they would surreptitiously join one of the young ladies from the "flock" and sneak to the belfry to pass a few moments in intensively explorative physiology. And the same hypocrites would blush at the mention of a Sunday baseball game. . . . If such things constituted virtue, I felt glad, with an unholy glee, that I was bad. For at least I had the peace of mind that comes from living an open life free from all sham. Perhaps pretense is necessary in emergencies, but as a regular garment it becomes too drab and sordid.

Fred had been in jail about a month before I could prevail upon my father to secure a release for him. The prison record held against him and although my single purpose in securing his freedom was to give him his well-deserved beating, I was disappointed in my desire, for when he was released, it was without my knowledge and he was sent out of the state.

Oakland had been exhausted, for me. There was nothing of interest there—and I sought other cities. Trips to San Jose, Sacramento, Santa Rosa and Fresno but sharpened my appetite for larger fields to explore. My father supplied what money I needed for current expenses, but I supplemented that with my own revenue. Once or twice he made vague suggestions that I start to work, but I could think of nothing I was prepared for and it was easier to drift about without the inconvenience of having to report at some job every morning. I did carry copy to advertisers of the Oakland *Enquirer* for a few weeks, but the fascination of seeing huge presses in motion, the activity of preparing a daily paper before going to press and the hustle and fighting of the newsboys soon devolved into a routine which made it just plain work.

However, I did have access to many large department-stores. With a fresh proof-sheet I would leave the newspaper office and visit the store to have the proof marked for errors. The time I passed while the advertisers were correcting their proofs was usually spent in looking over the store and making acquaintances. One large fur-store advertised regularly and I soon became familiar with the shop's interior—so familiar, indeed, that the manager thought nothing of leaving me alone in his office with the safe opened. I investigated it and found a considerable sum of money. Leaving it as it lay, I pondered on the situation and evolved a scheme whereby I could send another copy-boy with the sheets and have him meet the manager in the store, away from the office. Then watching my chance—the manager would correct his proofs on a counter or anything that disposed itself handily—I could sneak into the office and relieve the safe of its contents. The kid I chose for the job was a willing urchin. Fifty cents to deliver a proof and return it to where I agreed to join him was to him as manna from above.

The plan worked without a hitch. I changed from the usual gray suit I wore and my dark clothing attracted no attention. I got nearly five hundred dollars. My interest in proof-carrying waned. A new field of endeavor had opened for me. I tried similar schemes in the other towns and their successful operation gave me an independent income.

One evening I engaged a room in a fair-sized hotel on Washington Street and arranged with Red for him to come over with his girl and occupy a room on the fifth or sixth floor. He was then working with a "mob" of pickpockets—"putting his duke down." They responded to my call, engaged a room and stationed themselves by the window overlooking the street to await my signal.

Standing on the walk in front of the hotel, I lighted a cigarette, which had been agreed upon as a sign that there was no one but the clerk in the small lobby. Red phoned the clerk, who acted in the dual capacity of bellboy and clerk at that particular hour. He entered the elevator and ascended. I stepped inside, passed behind the desk and opened the unlocked door of the safe. The cash drawer and one of the compartments for the storage of guests' valuables were open. I benefited by this oversight to the amount of two hundred dollars and some jewelry. Red and I divided the money the following day and his girl got the "valuable packages." There may have been value in those rings and watches, but it was one of sentiment. . . . Ingersoll never manufactured a watch that would bring more than fifteen cents in a pawnshop.

[VIII]

I spent most of the money in frequenting expensive hotels, restaurants and theatres and in buying books, in San Francisco. I developed a mania for rare books. And I made the acquaintance of many clerks and dealers. Lying on the grass in Golden Gate Park, I would pore over the pages of a newly-purchased book, dreaming and scanning pages that were often of little interest except that they were old and smelled musty. There was one stretch of walk leading from a miniature garden that was a favorite retreat. There I repaired often to read or drowse.

One afternoon an elderly gentleman seated himself on a bench near by. He seemed, in common with others of his kind, to have nothing to do but sit on that bench and look about him. Small squirrels, friendly and tame from frequent feeding, were scampering about or posturing upon their haunches, their paws extended expectantly. He regarded them interestedly, then produced peanuts to coax them to him, the while breaking bits of the nuts and sampling them himself. I noticed that he divided each kernel with the squirrels. A rather companionable action, I mused. He continued this until the supply was exhausted.

While observing his actions I was amusing myself with various conjectures on his station in life. His clothes were clean and well cut. His shoes were polished and his hat was acceptable. What hair I could see was crystal-white and his face was freshly shaven except for a short, stiff, white moustache. Some philosophical old gentleman, one who had arrived at a period in life where he could relax from labor and pass his days in idleness, I surmised. A number of other possibilities suggested themselves, but I was unable to accept any character as satisfactory. Using the amusing antics of a frisky squirrel as an excuse to attract the gentleman's attention, I laughed. He turned half about and surveyed me, one eyebrow upraised.

There was a measure of haughtiness in his eyes that subdued my desire to laugh again. I felt that I had intruded; he gave the impression that he would not have seated himself there had he known of my presence. I had been rude and was being properly snubbed. Yet there was a hesitancy in his manner as he rose which lessened the force of his first glance. Again our eyes met and I was positive that he was interested in the volume which lay opened, face downward, on the grass before me.

"Gr-hump!" He cleared his throat. "Young man, sir," he stated, in deep, measured tones, "you startled me a moment ago"

Curious to investigate him, I expressed my contrition.

"That is very well—certainly I do not hold it against you. You appear to have a book before you. And from where I stand it impresses me as being an old volume. Is it, by any chance, a rare book?" His manner was that of a sovereign graciously allowing a subject to hear the royal voice. The play amused me and I entered into the part assigned me.

"It is, indeed, sir," I replied with what I intended for a humble tone. "The rather faint lettering on the cover announces it to be the *Anecdota* of Procopius and the second page proclaims that the book was printed over two hundred years ago. Should you care to see it?"

I have offered meat to a hungry dog and had him snatch it avidly from my hand. I thought of that when the old gentleman sprang to where I was yet reclining upon the grass and possessed himself of the book. His eyes were alight with a strange fire as he turned the book in trembling hands. His face was animated and his words jumbled. The transformation was so complete that I wondered over the reason. I had seen enthusiasm displayed by book-lovers, but this was an almost hysterical gladness.

"Procopius! Procopius! Well, well, well, well—gar-hump!" Again he cleared his throat and when I looked into his eyes, they were blinking rapidly in a losing effort to prevent tears from overflowing their edges. I saw him swallow as with a great difficulty, then raise his head and turn from me. So greatly was I affected by his agitation that for no explicable reason I desired to cry with him.

"You must join me on the bench," he said, with an attempt to regain his haughty mien. I was ashamed to have witnessed his naked emotion and tried to appear as though I had seen nothing out of the ordinary in his actions. When I was seated, he lapsed into a profound coma and turned the pages of the book after the manner of a man in a dream. I was sure he was not reading and yet he fingered the pages and appeared to be following some of the lines with his eyes.

I had been attracted by the book in one of the favorite stores when I had seen the old codger who owned the shop hide it from an inquisitive gentleman. I got the impression that it was not for sale and anything so valuable was worth looking through at least once, I had reckoned. Watching my opportunity, I had lifted the book from its place of concealment while the proprietor was engaged in conversation. And I had not made much progress in deciphering it up to the time the elderly gentleman had seated himself to feed the squirrels. But if it would afford him any great pleasure—and evidently it would, for he continued to stroke it lovingly, caressingly, stopping occasionally to emit a long-drawn sigh—well, he could have it. I was about to present it to him when he shook off the stupor that had settled over him.

Abruptly he changed his expression and presented a mournful mien.

"My young sir, do you appreciate that you possess one of the rarest of all books?" He seemed to regret that it had ever been in my hands.

I explained that I was trying to appreciate it, but that if it would make him happy, he was welcome to it.

The change that came over his face! A mounting gladness thawed his expression until it seemed to beam with some great spiritual light. He accepted the book, then appeared overcome by the greatness of my gift. Hurriedly he excused himself, for the afternoon, agreeing to meet me on the morrow. We parted and I wondered at the queer antics to which the book had incited him.

He presented himself promptly on the following day. I noted that he did not carry the volume with him, that he had several packages of peanuts for the squirrels and that he did not nibble each nut as he delivered it. But he was condescending in his manner and while I debated the propriety of asking his name and further inquiring into his antecedents, he abruptly dropped his reserve and became confidential.

I learned in quick succession that his name was James Wellington Boswell, that he came of an ancient and illustrious line (which he detailed at great length), that he was rated on the legitimate stage along with Sothern and Miller and that only the prejudice of a certain theatrical magnate prevented him from receiving due recognition of his histrionic abilities. He recited many plays he had graced, enhanced with his art and saved from certain failure by his personality. As he talked, I thought of the rapid change in his appearance he had wrought since yesterday and a small doubt was born in my mind; eventually the doubt became a certainty. He had made haste with the book to the nearest buyer and disposed of it, that "certain pressing needs might be provided for." He was "resting" between engagements at the time and intended to redeem the book later.

The delightful old fraud! His acting was not for my benefit; he had posed so much that the physical actions had worked in reverse and instead of being external evidences of his mind, the latter was functioning under direction of his outward acts. James Wellington Boswell he had labelled himself and he had the original James Boswell's eager desire for fame, or, having failed in that, a notoriety which would bring him before the public. His nose was hooked, but with a saving, patrician grace; and though he was not averse to accepting favors in the form of dinners or small loans, he had a habit of sniffing disdainfully if I was the least bit clumsy in the suggestion of them.

But he was surprisingly well acquainted with theatrical performers; unexpectedly, because of his long "resting period." He had not "trod the boards" in over ten years. How the interval was bridged would require a book in the telling. Sir James, as I soon dubbed him, not to his displeasure, was a constant diversion for me during the next two months. Following my absence from the city on a trip to one of the small valley towns, where I burglarized a store to provide money for our support, he would question me closely about my business. I soon was rivalling him in the variety and ingenuity of my evasions. He gloried in dining at the Palace Hotel, or Marquard's, or Solari's and he was never unwilling to give me in return the benefits of his reading and experience. Much of the latter I discarded, but he had an astoundingly accurate knowledge of books and authors. And never once did I indicate that I was other than a student with ample means, or that I believed him to be other than the particular character he was at the moment parading. An odd pair, but a mutually satisfactory one. Sir James really gave me more, in hundreds of mannerisms and poses, than I could have bought with ten times the money I gave to him.

Then one day he produced a letter from a girl in Seattle. Peggy, having met Sir James some months before, during a theatrical engagement, was then forming a barn-storming company and required him to act a given part in the play.

After considerable talk and preliminary skirmishing, during which he endeavored by implication to inform me of the immediate need of his talents in Seattle, he grew desperate. It was contrary to his principles to ask directly for a "loan." Purposely stupid and obviously missing the hints he threw in my direction, I delighted in seeing how long I could torment him in the polite manner he had taught me. . . . But his desire to travel north proved too strong for him to contain. When he was exasperated to the point of strangling me to obtain the needed money, I suggested that we both go to Seattle. Pleading a need of several days to prepare myself for the voyage, I started on a whirlwind trip in a drive for funds. The public was not accustomed to "drives" then, but within two days I had garnered almost three hundred dollars.

The residence section of San Francisco which borders the east side of Golden Gate Park offered most of my "quota." I believe I walked through at least fifteen houses within the next forty-eight hours. On the last evening, at dusk, I emerged from one house with a quantity of clothing in two suit-cases. It nearly caused my arrest while I was disposing of it in Golden Gate Avenue pawnshops. Two detectives, making a belated round of these places, stopped and questioned me when I left one shop. One of them entered to question the pawnbroker, the other remaining with me. I maintained that I was moving from one hotel to another and that all the articles belonged to me, but when they opened the suit-cases, the varied assortment raised further doubts.

The specter of the Oakland probation-release rose up and throwing all caution to the winds, I turned and darted off across the street at an angle that kept me in line with some children playing on the opposite sidewalk. I reasoned that the men would not risk shooting into a group—and I reasoned correctly. The detectives may have given chase, but in the gathering gloom I soon eluded their pursuit.

[IX]

Sir James and I sailed to Seattle on the *Umatilla,* a boat with an interesting history. Built for the Alaskan routes, it was a heavy rolling ship and provided a minimum of comfort. The small saloon was crowded with Shriners returning from a southern convention, some young teachers on a summer vacation trip and the usual assortment of passengers. To me it represented a picture of many possibilities—and I made the most of them.

Sir James, having decided to make me a brother actor, introduced me to recent acquaintances on the second day out, as though he had known them for years. I was a young dramatic student. I had a great future. He was personally educating me and as part of the program of my enlightenment he had condescended to allow me to appear in a minor production in Seattle. It was an amusing situation. I received considerable attention and appreciated, now, the reason why Sir James was wedded to that sort of thing. I wonder how much of the postures on board ships, in summer camps and boarding-houses has the same foundation that my claim to fame had.

A mock trial was organized by the Shriners and the suit tried was one instituted for heart-balm by a member of the teachers' group against Sir James. He accepted the position and, with judge and jury selected, the farce was enacted.

The ship was pitching about and the dignity of the court was seriously jarred. In the midst of an impassioned address to the jury Sir James suddenly stopped. The abrupt flow of his oratory was followed by a wild look from his eyes; then, tossing decorum aside, he dashed for the door to the deck and disappeared. . . . Some time later I found him in his bunk, pale and thoroughly miserable. But not because of his illness. His sole regret was that the wretched elements had deprived the good people of the ship of the privilege of enjoying his final exhortation to the jury, to vindicate him of the smirch cast upon his fair and illustrious name!

There is a delightful intimacy aboard ship. And I was not slow in turning the pastime into cash. While the intimacy was at its height between certain newly-met couples, I paid visits to staterooms from which the worshippers at the shrine of Aphrodite were absent. Consequently Sir James and I reached our port enriched by twice the amount with which we had left San Francisco.

The furor my pilfering might have created was over-swept by the announcement from the wireless-operator that war had been declared by England, as an ally of France against Germany. In the excitement aroused by that news I am certain that many passengers failed to notice their losses, or, if they did, they failed to report them.

CHAPTER 5

[I]

Seattle approached by evening. Gray, low-hanging smoke like dirty cobwebs filled the air. The water of the Sound, parting reluctantly for the prow of our boat, was oil-scummed and strewn with bits of flotsam. Long, tired-appearing steamers with chains through the scar-edged eyes of their hulls loafed at their moorings—neglected, seemingly long forgotten by their owners. Unpainted, ragged wharves jutted out over the water at irregular intervals, like teeth in a gigantic, broken rake. Dull-colored warehouses, rendered grotesque by the haphazard plastering of company names and pier numbers over their sides. And beyond, rising above them, a jumbled and inert line of roofs dimly discernible in the sordid grayness. Wheezing and puffing, a squat ferry churned its path to Alki Point, the blue-green brine swelling in its wake, trailing like a bedraggled bustle. From the funnel black smoke crept up to hang listlessly for a moment like a single dark plume before it was swallowed up by the somber smoke-blanket.

From a wharf not far from where our ship was being docked, there glided a slim, vibrant craft. Its trim lines, clean, white sides and evidences of polished brass compelled attention. As though happy to be leaving the depressing surroundings, it cut a narrow swath through the water and sped from the dock. Glass windows permitted a view into the interior of its upper deck. Warm and sticky as the late afternoon was, the coolness and comfort of the passengers seated on the rattan chairs within seemed to refute it. I expressed my envy of them to Sir James and inquired the boat's destination.

"Tacoma," he replied, delighted to exhibit his knowledge. "One of the two marvelously fast boats operating, which are a mark of progress for this—gar-hump—village."

I vowed that I would take a trip on that boat some day—and I kept that vow, though the trip was one forced by circumstances, which made it anything but pleasant.

Sir James had wired notice of our coming. The walk down the gangplank and into the roofed-over warehouse that served as a terminal was in the nature of a triumphal entry. We were met by a sextet of bewitching beauties. In the cone of yellow light from a flickering electric globe the faces of those girls shone resplendent from the crowd gathered to greet the passengers. The drabness, the smell of acrid smoke and the lassitude that had enveloped me was banished in the carnival welcome extended to us. Peggy formed the apex of a wedge through the crowd to us. Her smile was contagious. She radiated a fire and vivacity that instantly changed my dislike for Seattle. I had seen it through a fog—now it was revealed in sunshine and laughter.

"Dear old Bos!" She extended a hand to each of us. "I knew you'd come. With you the company is complete and—oh, you must meet the girls!"

Before she could turn from him to introduce the flock about us, he had leaned with courtly grace and kissed the fingers of her hand; then he beamed his happiness to meet "the girls." . . . While she did the Honors of introduction, I retained my hold upon her other hand.

Peggy was diminutive, but the inadequate sport dress and shirt she wore revealed much of a mature figure. Perhaps twenty years old, she had the assurance of an aged executive, yet blended her direct disposal of the formality with a naïveté I found to be wholly delightful. She turned clear, intelligent eyes upon me and for an instant I saw a gleam of calculation in them. She spoke and I was aware of a difference in her tone.

"He's so busy he's forgotten you. But he wrote me a long letter about you—and I've a part for you." She deliberately spread her charms before me, then asked: "Think you'll like it?"

Would I!

She knew my answer before I could voice it. "Of course you will," she said hastily, as Sir James deigned to turn again to her.

Mae, Patricia, Barbara and Lila were presented. So much activity, so much life, so much gaiety and so many agreeable hand-clasps—I reveled in the play. For play it was. That group was for ever acting. Even upon more intimate acquaintance, situations were created wherein each took an unassigned, but natural part and contributed to the progress of the moment's comedy or drama.

From the edge of the light-pool emerged three young men and an unusually robust girl. Ed, Dave and another chap. The girl was Tiny and though I knew her for several months, that was the one name by which she was called or referred to in conversation.

Ed, tall, massive, like a fair Norseman, had a direct, forceful manner. He shook my hand in the grip of a vice. Dave was a dapper youth; if the term "sheik" had been in common usage then, Dave would have merited it. He offered a limp hand, then pulled Tiny forward and almost pushed her into my arms. Squeals of laughter followed his buffoonery. Tiny bowed, made the best of her ability to smile, then affectionately laid one arm across Peggy's shoulders and drew her close.

"I'm glad he's young," she said to Peggy. "What should I have done if he'd been fat and forty?"

"Kissed him just the same," Peggy informed her. Then to me: "She's talking about her part—and she was scared to death that Bos was to play opposite her. But she's feeling better now—aren't you, Tiny?"

"Oh my, yes!" Tiny exhaled. Then confidentially to me, but in a voice that the farthest member of our group could hear: "I'm *terribly* romantic and it would have been too awful—"

I was uncomfortable and wondered why I should be made the goat. Sir James interrupted the detailing of what "would have been too awful" by suggesting dinner.

Chorus of approbation. With our bags carried by Ed and Dave and the ineffectual chap, we started from the pier.

My suggesting taxis to carry us uptown worked an odd effect. I was the cynosure of all eyes. I was yet to learn that no one in that crowd ever spent his own money for anything other than food or clothing. If another extended an invitation—all very well. But expenditure of capital was taboo. They were "resting" until the following week, when rehearsals would begin and the "angel's" purse-strings would be loosened. Having been accepted as one of the group, I had inadvertently isolated myself in my attempt to be hospitable.

Peggy came to my rescue. "Well, perhaps this once. How much money have you?"

Taken aback by the direct question, I mumbled: "Plenty."

"Perhaps we'd better count it. No one is entitled to more than is necessary while the rest of the artists are hungry. We have a community pool for our wealth. But you'll learn. How much is plenty?" She smiled and tucked her arm through mine as we paused on the pavement before a battered vehicle.

"Over a hundred dollars," I temporized in a whisper.

She released my arm and stepped back, surveying me in disbelief. Then, assured by my countenance that I spoke the truth, she stepped into the machine and posed, standing upon the cushions of the back seat.

"My fellow sufferers, gather nigh. He who ever directs our feet in the right paths, who ever guides us through temptations, who ever looks out for the welfare of hungry actors and actorines, who ever hears our pleas and responds to our supplications, He—well, He sent to us last week an angel and lo and behold! this week He has sent a missionary possessed of the riches of the gods! One hundred dollars! Coin of the realm! Our long fast is broken—we are about to repair to the nearest banquet hall and founder ourselves. Oh joy! Oh great gobs of luscious, dripping, joyously fried steaks! . . ."

She extended her arm as in benediction and although a curious gathering was collecting about us, she continued: "We thank Thee—yes, we thank Thee, but, O Lord, we're awful hungry—will You wait awhile until we get all filled up before we tell You how thankful we are?" She lowered her voice, tilted her head to await her answer, then murmured: "Yes, He'll wait."

An irresponsible, utterly mad crowd, we piled into that machine until the driver protested that he was not in the trucking-business. The springs did not break, however and amid much singing and bantering we arrived at a not too expensive restaurant. Even in her enthusiasm Peggy was mindful of the many meals the troupe would require in the next six or seven days.

The discussion with the driver took the form of a debate on the propriety of operating such an ancient machine. That the driver eventually got two dollars, which he accepted under protest, was due to the urgent desires of the girls and Sir James to enter the restaurant. Had time permitted, I believe we could have persuaded the chauffeur—as we did on similar, later occasions with other rented-car drivers—that we had conferred a signal distinction upon him by using his car. Powerful Ed could, in dire necessity, be depended upon to settle the disputes definitely and forcefully in our favor. In that restaurant I learned to order meals from the right-hand side of the menu.

[II]

The Bluebird was the name of the drama Peggy had written and was forming the company to produce. She had prepared other bits of stage stuff, but this was her first attempt to stage a four-act play. The "angel" had come out of the "north Countree with a poke of gold-dust washed from the mountains near

Nome." With him he had brought an unaccountable desire to put on the boards a play that would be billed as being managed by him. Peggy had met him during a boat trip two weeks before. He had, at one time, been unfortunately married and was hungry for "understanding." As Peggy phrased it to me during later moments of our intimacy, "When their wives don't understand 'em—I produce another show."

I held the notion that plays were organized in an orderly manner. How quickly that fancy vanished! The girls, Ed and Dave and two other young men were sharing a two-room apartment. Study of parts in the play occupied a major portion of the time. Acts were rehearsed, corrections made, criticism given—and rejected. Yet there was a carnival gaiety running through it all. Sir James, because of his age and partly because it pleased me to continue him in the rôle of a great actor whose merits were not generally appreciated, was located comfortably in a single room of the same building.

The angel appeared twice during the ensuing week at the apartment. But both times Peggy kept at his side and shooed away anyone who might inadvertently give him a different impression from the one she had implanted in his mind. The angel took it all very seriously. So deadly in earnest was he in the progress of the affair that even a joking remark about having to walk back from our road-tour seemed to hurt him.

For the final week Peggy rented a hall that boasted a stage and into dress rehearsal the group went. Most of the parts had been written with an eye to the costumes. This gave it a modern setting—for of what use is a pair of Romeo tights after the performance? Hence, at the angel's expense, the girls and men blossomed out in new street-clothing.

The show made a brave attempt to succeed. But after we had been away from Seattle for less than a month, the angel recognized the futility of supporting, at twelve hundred dollars each week, a show which produced less than half that amount at the box-office. He proposed to Peggy—who later mimicked his manner to Dave, Ed and me—and after her gracious rejection of his plea for her to come to the Land of Snow and Ice and cook biscuits for him, he vanished.

Sir James, wise in the lore of road shows, welcomed the advances of a matron who owned and operated a hotel in Centralia. We wanted to remain there and attend his wedding, but his "intended" crassly requested that we pay for our week's board and room. Like the Arabs, we closed our suit-cases and stole away.

Two of the girls formed a sister-act and booked out on a circuit with a southern terminus, they, too, recognizing the desirability of warmer climate through the approaching winter.

Again in Seattle, Dave, Ed and I engaged two large rooms. Peggy, Tiny, three other girls and two young men came there, having obtained our address from some mysterious source and the ten of us managed to live together for the ensuing month. The girls had one room, off which opened a kitchenette and the men had another, from which entrance to the bath was gained. The money I had retained enabled us to buy some urgently required beds and blankets. And that place soon became a refuge for any actors or actresses we knew who were "resting" between engagements. One or two of them would have a night's work at a motion-picture house—singing, dancing, or doing some specialty. . . .

A young violinist, whom Peggy found hugging his violin and looking forlornly into a restaurant window, practiced often in the room. Another couple, who later gained national fame as "Mercies and Girl," perfected their thought-transference act in that room. Seated back to back, with a long pendulum swinging from a specially constructed clock, they would count objects silently until each tenth one was reached. Then aloud and in unison, they would name the object in mind. By dint of constant practice they were able to attain a high percentage of thought-transference. At first they were prone to mistakes, but their perseverance was a matter for wonder. The girl was a pianist. Mercies would stand in one room and one of our number would whisper the title of a song into his ear. Immediately the notes came from the piano in the other room. They seemed constantly in harmony with each other. Even while walking past a street display-window they would glance into it, pass on to the next block and recite to one another the objects their eyes had registered.

Tiny *was* romantic. First Dave had been the delight of her heart; then one of the roomers down the hall occupied her attention; next Ed; and, sensing my approaching martyrdom, I laid ardent suit to Peggy. But Tiny was not to be thwarted. She gave me the full benefit of her yearnings in advice on the matter of my suit for Peggy. With the two rooms crowded—girls and men lying about on the beds, chairs and tables, even perched atop the piano, the two telepathic actors engaged in their endless practicing, the violinist tuning up or coaxing a melody from his instrument—Tiny would single out Ed or me and pour forth her tale of the men she had loved—and lost. A Freudian would have found interesting material in that fat girl, for not one tale in ten had any foundation except in some book she had read. Some of her stories rivalled the adventures of Boccaccio's characters in the *Decameron*.

Whoever rose first secured the best outfit for the day—that was the regular order of dressing in our apartment. The girls washed undies, stockings and handkerchiefs and plastered them on the windows to dry—to the mingled delight and chagrin of residents in the adjoining buildings. Strings from wall to wall supported clothes in various stages of drying. One night, I recall, there were almost thirty people in the two rooms. A show had gone broke, some of the performers were known to us and what was more natural than that we should share our quarters with them? Chairs shoved together formed beds, two ironing-boards laid over the bath-tub held another couple, four or five wedged into each of the large beds and the lounges held two apiece. But despite the crowding there was a respect for personal dignity maintained that spoke volumes for the people there. That there were suspicious-looking grass-stains on certain couples when they returned from an hour spent in the darkness of a park near by mattered not. We laughed, played, sang, annoyed the neighbors and believed that in some mysterious manner we should, some day, be formed into a company of stars and should write our names high in the heavens of theatrical fame.

I was absorbed in the working-out of the mind-reading act. This led to studying tricks of the mind and of sleight-of-hand and resulted in my going to work in a trick- and puzzle-store on First Avenue. Ed came to work there also. Between us we soon had an interest aroused in things magical that speeded up the trade at the store. That place became a forum for the young Magi, amateur and professional, of the city. I had ceased to prowl through residences. Peggy attracted me. I wanted to believe myself in love with her, but we had too many traits in common to permit this delusion. We did find a happy intimacy, but for the sake of some conventionality which neither of us could find words to express, but which we agreed was necessary to recognize, she declined to share an apartment with me; yet I was welcome in hers.

The two-room place degenerated into a nuisance. Ed and I were paying rent for it, providing most of the groceries, pacifying the landlord for the disturbance created. The jealousy and petty scandalmongering that are certain to occur in any group of young people made the air of the apartment difficult to live in. I soon was avoiding the place. As the really accomplished artists in the crowd drifted away to employment, the residue ceased to hold any attraction and Ed and I moved to a hotel apartment. Tiny joined a carnival company—as a snake charmer!

Dave drifted in and out of town, spending days during which he did nothing but lean over the counter at the store to talk or brag and to borrow a dollar from Ed or me. I spent many evenings with Peggy. She liked to read and I was glad to lie on the couch and listen. Through many of Dickens's books we progressed; some of Shakespeare held my attention—but I was restless. Zola's *Nana* we took to pieces, Peggy defending, I condemning. Then for a while we were engaged in the writing of a playlet. It was to condense, in a twenty-minute scene, the futility of trying to reform or change a girl by legal compulsion. With our faces flushed from the heat of our discussions over the presentation of the plot, we often sat up till morning.

[III]

Yellow soft lights set in purple shadows. Black employment-boards and luminous snow-covered sidewalks. A few huddled figures near the entrances to poolrooms and saloons. That was Washington Street. The distant tinkle of a piano from a girl show on the second floor of a gaunt building reached Peggy and me as we left the harsh noises of traffic about Totem Pole Square behind.

"It's like drifting into a side pool of some jungle stream at night," Peggy whispered. "Darkness and uncertainty—yet you can feel the vibrant life of concealed beasts about you. . . ."

We passed a half-opened door. Men in checked Mackinaws or huge overcoats were seated about dozens of card-tables. The flash of a tray-laden waiter's white coat seemed to blend into the steam and smoke strata above the throng.

A Chinaman shuffled by, almost brushing against Peggy. She pressed closer to me.

A woman, alert, fur-enswathed, emerged from one of the purple shadows. A sailor with his great blue coat unbuttoned attempted to embrace her. She peered apprehensively over one shoulder at the distant, lighted corner, then linked her arm through his and piloted his unsteady steps across the street. They vanished in the faintly outlined doorway of a rooming-house.

Suddenly blatant music struck my ear. A small band of soldiers of God had turned the corner and were bearing down upon us. One carried a flag, another blew a cornet spasmodically. One of the three females jangled a tambourine; the other two clanged cymbals. A large man and a fat boy supported a drum between them. The man beat the tightened skin in a vigorous effort to scare away any lurking devils—or ward off the chill of the wind—I couldn't decide which. In their wake trailed a few human derelicts. I drew Peggy close to the building, that they might pass on their way.

"O sinners, come and be saved," rose a female voice from amid the din. "Jesus died for you. Come! Come! Come and be saved!"

Others of the band took up the chant. The cornet expired in a wail. The drum beat out the rhythm of the exhortation. "Come! Come! Come and be saved! Come! Come! Come and be saved!"

The stillness, the mystery, the darkness, seemed to vanish before the onslaught of that valiant band. A few curious heads appeared from lighted doorways, leered, or made coarse jests—disappeared. A drunken lumberjack swaggered from one saloon and joined the stragglers following the band. Beside Peggy I stood quietly, listening, looking, trying to understand something of the spirit that impelled men and women to brave the elements and ribald scorn. Their display of effort was wasted—or was it? I recalled Bruce's interpretation of the Bible—"a beautifully written book . . . first prepared from the fables and myths of the preceding centuries." . . . Only a book? I asked myself. But what gave birth to the fables and myths? Was it possible that hidden within those pages there was a spirit of fire that warmed people so that they forgot their personal comfort? Had the fine fire of unquenchable belief that sustained martyrs through their torments been concealed in those writings?

The booming of the drum and the chanting of the group ceased. They turned a corner; some of the stragglers followed, others stepped into saloons, as though drawn by a magnet. What divided the derelicts in their choice? What held some on the trail of the religious band and what drew others aside?, I must have voiced the last question, for Peggy answered me. "Let's follow and find out."

"What's the use?" I said quickly. I was unwilling to admit her to my mood; was, in fact, annoyed that she had inserted herself so with such facility. It was an intrusion upon my mind.

"We're down here just to see what we can see—why not do so?" She elected to meet my action by closing her mind against me and her tone was that of a correcting schoolteacher.

The mission windows were white with steam. On the glass a brave chalk-design of holly-berries and green leaves surrounded staggering red letters: "GOD IS LOVE." Inside, a stove glowed in one corner. The warmth was pleasant—until I breathed the air. Long rows of benches, crowded with men and an occasional woman, extended from where we stood to a raised platform upon which a group sat, semicircular, under a cluster of lights. A man was speaking from the platform—in his hand a book.

"I'm so glad you've come," a light voice said. I felt Peggy's clasp upon my arm tighten. We turned to confront a fat, gray-haired lady who had materialized beside us. Her small eyes seemed to disappear as she forced her jowls upward in a smile. "Will you have a seat, please?" Taking our answer for granted, she guided us down the central aisle. Near the dais the benches were less crowded. I followed Peggy and received the brunt of the stares from turned heads.

With unnecessary bustling and gesturing the fat lady indicated our seats. I thanked her and she pitched her voice to a stage-whisper: "You're always welcome." Then she turned to beam at the man with the book.

Just in front of me sat a frail woman with a child on either side of her and in her arms she held a baby. Beyond her on the floor rested the drum and other instruments of the street band. A tall woman, whose hair looked like a cone set upon her head, was seated upon a stool before a small organ. The man on the platform nodded to her and the instrument awoke to life. I thought of my aunt's organ and wished for another kettle full of hot water. Then berated myself for the sacrilegious thought.

People rose from their seats, books clasped in hands held on a level with their chins. Someone had handed a book to Peggy. We stood holding it between us. Covert glances from those seated near us registered upon my consciousness. I exchanged a look with Peggy and was surprised to note the guilelessness of her countenance. Her upturned face held the serenity of Saint

Cecilia; then I thought of the visit from the angel and changed the comparison to the Madonna.

> *There is POW-er, POW-er,*
> *Wonder-working POW-er,*
> *In the BLOOD of the LAM-b. . . .*

It burst upon me like a sudden blast from a furnace. Instinctively I started. My thumb clenched the book tightly, the page was torn half across. With each repetition of "power" the very air seemed to vibrate. The walls of the room flung back the word and I was caught in a cross-fire of energy. My knee touched the bench in front of me and I experienced a tingling sensation. The combined voices swelled and assailed my ears in thunderous volume. From the platform the man with the book descended and possessed himself of the drum. In his ecstasy he shouted and beat the heel of his hand against the drum. One of the women from the semicircle joined him. Together they paraded down the aisle, singing and shouting: "There is POWER, POWER . . ."

The organist swayed and beat the keys with her hands, flail-like. Her elbows, extended like angle-irons, raised and lowered with the motions of a crippled bird in flight. I watched her, fearful that something was about to break. She jerked her head backward and added her voice to the bedlam. Two women waved books in a swinging motion and walked about on the platform, their faces flushed from the force of their singing. One of the children in front of me began to cry. His terrified face turned towards Peggy and she smiled at him. He put his hands against his ears, closed his eyes. Peggy leaned forward to stroke his hair. He grasped her hand and held it tightly, then opened his eyes and blinked to clear them of tears. His mother looked down upon him, half turned to Peggy, then shook the boy's hands loose. She frowned and the boy cringed. Peggy looked past me to the returning couple with the drum.

It seemed shoddy, cheap, devoid of all sincerity. There was an amateurish air about the actors that mildly disgusted me. I visualized our group putting on such a performance and the present one suffered in comparison. Then the song ended. A few beats of the drum followed the organ's cessation, as though the man had been unable to control his arm. A moment of silence. Murmurs from the audience. A hacking cough sounded from one side. It was repeated and caught up and spread in an epidemic of coughing and clearing of throats. Occupants of the benches shifted and scraped their feet as they sat down. The organist began another tune. From a half-darkened corner of the room, to one side of the platform, a young girl emerged into the light.

Instantly the sense of shoddiness, cheapness and insincerity left me. She was slender and pale of face, but possessing two unusually bright, dark eyes. There was a feline grace to her movements and as she faced the crowd, her lips parted in a smile radiating an almost divine gladness. I sensed Peggy's antagonism and knew I was right in my estimate of the newcomer's personality.

She had opened a book without looking at the pages and each touch of her fingers was a caress, imparting to that battered volume an importance that made me want to possess it. From her throat she poured forth a poignant sweetness that even the organ could not impair. In her notes there were perfume and flowers, bird songs and children's laughter; interwoven through them an indefinable quality like the mingling of goodness, purity and transcendental beauty. I was swirled away from the sordid room and transported to a fair, fragrant realm of rosy hues. Bathed in the glow of an ineffable light, I drifted on the billowy clouds of a supreme contentment. Comparative qualities ceased to exist: there was no meanness, hatred, or jealousy— love, loyalty, or confidence. I saw those emotions for the shallow terms they were. I had no need of them. I understood them for the poor names they were for our frailties. Past bewilderments melted under the gaze of my new comprehension. Below, in a murky valley, my acquaintances struggled. And I wondered at their willful rejection of the happiness that was mine—for it seemed they heard the voice to which I had listened and shut their ears against it. A great compassion moved me—then suddenly I grew afraid! It was not right that I should know such happiness. What had I done to deserve this? I doubted my ability to sustain the perfection of my mood. With my doubt was born a vague unrest. I sought to calm myself, but the restlessness grew. From the heights of my quivering uncertainty I peered downwards; gradually the cloud tilted and I drifted softly on to the emerald grass covering a mountain, which bordered the valley. I stood erect and strove to ascend my former billow, but the rose-tinted cloud melted, as though dispersed by my hands. The light grew less bright, then dim and when I looked up from where I walked, the first gleam of silver stars showed in the faint blue of evening sky. I wandered about, distraught, futilely trying to hold within me the joyousness of my waning contentment. But the more violent my efforts to retain it, the more rapid its passage. Abruptly I found myself on the edge of a great declivity. A moment I hesitated; the quick descent offered attracted me—but I drew back and made a final effort to ascend. Recklessness, engendered by my failure, brought me again to the abyss. A moment I stood resolute, then I danced, deliciously mad, over the edge of the precipice. . . .

"Won't you give your soul to God?" a voice pleaded in my ear. "Come to the mercy-seat—kneel and He will forgive you all. Come and we will pray for you."

I stared into the darkness of the uprushing canyon and it gradually took form. The ground was uneven and swelled in small mounds. The red-brown earth parted and I saw two small, white rows like bleached tombstones. Just as my crash was ringing thousands of bells about me, I shut my eyes, to reopen them immediately. I was staring into the face of the fat lady!

"Come," she repeated, "we will pray for you."

The singer was gone from my sight. The fat woman put her hand under my forearm and urged me gently into the aisle. Still unable to exercise my will-power, I went hesitantly, yet unresistingly. The short distance to the foot of the platform seemed to have stretched to an infinity. With unseeing eyes, but guided by many hands, I was brought to a small bench where the fat woman knelt and pressure upon my shoulder brought me down to a like position. Then with realization came a gratefulness for the opportunity to hide my face. I buried it in my cupped hands, my elbows resting on the bench.

Someone placed an arm about my shoulders and a husky voice prayed.

"Father, hear the plea of this boy—give him of Your goodness. Enable him to see his sins and strengthen him to fight against them. Dear Father, he is young, but he is willing to come to You and he wants Your help. . . ." On and on the voice pleaded with God to speak to me, to show me the error of my ways.

I was conscious of a new sensation. I relaxed utterly and allowed another to direct my thoughts. It was pleasing: this strange sense of starting afresh to invade an exoteric world. I thought of Peggy; a phenomenal contrition suffused my being. Then an utter meditative intuition possessed me and without any effort of thought the past and future, the antecedents and consequences of our liaison made their appearance in my mind. . . .

I was jerked from my mood—someone had spoken close to me and I removed one hand from my eyes.

". . . and this girl, O Lord . . ." Peggy was kneeling a scant three feet from me! Then I was not alone in the experience I had known. She too—

Seemingly hours later, together we walked down the street of purple shadows, black employment-boards and snow-covered sidewalks. . . .

I tried to speak of the illusion I had known, but I could not utter a word. I mused, suddenly ashamed of my past relationship with her; what must she think? And in answer to my thoughts she spoke, a delicious little tremble in the words. "What a wonderful evening!"

"Then you too feel—?"

"I do," she laughed. "I feel as though we can't get home quick enough to be the world's two happiest sinners."

[IV]

One morning I had returned from the saloon next to the trick-and puzzle-store, carrying the cash with which to open the store for the day's trade. While occupied with counting the silver into the respective compartments, someone came hurriedly through the doorway and passed quickly along the counter. His agitation was evident, my glance into the mirror informed me. Something familiar about the swing of his shoulders caused me to turn.

"Red! What are you doing up in this country in the winter?"

"Tell you later. Can you plant me somewhere in the back?" He pulled open his coat and I saw a black cash-box, such as the owners of small stores use.

Taking him behind a partitioned space, I learned that he and his girl had been out "heeling" on a store. She entered and occupied the clerk in conversation; Red sneaked behind the counter and stole the cash-box. The clerk had seen him leave the store and had set up a cry. Red had run and turned into the first store that seemed to offer protection, as the snow was inches deep on the sidewalk and he could not make much speed running. He had intended to dash through the store and gain safety in the alley behind.

After the first excitement had waned, he seemed amused at the job I held. He suggested my returning with him. I explained that Ed and I had an apartment, that we were practicing an act and that I was about to be married and settle down. As I detailed my plans, they took form in my own mind. Prior to that morning I had not thought of them other than as hazy possibilities. But putting them into words seemed to give them form and soon I had convinced myself that Peggy and I were ideally mated, that I could earn enough by acting to support us until we finished writing our playlet. Then she and I would cut loose from that part of the country and travel over the United States, Canada and perhaps the Continent. Red listened and smiled.

"You get some of the craziest notions—for a guy that's not using stuff."

A week later I opened the store about eight o'clock, as usual. Two hours later Ed appeared. His eyes were large and he glanced often over his shoulder at the door.

"Listen, Ernie," he said, twisting his hands and snapping his fingers together nervously. "You know that dago I sold some marked cards to last week?" I nodded. "Well—" Ed paused, clearing his throat. "Well, I've had some trouble with him—and I've got to get out of town. Let me have what money you can and I'll send it back to you. The *Congress* leaves for Frisco in less than an hour—I can just make her. Don't tell anyone you saw me, or where I'm going—not even Peggy."

I was burning to ask him many questions. But his agitation increased so rapidly that I sensed the reason for it. I emptied the register of cash and gave it to him; he dashed out of the store.

About noontime, just before the owner of the store was due, two plain-clothes men entered. I recognized one of them as the officer assigned to cover that district. He frequently passed the store, hut this was the first time he had entered. They both exhibited a haste that warned me of some impending trouble.

Briefly they questioned me. I was about to refuse an answer to any of their questions, when I sensed that this was no small matter they were intent upon learning. Compromising to the extent of giving them only information that was known to my employer, I gauged my answers to conform to my resolve. Yes, I lived at a certain address and in a certain apartment. Yes, I slept there last night. I had left the apartment about seven-thirty. The clerk on duty at the desk would tell them that, I reasoned. Did I know a certain gambler who was known commonly as "Dago"? No, I had never heard of him. Had I seen my room-mate since I left the apartment? To deny that would have been to say that Ed was in the apartment when I left. I decided to say no more. They would not tell me the reason for all the questioning and I chose to become obstinate. Angrily they arrested me and escorted me to my apartment.

Since then I have visited slaughter-houses, but the sight that met my startled gaze that morning rivals the most bloody scene. What had been the Dago was slumped down by the foot of the bed. The sheets were streaked with crimson. Blood had been flung, as from a brush, across one wall and flecked the face of the mirror on the dresser. I could visualize Ed using his tremendous strength to throw that body about the room. Chairs were overturned and there were large, dark stains on the light-colored carpet. Ed had evidently fought the Dago with every object he could lay hands upon. That the fight started before Ed had dressed was shown by the blood on his discarded pajamas. The actual murder had been effected by use of a razor and to my horror I saw that the head of the man upon the floor was nearly severed from the body.

Relying upon the ancient formula that a murderer will confess when confronted with the corpse of his victim, the officers shoved me about the room, forced me to step in moist blood, lifted portions of the sheets and dangled them accusingly before me. I was terribly ill. Twice I vomited and although on the verge of fainting, I exercised what will-power I could command to prevent it. But only because I was fearful of babbling something while semi-conscious. Now that I knew the reason for Ed's flight, I *had* to remain silent for the three days necessary for the *Congress* to reach San Francisco.

Later I was removed to the City Prison. A check-up on the movements of the deceased on the fatal morning revealed the fact that he had been seen alive at eight-thirty by the clerk of the apartment house. Further investigation produced the fact that I had been in the saloon as usual to get cash for the store register at the usual time—about eight o'clock. The authorities were convinced that I had not committed the murder. But they spent the next week beating me and kicking me in a futile effort to make me talk. For seven days I was allowed nothing to eat but bread and water. I have a scar over my eye as a token of some officer's affectionate shoe's caressing my face while I lay on the floor, having been knocked off my feet by a viciously delivered blow to my mouth. I believe there were clubs used—after conscientious upholders of the law had bruised their hands on me. But I cannot be sure, for after the first forty-eight hours I lost account of any specific beating: it intruded only into my consciousness when a let-up of two hours or so in the torture permitted outraged nerves to recuperate sufficiently to register fresh pain.

[VII]

Peggy secured my release from that jail. She was without any money. Going from one attorney to another and talking with them, she found one who would prepare a writ to have me brought into court—and she paid him his price.

The judge who ordered the police to file charges or release me read a lecture from the bench on the need for help from all citizens in maintaining the dignity of the law. That one of my eyes was swollen shut, that my lip was split and that I was dirty and unshaven and must have shown my hunger, all these evidences of the "dignity of the law" in the treatment of a citizen did not enter his tirade.

Walking from the courtroom with Peggy, the attorney whispered that I had better leave town or the police would hold me as a material witness. This precipitated our flight, though I believe that the attorney, that noble representative of "rights of the people," did not anticipate Peggy's leaving with me.

The owner of the store, a rotund Bohemian, accepted my explanation that the missing cash had been lost by me on my way to the police station. He gave us fifty dollars and wished us well. With what clothing we could crowd into two suit-cases, the unfinished playlet and a few of Peggy's books we went to the Colman Dock and rode to Tacoma on the very same boat I had seen months before as Sir James and I entered Seattle.

[V]

The vicious treatment accorded me by the Seattle police awoke within me the first consciousness of organized society as an antagonist. Previously I had pondered on the actions of people in business, officials and members of that nebulous stratum the upper world, but only for the contrasts those actions afforded me in comparison with what they should have been. That there were hatred, prejudice, malice and other obnoxious traits in people was a matter of regret to me, but I had either refused to believe those attributes were real, or had disregarded them and taken for my own use only such of their other qualities as were acceptable. Beating and brutality opened a new vista into an alarmingly hideous world. I tried to retreat from it, sought to make it revert into some nightmarish stuff. My efforts availed me little until I had accepted the police and all persons connected with courts or the administration of law, as enemies. Then I could shove it away from me and it ceased to be the burning torment it was during the month or so that Peggy and I lived in Tacoma. Burglary provided an outlet for the spirit of revenge that rose within me—serious burglaries—not the curious visits to homes I had been making in California.

I retreated further into the world of my own creation. And from some prominence jutting above the rosy clouds of that domain, I surveyed the town of Tacoma as a field for my exclusive plundering. I was a man with a mission. I knew some of the heretic ecstasy of a crusader. I had been grievously wronged—I was imposing a just retribution on the creatures who had persecuted me. They believed differently from me. Who was to determine the propriety of my acts? Taking the history of Christianity, the conquest, or, more fittingly, the rape of this country from the Indians, as my guide, I found that I was not only justified, but performing an exalted work. I do not believe that phrases it completely, but I saw it in the thought-forms that the preceding words convey.

My persistent pilfering soon aroused the two daily papers to condemnation of the inactivity of the police. There were editorials demanding some show of intelligence from the guardians of the peace. My egotism swelled as these papers united to protest the inability of the police to catch the burglars who were making nightly inroads upon stores, offices and residences. It is curious how a city will attract other crooks by the constant playing-up in its papers of the activity of some peculiarly elusive thief. Soon Tacoma was submerged in what the mania for catch-titles has been pleased to term a "crime-wave." Doubtless many of the crimes committed were begotten by the hysteria which mounted during that month to a crisis.

Residents who had not been allowing their desires to steal to find outlet answered the suggestive news-reports and did a little burglary to help the general cause along. Odd as this may sound, it is absolutely true. Constant suggestion will bring a man to the commission of an act that he could no more than conceive as an abstract proposition otherwise.

Newspapers employed at that time the adjectives "daring," "elusive," "clever," "mysterious" in their descriptions of crimes. What average moron who finds the bulk of his reading in the newspapers but will respond to such insidious suggestion? To be an elusive burglar, a daring robber, a clever forger, to outwit the police by being mysterious! The craving to climb out of the rut of everyday routine and be "different," even if only for a night, is universal. Hence the city suffered from many crimes, until the crisis was reached. The chief of police resigned. The new chief arrested as many suspicious characters as the jail would hold. Emergency patrolmen were scattered about the residential district and the roofs of the stores were illuminated by huge search-lights.

For two weeks I continued, but burglaries decreased almost overnight after the first beams of the lights were played about skylights and other possible means of entrance. I was not stealing much in cash and I eschewed jewelry and clothing. But continued prowling through stores that were supposed to be closely guarded supplied the papers with a sufficiency to enable them to keep alive an issue that they seemed loath to relinquish. Columns had to be filled—what better than criticism of public officials?

Peggy finally prevailed upon me to leave before being caught. She did not approve of my depredations, still—clothing *is* expensive, meals must be provided and in the face of such logic as this she allowed me to convince her—over her not too strenuous protests—that there was nothing actually wrong in my actions, if I did not bungle some affair and land in jail.

We worked on the script of our playlet and finally hit upon the title of *The Man Beast*. I was the Beast when it was later produced in San Francisco. . . .

CHAPTER 6

[I]

Christmas was approaching when we arrived in California. Although uncertain as to whether I was safe from the effects of the violated probation in Oakland and somewhat worried over the possibilities awaiting me if either of the officers from whom I had escaped in front of the pawnshop, months past, happened to recognize me, I was yet willing to risk a return to San Francisco. The greatest factor in my decision was the belief that I "belonged"—in a measure at least—and hence should rate another probation-release. Were not political favors owed to my dad? Was I not my father's son?

We first took the playlet to Paul Geirson, a florid-faced, bushy-haired windbag who conducted a dramatic school. Our object was to secure his aid in producing it with some of his pupils. The parts required three other women. Geirson recognized the merit of the thing and temporized by saying that he would try it out in his school. For two weeks we went daily to see him. He was either "out" to us, or actually absent from the city. In the interval we had opened negotiations with Sid Grauman, who was then manager of the Empress Theater, one of the old Sullivan and Considine string of vaudeville houses. He was willing to help us put it into rehearsal and suggested players for the other parts. Unable to secure the return of the script from Geirson, I brought into play my ability to make an unconventional call. I scrambled over the roof and down into his office, ransacked his desk, secured my object and, lest the call point too directly to me, scattered all his files and papers over the floor. He proved his ability as a showman by announcing to the press that manuscripts worth thousands of dollars had been stolen!

[II]

The Man Beast was produced the first week of the new year. It was in tune with the public mood then and scored a success that rather surprised Peggy and me. A girl working on a baby-dress, while her mother washed clothes, opened the act. Enter an expensively clad matron and a younger woman, bent on conveying the girl to a reform school because she will not divulge the parentage of her expected child. Discussion of morals and portrayal of the poor working-girl's slight chance to happiness under existing restraints brought cheers from the gallery and a raise in salary for us. Enter the son of the matronly lady. His recognition by the girl was the high point of the play. His fiancée swoons and his mother attempts to hide the smirch on the family escutcheon by offering to have the law's decree rescinded and the poor girl sent to some obscure part of the country. Heavy curtain-speech from the mother, bent over the wash-tub, on the elasticity of the law and a final line: "To hell with the State! The girl and I can work out our own salvation!" Not so good now, but a riot then.

The opening was on New Year's Day. Warden Johnston of San Quentin had arranged with Sid Grauman to bring the entire bill of acts over to the prison that morning. We met at the Ferry Building and arrived at San Quentin Prison about seven-thirty. Despite the early hour, there was not one protest from the performers. Rather, there was in that crowd the visible gladness which has ever marked a charity performance. Men shut away from the world were to see their first real show in years.

It was in that manner that I had my preview of the place which later housed me for many sedentary years. At one end of a low-ceilinged hall, which had once been a dining-room, a stage had been built. Watching the men in the audience while the first acts were presented, I was struck by the whole-hearted joy they expressed over the slightest mirth-provoking remark. Their approval of each act was thunderous and sincere. They were loath to permit a performer to leave the stage. I noticed that many of the men wore stripes and was informed by a convict stage-hand that they had at one time or another exhibited too much pep in their desire to leave the hospitality of the institution—and, failing, had been changed from blue-gray clothing into the more noticeable black and white stripes. The faces I could see in the light reflected from the stage were different from what I had expected. There was not one countenance that impressed me as being "criminal" in the accepted picture of the word: lantern-jawed, with low-placed ears and low of brow.

Awaiting the time for our act to go on, I mused on the curious position I was occupying. A thief many times over, I was yet able to leave that place and the two thousand other thieves when the show was concluded. And I wondered how many people who visited that place had similar thoughts. I classified all the prisoners as thieves, but my ignorance of prison populations caused me to do a minority an injustice. There is a small percentage of men in prisons who are "not there for stealing, thank God!" They form the nucleus of the religious organizations; they are the stool-pigeons and general nuisances and they will tell you in apparent sincerity how they were "framed" by vindictive "kin-folk" who wanted their property, adding, if you have not started to leave them, that "anyway, I shouldn't be here, because the girl was willing. But her mother swore that the girl was only twelve—and she looked every day of fourteen!"

The closing line of our act almost caused a riot. When Peggy's cue gave her pseudo-mother a chance to shout: "To hell with the State!" pandemonium broke loose. What a choice morsel then! It would have constituted an act of treason three years later....

As I left San Quentin that noon and hurried beside the others to catch a ferry back to San Francisco, I was resolved that I would mentally sign a peace pact with society and continue in vaudeville. I had been fortunate in avoiding arrest many times and I was of no mind to tempt Fortune further.

The Man Beast played three consecutive weeks at the Empress. It was posted on the billboards about town like a circus. The heartening success seemed to assure the future for Peggy and me. I had found a legitimate work that was intensely interesting, yet allowed me leisure for further development.

But the very success that had seemed to open up an attractive, legal livelihood proved my undoing. Although I was using an assumed name on the program, some of the friends I had in Oakland attended the theater and, in the manner common to those who get you killed while trying to do you a favor, they spread the report of my appearance. Friends are like that—especially the friends of a thief. Anxious to the point of imbecility that he shall be given full credit for his accomplishments, they will mention his name in connection with some crime. Their intent is to show his cleverness. Their accomplishment is to show the police the way to him. The result of the talk over my stage appearance was that an efficient detective arrested me after an evening performance. I had violated probation and I was called to account. The violation consisted in my not sending in a written report regularly, to fill the file assigned to me when I was released from jail.

Although I argued that I was then engaged in a lucrative profession and that I was destined for better positions as my ability increased, my argument was turned against me. The very fact that I had performed in that arena of the devil and in an act that was destructive to good morals, according to the officials, was prima facie evidence that I was a subject needing the training that only a reform school could give. Had I been previously employed digging ditches for a dollar a day, instead of acting in vaudeville for sixty dollars a week, they would have overlooked my neglect to report and considered me a rising young man.

I tried to persuade them to my point of view, but I lost that argument. My father, however, arranged for me to be sent to southern California, to the George Junior Republic—a self-government school—which sometimes accepted delinquents from the courts. This, he explained to me, was vastly different from being sent to the state reform school.

[III]

The probation officer, a chap with a keen appreciation of a youngster's problems, but hampered in his desire to handle certain cases by the senseless routine of his office, accompanied me to the boat that was to take me to San Pedro.

"You are being sent down there alone. I shall not even inform the captain of the boat that you are under commitment. Now, give me your word of Honor that you will report to the officer from the school and that you will not try to avoid him. He will meet you at the dock."

He had a pleasant smile as he extended his hand. What boy of sixteen would not respond to such an appeal I was on my Honor! I clasped his hand and pledged myself, adding that if I missed the official, I would go straight to the school by myself.

Although he left the ship fifteen minutes before sailing-time and I was sorely tempted to sneak ashore and rejoin Peggy, that phrase "on your Honor" loomed large and I respected it. I have often thought of that incident since then. A similar situation occurred to a man I met in prison: he had become separated from the sheriff who was taking him there for a fifteen-year sentence. Knowing the sheriff as a man reputed to be "square," the prisoner had felt impelled to deliver himself to the prison. He had served five years when I talked with him and in reply to my question whether he would repeat his performance, he said: "I'll tell the world I wouldn't—what an eighteen-carat sap I was!"

But my reasons for agreeing to deliver myself were not altogether altruistic. I had been assured by my father that I would not be left in the school for long and I visualized the future in terms of the theatre. How would it be possible for me to appear upon a stage if I were a fugitive?

I missed Peggy's companionship. We had come together so easily, there had been such a natural acceptance of each other, that I was not aware of the place she really occupied in my thought until we had been separated. On the trip south I spent the greater part of the night walking about the deck and devising schemes for rejoining her soon. The show was billed to appear in Los Angeles within a month. I might prevail upon the school authorities to allow me to play with her during that time! I had much to learn about the management of schools for reforming boys. But at that time it seemed logical: I desired it, it would mean a great deal to me—why should it not be so? Having twisted the future to fit my idea of how it should unfold itself, I retired. I was lonesome that night and just before daylight, when I finally dozed off, I experienced a return of the bitterness that had filled me because of the police brutality I had suffered in Seattle. To that I attributed my present position—my isolation from Peggy. Although I had been separated from her but three days, I had colored our time together with the rosy-tinted delights that one never knows except in retrospection. Trivial moments of happiness with her returned as transcendental joys. The longer I dwelt upon them, the greater became their allure. I had never known what living meant, until I met her! And, with our act a success, we had built wonderful plans—to enjoy together—but the affair in Washington State had forced us from there and into the arms of one of my past crimes and what had loomed so attractively was now shattered. My decision to meet the school officer wavered as a flood of bitterness all but mastered me—but I had given a pledge of Honor! In futile circles I sought to find the end of my Gordian knot. One moment I had justified to myself any action that would bring Peggy and me together; the next I berated myself for even entertaining the thought of not keeping faith with the man who had trusted me. . . .

[IV]

When the ship docked, I went ashore. Waiting until most of the crowd had dispersed, I sought out the officer. Fully an hour passed before he arrived. When he saw me, he made a quick comparison of a photograph that had been sent to him by mail, then swooped upon me like a chicken-hawk. His nose was long—like the beak of a fowl—his thin lips and lack of chin marking him for the small-spirited creature his actions displayed. I resented his attitude towards me, for he radiated a distrust. That I could have avoided him seemed never to have entered his calculations and he walked close to me as though fearful that I should run away at the first opportunity.

"Big for your age," he remarked, "but that won't hurt none—you can mix more concrete than a little fellow." He exposed tobacco-stained teeth in what I assumed was an attempt to smile.

"Mix what?" I asked.

"Concrete! Building a new hall now. All the boys work on it—that is, most of them. Best place for you—learn a good trade. Don't turn up your nose that way! Do you think you're better than somebody else?" He snapped out the question, daring me to assert that I was.

"No, but I thought this was a school—classes—all that."

"Well, we'll do your thinking. Concrete is where you go. The court sent you here and you're going to learn to work. This is a self-supporting school. You can earn nine dollars a week—and if you're careful and do your own washing, you can save two dollars almost. Some of the boys save enough to buy their own overalls. You'll have to get rid of them clothes you're wearing and I suppose you got more in your bags, but you can't be no better'n nobody else—you have to *earn* your money here."

The sharp contrast of his description of the treatment I should receive with the plaudits and attentions of theatrical folk was far from being attractive. Earn nine dollars indeed! I had more than twice that in my possession at the moment. What reason for not being "better'n nobody else"? I *did* feel superior to any boy of my age—I had played the part of a man, both on and off the stage. I was able to take care of myself—and he was going to teach me to mix concrete.

I thought of the expression Sir James's face would show could he have listened to my present mentor's talk while we rode to Los Angeles on the electric car. The probation officer had told me it would not be difficult for me to get along at the school because of my older appearance—and here that very experience was being used against me, for when I outlined briefly my past occupation, the school officer frowned and said: "If that's what you was doing, it's high time they sent you down here where we can get you away from them influences. You ought to know that you got to work for everything you get in this world. Look at me—I've worked all my life" (he was about forty years old) "and you can see from my hands how hard I labored. See them calluses? Well, I didn't get 'em at no theatre and look at the position I hold now!" He straightened his shoulders and elevated his chin. "I'm in charge of the whole farm at the George Junior Republic."

An auto met us at Pomona. We reached the school late in the afternoon. Just as we entered the grounds, the officer gave me a bit more information on the operation of the school and paved the way for me to make a decision that I had been seeking desperately to justify.

"We ain't got no walls about our place," he said. "If you want to run away, you can—but just you try it! We'll get you and..."

But I had ceased to listen to him. He had solved my problem. Had he said I was Honor-bound to remain, I should have been sorely beset. But he had thrown down a challenge! "Just try it!" Would I! The probation officer had only pledged me to report to the school. I had done that—now I was free to accept the taunt of the officer—and I did!

About three o'clock next morning I lowered myself from a dormitory window, gained the ground and escaped in the fog that had mercifully risen during the night. Some boy, infatuated with the privilege of earning nine dollars a week, was unable to understand the imbecility of one who was not so enamored and sounded an alarm. I don't know what effort was made to recapture me, but I reached Los Angeles the following afternoon.

[V]

I secured a cheap room in an obscure hotel and lived as economically as possible. I passed most of my time in my room reading. Peggy and the company would soon be in town, I reasoned. I would fill my old part; we would route the show out of the state. The money I had was soon spent. I did not want to steal. I had seen the results of persistent stealing, in the prison and I had glimpsed a place that seemed even more terrifying—where they taught one to mix concrete! In both places I had experienced the feeling that life was a rather useless spark to one confined in them. As a result of my resolve to build my future on histrionic ability I forced myself to live on free lunches from the saloons along Main Street. What exercise I took was taken in the alleys and in places where I could not be apprehended. It seemed to me, in my constant depression, that every passing citizen eyed me with suspicion. And to lessen chances of detection I studied my facial expressions in long periods before a mirror and schooled myself to hold an innocent countenance, which later saved me much trouble.

But bartenders are hard-hearted individuals—they ordered me away from the lunch-counters when I failed to buy a drink. One night, hungry, yet unwilling to steal, I tried begging. I started to ask fifty people to hear my tale of woe—and was never able to open my mouth. As I would approach some man, my opening question trembling on my lips, I would suffer a drill that froze my vocal organ—and in silence I would pass him by.

Returning to my room, my hunger unappeased, I brushed against a woman in the dimly lighted hall. A member of the world's oldest profession I found her to be. My mumbled apology formed an opening for a quick acquaintanceship. I accepted her invitation to enter her room. Although I fully expected her to wax furious when she learned that I was without funds, I was lonesome and desperately desired to talk with someone. A few moments of desultory fencing and she knew my status.

She was a battle-scarred old harridan, but the cloak of her occupation fell instantly. "Well, for the love of Christ, kid, why didn't you say so! Here!" From a stocking she extracted a few crumpled bills and extended one to me.

For a moment I hesitated. That soiled bit of green paper seemed symbolic of something unclean. Chagrin, resentment, a prudish disdain filled me. I hated myself for being in such a position. The ready sympathy of the woman was lost upon me—I saw the action only as one wherein I played a despicable part. Yet I was unwilling to insult her.

"Take it," she urged. "It's only a dollar, but I didn't have any luck tonight. Tomorrow, maybe—"

Snatching the bill, I fled from the room and out of the hotel. Twice I started into a restaurant. Twice I turned about and continued down the street, then stood on a street corner for a quarter-hour. I was hungry, I said, I just had to eat and one dollar is like another—but was it? The internal argument swerved from an attempt to satisfy my hunger to the lack of principle I displayed in accepting the money.

It was nearly one o'clock when I stood before a restaurant again. There were few people at the long counter and none at the tables. A man brushed by me and entered. His walk and form were unmistakable—Ed!

He had hardly seated himself when I reached his side. Gone was all thought of food. I was wanting to extend my hand and tell him of the many things that had intervened since he fled Seattle, but as our eyes met, I refrained. There was a startled expression in his face that seemed not born entirely of our unexpected meeting. It struck me as being a set expression—weeks old.

The waiter finally dispatched with our order, I turned to Ed. "Well?"

"Going to Australia—next week—enlist in the army—better come along." He jerked out the words as though he had spoken against his will. I had a quick mental flash of him during the weeks past: secretive, morose, fighting against he knew not what.

"Perhaps I will," I replied. "How can we get there?"

"I can fix it for us two to work on a boat. Then we can say we're Canadians and get into the army—anything is better than this—" He opened both hands and laid them palm-upward on the table.

Suddenly I knew a superiority. Whereas I had been desperately lonely when I had left my room, I was now glad that I had not the torment that caused Ed, in his anxiety to rid himself, to welcome the chance to share it. I believe the feeling I had then was the same as certain welfare workers know when they come into a crowded jail-corridor to tell the inmates how much better it is to live an honest, upright, Christian life. I felt a security in knowing that, regardless of how much I must contend with in avoiding apprehension, Ed had a hundred more terrifying specters to fight. . . . But he was my friend. He and I had shared the scant offerings of life together and I was ashamed of my thoughts. Australia! The very name spelled adventure. I was not greatly taken with the idea of entering the army—I had heard that they rose at day-break—and that would dispel all romance of war for me. Then the thought—Peggy!

I reconciled the thought of her with Ed's offer in the manner best calculated to make decision easy: a week must elapse—I would see what happened in that time Ed paid for our scant meal. Together we repaired to my room. He had a few dollars in his possession, but his wardrobe consisted of the clothes he wore. While we talked, harsh voices from the hall interrupted us. Ed's face went several shades paler.

"Don't be making a rumpus, Kate, you old tramp. You been up often enough to know it ain't no use arguing."

Switching off the light in our room, I peered over the transom and down the hall. Two men stood in the lighted doorway of the woman's room. She who had befriended me attempted to break from them. "Better come easy," one of them said, jerking her to him.

"Aw, leave me alone," she pleaded, "I ain't well—and I ain't been on the streets for most a week."

"Don't be tryin' to bull me. I saw you myself. Come on—"

"Well," the other man drawled, "well, she might be able to—"

"Post bail?" Kate asked listlessly. "Say, I ain't got but three dollars—and you'd want more'n that, wouldn't you?" she concluded with a trace of hope in her voice.

"We don't want none of your three dollars, Kate," said the first man, "but we gotta take you down if you can't put up at least twenty-five bucks."

"Aw, you guys—where'n hell would I get twenty-five bucks?" Kate stepped between them. They escorted her towards the stairs and I heard her say: "You got fifteen from me last time—and that was—"

"Shut up!"

Ed whispered to me from the darkness of the room. "I thought they was after me. It's a shame to be grafting off a poor woman like that."

My hand stole into my pocket and touched the crumpled bill.

"Twenty-five dollars," I mused. Suddenly I was angry. Quickly I explained to Ed what I knew of the woman. I resolved to go out and steal the twenty-five dollars as soon as I could and I urgently offered Ed the opportunity to accompany me. With the determination to repay the woman's kindness came a lightening of the depression that my earlier meeting with her imposed.

"Steal from a house?" Ed said. "That's not right. I didn't know you did things like that."

His attitude was sincere, but at that moment I wanted to punch him. Almost cutting off a man's head a few weeks ago and now protesting against mere burglary. He was what is known as an honest man. Work of any legitimate nature was acceptable to him, but at the thought of dishonest work he revolted.

I had to get that money. Though I would not steal for myself earlier in the evening, I now felt the incentive to get the money which would release that woman from jail and restore some of my self-respect—odd way of arriving at a conclusion. But I had received contaminated money; I could compensate for the gift only with money in kind.

I had a rather exciting time in obtaining that money. In the bedroom of a residence I annexed a pair of trousers with a gratifyingly heavy purse inside. Replacing them on the chair, I must have caught a suspender strap over my foot. As I took my first step away, the trousers toppled the chair to the floor and the sleeping occupants of the bed awoke to emit lusty protests against my intrusion. I slid down a flight of steps and nearly made a new doorway through the side of the house, in getting out of it. Running across the lawn, I greatly increased my speed when the householder began to fire a revolver into the air.

From an all-night drug-store I telephoned the police station to ask if bail was set for—and suddenly I realized that I knew only the name "Kate." Chancing it, I asked the officer the amount of Kate's bail. He knew her, laughed and asked if I was waiting for her.

The first faint light of dawn was outlining the furniture of the room when I rejoined Ed. I had sent a messenger with the money to post Kate's bail and while I undressed, I heard her come up the stairs and enter her room. . . . Ed was nervous and when I showed him the rest of my money about eighteen dollars—he frowned on my act. But I was tired and I drifted off to sleep while he whispered his fears to me.

It was close to noon when I awakened. Light from a partly opened window showed Ed's face pale and his lips trembling, as he breathed unevenly. I raised myself on one elbow to peer more closely at him. He emitted a sigh so tremulous that it gave me a queer sensation about my heart. He lay like a man slumbering under a powerful drug and subconsciously struggling against it. I shook him. He opened his eyes, started slightly, then recognized me. Disturbed, I rose to dress and again tried to rouse him, but he protested weakly and closed his eyes. He was lying flat upon his back and when I suggested his coming with me to a restaurant for breakfast, he turned his head to one side. The response was that of a man utterly exhausted and absolutely indifferent to all interests.

When I returned to the room late that afternoon, he was lying in the same position. My efforts to arouse him were of no avail. Alarmed over his condition, I brought a doctor and learned that Ed had "a slight fever and had better rest for a few days." After the doctor left, Ed tried to turn over, but something prevented him. I had the notion that some gigantic spike had been driven through his chest, holding him to the bed. I turned him and tried to make him talk. He would make a clicking sound with his tongue, refuse more than a meagre swallow of water, then relapse into his former position. When his fever mounted, he grew delirious and twisted about like a spent beetle on a pivot. At about ten o'clock he grew quiet again. At midnight he was dead.

Despite his powerful body he had been but a child mentally. His fear and his inability to control it, had killed him. His was the most perfect case of fatal suggestion that I've ever witnessed. I did not think of it as such then; rather, I was terrified to the point of being unable to leave the room until morning. Throughout the remainder of the night I sat and pondered. All the thoughts that raced through my mind are impossible to recount now. The sorrow and pity I felt for him were submerged in the terror that would allow me neither to cover his face nor to leave the room. As I regarded him from time to time, he seemed to grow smaller. Beneath my gaze his face shrank and his form collapsed. I would force myself to look away from him; then, with no desire to do so, I would find myself contemplating him again. And with each eye I saw him differently. Closing one eye, I could focus only a portion of him; then when I opened it, the form seemed to move; and with the other eye closed, he assumed a different position. Yet the inanimate body appeared to me as always having been void of life. The chap with whom I had laughed and worked, the same smiling, good-natured Ed who had acted his part in *The Bluebird* with a fervency that seemed to promise a splendid future—all that held no relation to the shrinking form upon the bed. The thing that lay there was inert and gruesome.

I pondered long on the change that occurred to make his once lively body assume the guise of some hideous and repulsive thing. That he was simply dead did not suffice. Even while I stiffened in my chair in the horror of my position, I wondered just what had left him and where it had gone. To lie down and kill oneself by thinking about death was too easily understood—I wanted a more involved explanation. "He is dead," I would say to myself and then I would repeat the word "d-e-a-d" and picture it, as on an electric sign. One letter winking out to be followed by another, then the whole word flashing bright and sharply outlined against a black canopy. The dazzlement seemed but a ruse to prevent my seeing into the darkness beyond. I puzzled my brain over the problem and attempted to discard the word for some picture that would lessen my bewilderment. Then, finding myself gazing fascinatedly at his face—dead! dead! But why? For what purpose? "An eye for an eye?" No! I would not believe that and yet—? To be strong and able to walk about one evening and at almost the same hour the next evening to be dead! It was unreasonable. And he had done it himself—no one had lifted a hand against him! I recalled the telepathic act and the tremendous power of thought-transference. But that was disciplined training of the mind. The regularly swung pendulum had enabled Mercies and his girl to memorize their subjects. But Ed! His was the untrained mind counting only one subject! I could see a word on a long, twisted rope—swinging out into some obscurity and returning to glide past is eyes. The word on the rope was "MURDER." And with clock-like regularity it swung before him. Into the darkness—out into his vision. Again and again it was before him. Evenly timed, precise and maddeningly gauged, it must have beaten against his sanity until that fragile bulwark crumpled. His utter lack of mental power to dominate the swinging of that word, his inability to substitute another thought for it, had, like drops of water against a stone, worn away his resistance and—again I was staring at the form! I shuddered and, failing to shake off the horror of my own thoughts, sought relief by retreat from the reality of the situation and achieved a comparative equanimity—just before day-break.

. . .

[VI]

Having broken my decision not to steal and being again in funds, it was natural that I should continue. Los Angeles seemed to be made for a burglar's operation. Everything combined to assist me. The mild climate enticed many of the residents from their homes during the afternoons. With an order-book in one hand I approached many cottages and bungalows, ascertained their state of occupancy and entered those temporarily vacated.

When Peggy arrived, I was in possession of about three hundred dollars and a presentable wardrobe. Although I had seen posters of *The Man Beast* for several days before the act actually appeared, they seemed not to concern me. For some reason the fact that I was fugitive from the school gave me the feeling of being removed from the sphere in which I had formerly moved so confidently.

Unable to locate her at any of the leading hotels, I waited until after the first matinee to talk with her. To pass the time I attended the show, mentally reciting the lines to assure myself that I had not forgotten my part. The man who was playing in my stead was a handsome chap; even without stage make-up he would have presented a striking appearance. I knew a vague jealousy. As I watched him perform, that jealousy became more than a passing emotion—it seemed to take form. A prey to my imagination and being a very human young man, I credited him with usurping my place in the affections of Peggy. It is natural for a man to render the worst possible interpretation of such a situation. The egotistical assurance that runs beside it says: "Such a thing couldn't possibly happen, bub—" And in the conflict of thoughts I found a tormenting pleasure.

She stepped from the stage-door and stood still a moment, as though undecided where to go. She was dressed in a new sport ensemble; her eyes were yet lighted from the emotion of the final scene, with an air of confidence and independence previously not so distinctly hers. I saw her as a desirable creature from a different and seemingly remote, part of my life. She had not yet seen me. Thinking of the reception that would be accorded me upon our reunion, I had visualized it in terms of emotions. Colors, lights and shadows; soft words and over it all an enchantment of some hidden music. Here the harsh street-noises intruded, the scarred door framing her detracted from the picture and her attitude of being totally oblivious of my proximity contrasted so sharply with my expectation that I felt cheated. Curious, how anticipated meetings are at variance with their actual consummation.

She turned towards me and I stepped before her. She raised her eyes and with recognition came a startled look. Her left hand rose in an unconscious gesture of warding off a blow. The third finger was encircled by a plain gold band. The features of her face grew indistinct—my eyes were blurred to all except that bit of gold. I must have said something about it. I continued to gaze at the dull gleam from it as though hypnotized.

"Didn't you know?" Her voice reached me, carried on roaring waters that threatened to burst my eardrums. I shook my head. I was incapable of speech.

"Why, Farral and I were married—two weeks ago. He's with the show and is playing . . ." But I had turned and walked away.

[VII]

Humiliation and a growing hatred filled me. The greatest tragedies of life are not the cataclysmic destructions that devastate one's home, one's business, or one's family. Rather, it is the little incidents, trivial in the retelling, that wreak the greatest havoc. The loss of confidence in a trusted friend or lover is, perhaps, the most chaotic catastrophe a young person may know. To have given freely and without restraint and to have received, seemingly, from the loved one the same degree of affection; then to have that confidence discarded—made a mock! For with the realization that Peggy was irrevocably gone came the belief that I was passionately, madly, in love with her. The thought of the gleam of calculation I had caught in her appraisal of me at the time of our first meeting returned to me and I put it from me as a trick of my imagination. No! No! She had not willingly married another man. There must have been some coercion, some fearsome pressure put on her. That the hours we had spent together meant so little to her that she could forget them within two weeks was impossible. Consideration of this affair now makes the reason for my disturbance all too plain. But at that time it loomed as a black wall before me. It was the end of all dreams, the utter and complete destruction of the future. Life held so little when one was alone—and lonely. Of what use to carry on? . . .

Aimlessly I wandered about the sidewalks. Gone was all thought of time. Although I kept a watch for anyone who might seem to be paying me undue attention, it was with a tiny speck of my brain. I was abjectly miserable. With Peggy so definitely removed from me, I found her more desirable than ever. No one could ever replace her. I should spend the rest of my life in wearing a mournful expression and sighing—sighing prodigiously, with the whole weight of my dead love pressing out each sigh. I tried it—and achieved a gratifying feeling of despondency. For perhaps two hours I walked about town, sighing and looking into store mirrors to determine whether my face was sufficiently mournful. I made one of those momentous decisions and determined that for all time I would bemoan my fate.

Then I discovered that I was hungry. Food? Why, even to think of such common material while sorrow was upon me brought a sense of inward betrayal! I, enter a restaurant and eat? Sit at a table and order a meal as though my soul were not slowly dying? No—no—no—a thousand times no! I would, instead, walk until I became faint, then fall in my tracks and be taken to a hospital, where I could be comfortable while I slowly pined away. But my feet protested against further pounding on pavement; I compromised. With the thought of resting only until I could continue my walking I sank into the seat the waitress indicated.

Late that evening, restless and not knowing exactly how I should conduct myself to extract to the last bitter drop the deadly poison of self-sympathy with which I was determined to exterminate myself, I boarded a street car, bound for Hollywood. I must have an audience to appreciate my suffering. Lacking a stage, I chose a prominent seat and slumped so far into it as to attract attention. But people are so indifferent towards another's grief! As I passed a street carnival, the thought occurred to me that I would be more profoundly depressed were I in the atmosphere of our former happiness.

Leaving the car, I strolled by the various attractions. Entering one after another by muttering the magic word "Shill" to the ticket-taker, I had almost exhausted the offerings when I saw Tiny in a snake pit. There were few people watching her and shortly they departed.

Our recognition was mutual. Holding a large, sleepy snake in one hand and treading clumsily over the others, she gained the edge of the canvas pit and greeted me effusively. I was glad to see her, though slightly hampered in my attempts to tell her of my great sorrow by the careless manner in which she waved the snake about to emphasize her remarks. She had fresh versions of her thwarted love-affairs to tell me, but she balked my efforts to reveal to her the battered condition of my heart. Misery loves company, but not when two miserables are trying to pour out their own troubles at the same time. I left soon after a crowd gathered and the owner of the pit had directed Tiny to have the snakes do their tricks for the cash customers.

[VIII]

Next morning I took stock of myself. That I had lived through the night was a disappointment. But since I was alive, there was nothing I could do about it. It was ten o'clock. The bed was comfortable. The service of the first-class hotel was mine by a mere indication of what I desired. Counting my money gave me no pleasure—I wished mightily that I were back in the little room in Tacoma. But in the light of a sunshiny morning the gloom that had enveloped me the previous night was not so thick. As I lay considering it, it suddenly seemed terribly far away. Yesterday! Why, it had taken its place with a thousand other yesterdays.

I decided, with one of those decisions that I was constantly changing, that the rising moon should look for me in vain. But where to go—what to do? What there had been in store for me had soured in the keeping. The authorities from the George Junior School might be searching for me and it was an act of wisdom to leave Los Angeles. But in what direction? Mexico? Full of *revolucionarios!* Australia? A war and the prospect of being a soldier. San Francisco? No. Seattle? Well, the boat trip would be pleasant—but no. Go east—where? From the recesses of my mind came the same urge that had prompted Buddy and me to reach Chicago. That was it—Chicago! For no particular reason—just because it was away from Los Angeles. . . .

Having mentally made the journey, discarded all thought of the trouble I had been through on the Pacific Coast, I rose and dressed. In my new objective there was a lure that allowed me little time to prepare. By telephone I ascertained the train schedule and learned that I could start within the hour. Hastily I packed and summoned a taxi. I was alive with enthusiasm.—

nothing could be accomplished quickly enough to please me. I urged the driver to greater speed, promising to pay his fine if we were stopped. To reach that train and be actually started on my trip became an obsession.

Just as I left the cab, an officer arrested me and half an hour later I was in the City Jail.

[IX]

"You shoulda known we'd get you, kid," an officer remarked as I was being held in an ante-room. "Why, we've had pictures of you for a week. And you've been doin' a lot of prowling too—haven't you?"

"Prowling?" I looked as innocent as I could. "What's that?"

"You don't know, of course," he answered, with heavy sarcasm. "Say! most of the beefs from the residence section give a description that tallies with you to a T."

I protested my innocence and professed ignorance, but he showed me a photograph from the Berkeley police and asked if I had ever heard of the George Junior. I evaded his question by saying I had not met the young man and then asked to see an attorney. At tins display of jail knowledge he laughed and informed me I'd need several lawyers. He entered my name on the register as being held for suspicion of burglary, then locked me in a "tank." The swift change from an anticipated trip to Chicago to the filth and close confinement of that jail was the beginning of a series of such changes. After that and for years, I did not know any sensations but those of great rapture or abysmal dejection. High lights or shadows there were no middle strata.

An attorney talked with me that evening and the fact that I had more than two hundred dollars—which was speedily transferred to him—resulted in my release the following morning. As he explained the procedure to me, it amounted to "seeing the arresting officer," neglecting to inform the school authorities of my apprehension and filing a writ in the Justice Court. That the law allowed the police to hold me seventy-two hours as a "suspect" while they assembled evidence against me mattered not. The attorney "spoke" to someone who had preferred a charge of burglary. In court the attorney asked for evidence to be produced and none was forthcoming. The judge ordered my release. One parting bit of information from the barrister made plain to me why I was leaving the jail free instead of being returned to the school.

"Never be broke when you're pinched, kid. We can do nothing for you if you are. You better be careful—but if you stay in town to 'work,' and do happen to need me—well, here's my card."

Yet many people profess to be puzzled at the increase in crime!

CHAPTER 7

[I]

My father's stenographer discreetly closed the door she had opened to admit the probation officer with me.

"You're in a bad mix-up," my father stated after we were seated.

"Looks that way," I admitted and wondered over the presence of my "Wallingford" mayor in the room.

"Yes," continued my father, "you have been away from that school for almost a year—heaven knows where. What have you been doing during that time?"

Before I could reply, the probation officer said: "There's little that he hasn't been doing. The police reports on him show that he's been in jail in Los Angeles, Fresno and Sacramento. But he always managed to get out before they discovered he was wanted by us. It's a shame! You have a great lot of worry right now and that he should add this latest scandal—"

The latest scandal consisted in being overpowered in a San Francisco house after a fight with the owner. I had tried to leave when he awoke from an afternoon sleep to discover me, but he had effectively prevented my doing so. It had been but a matter of an hour after I had been delivered to the police before they communicated with Oakland and established the fact that I was a probation-violator and also an "escape" from the school. My father had set in operation some political machinery that brought me to Oakland. The probation officer had escorted me to my father's office before taking me to jail.

"Why didn't you stay at that school?" my father asked.

"Because I didn't want to," I replied truthfully. "They were going to make me mix concrete—and I didn't want to mix concrete."

Wallingford frowned and said: "It was my belief that they had a variety of trades to offer a young man."

"Well, I might stay a bit longer and see what else they have to offer," I suggested, wanting to make my return to the school as certain as possible. The three men exchanged glances. I beheld a significance in their eyes which indicated that I should not be returned to *that* school.

"You should be learning a trade," said the probation officer. "You are of the size and appearance of a grown man and you aren't able to do a single honest turn of your hand."

My father was studying the end of his cigar with rapt intent. He seemed to be considering a line of procedure. Like a teacher outlining a problem he presented a program and when he spoke, it was to all three of us.

"The furor created by your escapade in San Francisco will die down in a few weeks. We implied that we would send you to the reform school and the authorities over there released you to us. Now, what assurance have we that you will not start another rumpus in the event that you should be readmitted to probation?"

"Dad, I don't want to do any more stealing—I'm sick of it. There was a sort of attraction about it—at first—but that's gone. During this past year I've been so darn sick and disgusted with the whole mess that I'd have given anything to get squared up with everyone and not have that probation hanging over me. I can't tell you all the places where I've been or all the money I've spent, but I can tell you this: living in hotels, going to shows and just bumming around gets awfully tiresome. Sometimes I've come to my room and sat there for hours. Just sat in a chair and stared at the walls, not reading or even doing much thinking and the whole time I didn't know what to do with myself. It got so bad that I couldn't even entertain my own company— everything was flat and stale. It seems as though I've been living a million years—and yet haven't done anything that is worth thinking about . . ."

"Aren't you feeling rather sorry for yourself?" asked Wallingford.

While I had been speaking, I had seemed to glimpse some explanation of the thousand problems that had perplexed me in my year of wandering, but with the cynical interjection came a quick reaction. If he felt that way about it—all right!

"Yes, I guess I am." I looked at my father. He was still regarding the tip of his cigar.

"It seems to me," he said, turning the cigar in his fingers slowly, "it seems to me that you are ill prepared to earn your living. Now, if you could manage to stay out of jail for a few months and would study and apply yourself, you could overcome that fault. But we can't risk it—just now. I'm going to tell you just what we have to face and you can understand how we must proceed. His Honor"—indicating Wallingford—"is now campaigning for re-election. I am managing his campaign. The old judge who released you is up for re-election, too. Now, it would not be of any great importance if you were released again, except that the opposition would seize upon it. They would make capital out of any such action. They would point to it as evidence of the future intentions of our administration. If the son of the campaign manager is so leniently dealt with, what can the people expect of their interests when franchises and so forth are being granted? Can't you see the papers blazoning that in great letters?"

The probation officer looked at me and we nodded in unison.

I accepted the decision that was made soon after that. There was nothing more said of my training for future citizenship. I must accept my lot in the spirit of one who is sacrificed. But it was made plain to me that I should not have had to be sent to the reform school had I been arrested at any other time than during the heat of a political campaign.

In the reform school I met Buddy. He had been there for almost two years. He had been sent to some religious parental home when his mother parted from his father and from that place he was farmed out to an elderly couple, who took full advantage of him. He worked long hours and was frequently beaten. The reform school had sucked him into its maw a few months after he had run away from the intolerable conditions of his servitude.

Situated on the edge of the Mother Lode country, just where the Sierra Nevadas tumble down in broken confusion before flowing out into the level plain of the San Joaquin Valley, the Preston School of Industry surmounts a prominent hill, a gigantic red splash of brick buildings against the blue sky. Like a fiery, age-old beast, it glares down upon the town of Ione, California, sprawled at its feet.

What the purpose of that school was I do not know to this day. I went there with the resolve in my mind to learn some trade—to discard completely all thoughts of illegal living—to absorb some ideas that would release me from the morbid anxiety which had constantly depressed me; that was the mood with which I accepted my commitment. . . . I found meanness and hatred. The very officers who were presumed to direct and instruct were lacking in the essential abilities that should have been predominant in their characters. The language they used in speaking to the boys was full of profanity. With fifty other boys I was herded into an ill-lighted basement each evening. There we sat on benches, for three hours, often deprived of all reading-material because some petty annoyance had, in reprisal, been put upon the officer in charge of us. In the dormitories pederasty was nightly practiced. The night-watchman seemed indifferent. For weeks he would do no more than chase an amorous older boy from the bed of some youngster. Then, waxing virtuous, he would deliver a tirade against all boys who even thought about such practices. While the boys stood at their respective bedsides, naked, he would walk about and lecture us on the evil of our ways. Having temporarily induced the mood he sought, he would order us to bed. Securing the huge lock on the door, he would disappear into the hall. Half an hour later he would reappear, listlessly resume his seat and soon fall asleep. . . .

Because of my escape from the other school I was immediately labeled "suspicious" and hence put to work with a pick-and-shovel squad under the watchful eyes of three officers. This brought me in contact with most of the boys who, making the only gesture they could against their environment, had escaped, to be recaptured, or had failed in an attempt to get away. Barry, he who had first provoked me to laughter when he shaved off his eyebrows, was in that company. He had lost his happy attitude. He was sullen and spoke only grudgingly to me after our first talk. He was planning for the time only when he would be released, so that he might "get even" for all the beatings and tortures he had suffered at the hands of the authorities.

Curiously enough, I found an odd pleasure in working! The physical exercise provided an outlet for the energy I had stored within me, which I had been unable to direct. But the very release it provided seemed to increase the mental alertness that kept me ever aware of a thousand trivialities. To work with a mechanical motion soon became easy and hence I went on long flights of adventure in my imagination. There was no attempt made to control me, beyond being certain that I was among the other boys. For two months I followed that work as it progressed along a deep ditch. I entertained a queer notion that if I applied myself diligently, I should be permitted to go to another company and enter a trade. I had no preference, but the constructive work of the carpenter-shop rather appealed to me.

During an inter-company baseball game Buddy and I had our first long talk. I was startled at the difference in our mental qualities. Having carried the picture of my little playmate for several years, I was not prepared for the change that time and environment had worked in him. He had but one thought in his mind: to get out of the school! There was absolutely nothing else that interested him. He did not read, even though he had learned to do so at the parental home; and he could not take an interest in his work, for he was polishing floors and making up beds in one of the dormitories. The months spent at the school had been lived just as he was living when he said: "If I could only get out of here!"

After our conversation I grew fearful of what might happen to my mind if I remained too long at the school. I wrote to the superintendent and requested permission to have some books sent from home. He replied, after ten days, that I could draw books from the well-stocked school library. I did, but the adventures of the Rover Boys and kindred spirits failed to interest me.

Life at the school was a dull, senseless routine. Work became a nuisance. I would spend one week digging out a ditch, shoveling the muck to the edge—then occupy myself the next week in shoveling the dirt back into it. There was no reason for so doing, except that I was ordered to do it—under threat of corporal punishment. The officers vied in devising schemes that would entail the maximum amount of labor and accomplish the minimum of progress. Work was demanded of the squad with which I labored only as a means of keeping us employed. There was not one iota of intelligence displayed in ordering a boy to shovel dirt from one pile only that it might be shoveled back. I speedily developed a loathing for all work—it was senseless. . . .

[II]

"Six months of wasted effort," I said to myself one morning. "I'm going to leave—beat it, get to hell away from this place."

Recalling that decision now, the only criticism I find to make of it is that I waited six months to put it into operation.

The day was born early and the air in the dormitory, even before the signal to arise was given, was heavy with warning of the heat being developed. Restless movements among the sleepers—as though they tried to shudder off the weight of their slumber. Gazing from one window, I saw the white smoke of a distant gold-milling plant curl upwards. Against the broken, ragged-topped range of mountains it showed like a great phantom finger—beckoning, enticing. Nearer, the first shafts of the sun were brightening the dusty green trees from their blanket-like covering of the valley into the individual tips of pine and oak. An automobile chugged over the road bordering the school grounds, raising a small cloud of slow-moving dust. The crunch of gravel under officers' feet, as they assembled before the building, reached me faintly. The whistle to rise was given. I cast a last glance at the smoke finger and bounded from my bed—vibrant, eager, impatient that I should have to wait almost an hour before making my opportunity to escape.

After breakfast I feigned illness. An officer took me to the hospital and left me in company with several other boys. Another officer watched us while we awaited the arrival of the doctor. The hospital was on the third floor of the main building. We sat on benches along the hall, near stairs that let down into the administrative offices. Buddy was seated near me. In a few words I told him of my intentions. He advised me to wait until I had a better opportunity. He was certain that I could not pass through the offices below without being detected. I was adamant in my resolve. He told me he had but a few months to serve before he would go free, or he would join me. Watching my chance I crept to the stairs, descended three flights and surveyed the long hall to the main entrance.

A matron was directing the efforts of several boys while they polished the floor. Doors opened off the hall. A few officers passed from one room, through the hall and disappeared into another room. To be caught standing where I was would allow but one interpretation—the correct one. I removed my shoes and in stocking-feet walked noiselessly to the nearest boy. It was Barry! He had been transferred from the other company that morning and put to polishing floors. The gods were with me. He realized what I was trying to accomplish and at a sign from me he surrendered his polishing rag and stole to the stairs. On hands and knees I applied the rag vigorously, edging towards the matron. She stood where she could observe a boy who was working in one of the offices. As all the boys in the hall had their shoes off, she felt reasonably sure that none would attempt to leave the building. My shoes were stuffed into my shirtfront. By keeping my face averted from her I was able to work to the front doorway. For a moment she stepped into the office. Instantly I was out on the porch. An officer was coming up the steps. I dropped to my hands and knees and applied my polishing rag to the tiling of the porch floor. The officer paid me a casual glance, then entered the building. I broke a shoe-lace in my haste to get into the shoes. Making an emergency repair, I rose and ran across the road. The hill sloped gradually away from the building and was thinly planted with shrubs and small trees.

A return of that surcharge of emotion which had thrilled me on the occasion of my first burglary filled me now. A wild recklessness speeded me onward as I leaped over bushes and slid on loose ground. There was an open space of two hundred yards to traverse before crossing the road, to gain the comparative safety of the thick, high brush and trees of the mountain-side. I imagined that my escape had been detected and that officers were even then mounting horses to run me down. I could picture the commotion in progress: the matron shouting to the officer in charge and he in turn telephoning to farmers in the vicinity, ordering them to head me off and capture me. As I raced over the clear space, I expected to hear the report of a gun. I remembered the fate of another chap, who had been shot to death by the officers during an attempted escape—and I ran the faster. The shoe with the broken lace slipped from my foot and was kicked yards ahead of me. In my panic I started to run past it, then my reason commanded that I pause long enough to retrieve it. Over the rough, hard ground I bounded, carrying the shoe in my hand. Diving into the first shelter that offered itself, I forced my way through the brittle brush and turned about to gauge the proximity of my pursuers. I was little short of astounded when I realized that I was alone. The hundreds of imaginary pursuers I had mentally conjured up nearly forced me to deny the evidence of my eyes. I was alone, unpursued, yet in company with so many conflicting thoughts! "You are never less alone than when you are alone," Bruce had said. And I had a host of companions that day!

Months later I learned that Barry had resumed his place on the floor as soon as I had made off through the front door and the matron had been satisfied to count the number of boys present in the hall without verifying their identities. How many specters and anxieties does a man fight and flee from, which have no more reality than the "pursuit" I feared that day?

By the straightest line possible I was forty miles from Stockton and equally far from Sacramento. I had the choice of two routes: one through the brush and trees covering the mountains, the other across the valley. Knowing that officers from the school would soon be posted at the cross-roads and bridges, I elected to remain in the covered country and take a semicircular course that would bring me to Stockton. One foot was severely bruised and began to swell soon after I had climbed the first slope into the mountains.

Holding as nearly as possible to the smoke I had seen from the dormitory window, I traveled nearly twenty miles by evening. The heat increased until it was actually scorching, when I exposed myself to it while crossing a cleared space. I followed a river for several miles. Deep-cut in its gorge, the steep sides were difficult to scramble along. The width and rush of the water made crossing its rock-strewn current a mad risk. Near an abandoned placer I found the river bed widened and made shallow by the gravel sluiced by the miners from the lulls. Some ramshackle buildings on the opposite bank offered mute token to the blasted hopes of the Argonauts.

Disrobing, I tied my clothes in a pack and secured them on top of my head by my belt-strap. Entering the cold, clear water, I experienced a delightful, cooling caress as the current swirled about me. After the day of walking and running, the refreshing effect of that bath was the equal of two full meals. Nearing the opposite shore, I stepped into a hole and before I could regain the surface, I was carried downstream some fifty yards. My clothing was soaked, but I had gained that part of the country which would permit me to continue on to Stockton without my having to cross a bridge. Frequent talks with other boys who had attempted to escape had not been in vain.

I avoided the gold-milling mine buildings from which the beckoning finger of smoke had shown. The country beyond was uneven. Ranches there offered fruit for the taking. About ten o'clock I was following the rails of a branch railroad that I believed would bring me into Stockton. I had just passed a white board with two black letters inscribed thereon: X.W. "Crossing— whistle," I murmured to myself and paused, debating the advisability of circling the crossing. While I considered the possibilities of officers lying in wait at the crossing, a machine dashed down the road and stopped. An officer flashed a light on the soft dust, inspecting it for shoe-marks. The soles and heels of my shoes had a deep cleft cut in them and there were hobnails driven into the leather in such a manner that walking on impressionable earth would leave two initials: P. S.

Another officer joined the first. In the night's stillness I could plainly hear their voices. No, I had not passed there, they decided. The second officer drew from inside the machine a blanket and a shotgun and after inspecting the best place for his ambush he laid them down under a tree, a few yards from the track. The machine turned about and headed for the country through which I had traveled that afternoon.

I crouched down between the rails. With the noise of the car's engine gone, I imagined I could hear the officer breathing, To my left was a small bank with a few bushes growing upon it. Quietly I drew myself up and lay prone behind one bush. I feared to attract attention should I try to get away from there.... I was tired. The day had been replete with excitement. After the regular hours of the school, devoid of all thrill, the emotional state I had that day sustained refused to carry me farther. I drew a rock to me, pillowed my head upon it and decided to wait a few hours before moving on. The officer ignited a match and applied it to his pipe. I saw into the ruddy glow it made against the darkness and discerned the features of a round-faced officer who was notoriously mean in his treatment of the boys. I definitely decided not to move.

That night was still and soft and languorous. Overhead a gorgeous California moon was at its full and flooded the country with its radiance. Endless veils of saffron and silver hung across the heights and touched with liquid gold the pine-trees, the distant, stately redwoods and the shimmering leaves of an orchard near by. Beneath the foliage the shadows were dark in patches and again were filtered through with moonbeams until exquisite with dainty mystery and symbolism. Lulled into a feeling of security by the sweet perfume from the orchard, I discarded the reality of my position and relaxed utterly. In giving up so completely to the beauty of the night I ceased to think of the officer's proximity. No one, I fancied, could fail to respond to the charm of the night; no one could be so brutal as to renounce this fairy pageant that he might return to the sordidness of an ugly group of brick buildings....

An ant nipped my ear and brought me to consciousness. I brushed it away and sat up. Morning had brought an awakening of animal life. The stillness of the night had vanished. Peering between the leaves of my concealment, I saw that the officer was in the same position as before, but dozing now. Crawling stealthily backward and keeping the bush between us, I retreated a hundred yards, then stood erect and struck off on a tangent. That day I walked almost thirty miles. It was impossible to follow any road and to appear at a farmhouse would be to notify the authorities of my position. By a devious route I traveled toward Stockton. I had eaten nothing and was suspicious of the water the almost dry creeks offered. Stagnant water near a shady stretch of fields enticed me to dig a small hole near it and after the hole was filled, I drank sparingly. The foot that was unshod in the early part of my escape was causing me considerable pain. In the haste of my departure I had trod unmindfully over sharp stones and stubble and my foot was swollen with bruises. The sun had burned my forehead and it throbbed intolerably. I still wore the hickory shirt and faded, blue denim overalls of the school uniform, so I could not even risk asking for water at a farmhouse. During the afternoon I walked across a level plain, which, I imagined, was bringing me closer to my destination. Just before dark I struck a railroad track and, believing it to be the same I had left that morning, I paralleled its course. Shortly it led to a small settlement. From a secure distance I read the sign on the station: Milton! I was thirty-eight miles from Stockton and almost fifty from the school. I had come in a straight line, though not in the right direction!

Knowing the usual locations of officers who were sent to capture a boy who had escaped, I felt safe. I had slept near the farthermost out-guard they posted. I was free to walk down the track and go to Stockton. I was hungry, but not insistently so, for I had lost considerable interest in food while at the school. The peculiar manner in throwing it upon the tables there had made it appear a sort of necessary evil. The twenty-odd houses of Milton must hold *someone* who would listen to the plea of a young man temporarily out of work. I approached the kitchen of a two-storied building that appeared to be a hotel. The result of making friends with the Chinaman peeling potatoes in the rear yard was a sandwich—a thick piece of cold bacon between two slices of stale bread.

Invigorated, I directed my steps down the track and kept on until almost midnight. My ankle had swollen so that I could wear my shoe only by sheer determination. Once I rested and my foot stiffened so quickly that I was unable to rise for half an hour. I thought of trying to start a Ford after it had been left out in the night.

From where some sheep were milling came a tiny light. Investigating, I found a herder, a man who, without being too inquisitive, managed to convey to me his full appreciation of my predicament. I slept the remainder of the night on some sacks, but the closeness of the sheep made a violent contrast to the previous night.

Uncertain of the real intention of the night-watchman, I left early and so entered Stockton, breakfastless, about noon. Going to the steamer docks, I tatted with the mate of a boat that would leave for San Francisco that night. He listened to my tale of having lost a job in that town and wanting to get home to San Francisco. But too many men were making a practice of bumming rides, he asserted. However, if I would come to the boat dock before the steamer left, he would see what he could do for me.

To walk the streets would have been to incur certain arrest. I was tired and exhausted. I started to make a burglarious call, but decided against it when I nearly fell asleep in walking from the dock. I managed to get down to the river bank a short distance from the town and found a place where I could rest. I was totally "out" for several hours.

Returning to the dock, the mate gave me a broom and instructed me to sweep off the walk near the gangplank. Passengers were boarding the boat and for an interminable half-hour I experienced the most poignant torture imaginable. At any instant some officer might recognize me. It was the third day and the school authorities would probably have men at the boats in both Sacramento and Stockton. My acute consciousness of others' movements, the light-headedness induced by my long fast, the thought of the beating that I should receive upon apprehension and the pain from my injured foot put me to a test of self-control that, visualized in advance, I should have sworn I could not have exercised. Sweeping, the while expecting to have someone touch my shoulder and inform me I was under arrest, nearly paralyzed my muscles. But I cleaned the indicated place and gained the lower deck before the boat left.

There had been feverish activity by the stevedores to get the cargo trucked aboard. Now they were resting, with the exception of a few who piled sacks of potatoes one upon the other until they almost touched the floor of the upper deck. Great, perspiring, hairy-chested beasts. Some were naked to their waists. Others puffed avidly on cigarettes. A gong sounded and they made a rush for a narrow door. I followed, hesitantly. Peering into the room, I saw huge plates piled high with enormous quantities of food. The steam from it hung over the tables. A gigantic Italian seated near the doorway lifted his eyes as he shoveled an incredibly large spoonful of potatoes into his mouth. With his other hand he reached for a loaf of bread and broke off a chunk to dip into a pot of gravy. He dropped his spoon, grabbed for a plate across the table and emptied half its contents into his plate. He looked quickly over his shoulder at an approaching waiter; then he saw me. With the bread in his hand he motioned me to enter and indicated a seat near him. The movement of the boat was uneven. I had doubts about the wisdom of eating just then. However, I accepted the invitation. Most of the light was supplied by two lamps suspended over the table. The shadows cast upon the faces of the men as they wolfed their food gave them a sinister appearance. There seemed to be but one thought in their minds. They jabbered and shouted at intervals, but held their mouths close to their plates. There was a primitive gusto in their actions. Holding one chunk of roast meat in toil-stained fingers, the huge Italian chewed *away* half of it, dropped the remainder to the table beside his plate and drew the back of his hand across his lips. He smiled at me and his mouth showed the lacerated meat as a repulsive mess.

Someone dumped potatoes, a great handful of spaghetti intershot with tomatoes that looked like streaked blood and a jagged piece of bread on an aluminum plate before me. A quart of coffee in a tin cup was set beside it. Suddenly I shook off the qualms I had been entertaining. Consciously I lowered myself into the bestial mood. The squeamish feeling in my stomach vanished and I consumed all the food I could hold—which was a good deal.

For an hour I sat near an open port-hole and watched the high marsh-grass and tule-weed glide by. The boat turned and twisted as it followed the winding course of the river and frequently I could see lights from houses winking across the water. To be in one of them—to have all the past months of hatred and meanness forgotten! I was traveling, but not towards any definite object or place. There is a vast difference between going to a welcome and leaving a curse. Anticipation of joy awaiting us heightens delight, but to be moving only because one is impelled to do so—that is quite another matter!

Feeling drowsy, I crawled on top of the sacks of potatoes and found there a scant two feet between their upper row and the lower floor of the deck. For a while I lay listening to the throbbing of the engines, the sharp blasts of the whistle and the chance scraps of conversation from deck-hands as they moved about. Then, from directly over my head, came piano music. I had been away from music for months. It thrilled me and I imagined that I was experiencing a delusion. I had been through so many varied emotions within the past sixty hours that I could not be certain of my own senses. Placing one hand against the rough timbers, I could feel the regular beat of the rhythm some pianist was evoking from the instrument. The passengers evidently found the entertainment pleasant, for the music continued almost an hour. To me it was a stabilizer. It gave form to a condition of my mind that was threatening to spread out and overflow. It held in check the impulse to jump from my berth and shout that the world was crazy, that life was meaningless and inconsequential and that the more one thought about it, the less assurance one had of any plausible solution! I wanted to sleep, but the whirling of events through my brain was a phantasmagoria of impossibilities. I could not have lived through the disconnected and jumbled scenes—yet I had. I retreated from them, denied them, sought to induce the mood that had carried me over the dulling workdays. All the harmonies of the piano reached me and though I have since heard some of the greatest artists, none of them have induced the contentment that then settled upon me. There was something of a liturgical response in the answer I made to the soothing vibrations of those notes.

I imagined a woman to be playing. I pictured her—and she became the girl who had sung in the Seattle mission. My mind thus veered from the escape and soon I was reliving other days and building delights to duplicate them. Before I slept, I had thrown all thoughts of the school into the limbo of unpleasant experiences. This has happened often since then. Just as Buddy and I had inverted the experience with the vicious black man in West Oakland. I am through with it. I have extracted whatever it had of use for me—the rest is waste; *ergo,* I throw it away.

[III]

During my year of travel, after I had left the George Junior School, I had met a man who was acquainted with Red. This man was Dan and when I reached San Francisco the following morning, I went to his home. There I learned that he was in prison, serving a four-year term. He had been caught without sufficient funds and was paying the penalty of being broke. His aunt supplied me with clothes and one hundred dollars and gave me Red's address. He was in Milwaukee. I took the money, deposited it in a bank, received a check-book. In the reform school I had become interested in the cashing of checks as a new phase of stealing. It seemed of a higher tone than burglary. Also, I had lost some of the confidence that I had formerly possessed in abundance. Those few months at the school had worked many minor changes in me that I was not aware of just then. Gradually they appeared.

Fortified with the check-book, I made a round of stores and small saloons and cashed about two hundred dollars' worth of checks. The following morning I drew the original hundred from the bank before the checks could be presented.

To join Red was the thought uppermost in my mind. I retained the unused portion of the check-book. I distributed checks down through the valley towns until I came to Fresno. There was a fascination about selling a worthless piece of paper for seventy or eighty dollars to some merchant who was overanxious to sell a pair of shoes. I bought all the clothing I could possibly use, in that manner. Hats, haberdashery, everything but a suit-case. The psychology of buying an article that indicated travel worked against me, I reasoned. In Fresno, a bit uncertain whether the local police would remember me, I debated the advisability of giving the town a whirlwind selling-campaign. For that was the manner in which I operated. I would be up early, start out with a dozen checks signed and ready for endorsement. Entering the first likely-looking place, I would allow the proprietor to persuade me to purchase an article. Hesitantly I would produce the check.

"I'd like to have that hat, but—" and into view came the check.

"It would fit you excellently," the salesman would reply.

"But you don't know me—and I've only this check. . . . Of course—No, I guess I'd best wait and get the hat later. I'll be back this afternoon."

His sale gone in that "I'll be back," the salesman would invariably extend his hand for the check.

Then I benefited from the times during which I had schooled myself to hold an innocent countenance. For, as he would scan it and then lift his eyes, I would interject into his decision the remark: "Well, if you'll cash it, give me a pen and I'll endorse it." Extending my hand with the words usually produced the desired result. He would accept the paper after I had endorsed it.

Then into the next place. Others in turn. With each succeeding store some force was generated within me. I worked almost mechanically. Watching the eyes of the salesman, I could in nine cases out of ten make the proper and effective suggestion at the decisive moment to bring him over to my desire.

By noon I was working at a speed that carried me on, over minor objections and by evening I was going so fast that I could have sold the most difficult clerk in town some worthless paper. The same force was used in foisting Liberty Bonds during the war—the same domination of another through suggestion. That there was the powerful factor of patriotism on the side of the bond-salesmen made their jobs mere child's-play. To take advantage of a difficult clerk, I found, was easiest early in the morning, just after the store had opened. The phlegmatic operation of the average mind prevents its working very rapidly until the man is awake for several hours. It was a curious, practical study of human nature—in one phase. . . .

In Fresno I concluded to make a single attempt. The chances of police recognition, were I too long about the town, were great. Hence I prepared a check for twelve hundred dollars—it was drawn upon the original San Francisco bank, but enclosed in an envelope that was addressed to me at a local residence. The cashier of the largest bank was pleasant when I told him I had recently moved to Fresno and wished to open an account. I explained that I had come from San Francisco and that I had sold my automobile and had just received the check for it. He observed me as I drew out the paper, accepted it, gave me a deposit book and informed me I could not draw against the account until the check had been forwarded to San Francisco and returned. He was very agreeable and introduced me to an assistant—a severe-visaged woman who wore glasses and held her lips in a thin, compressed line. I had counted on securing the money from the assistant and this rather formidable person disconcerted me. Nevertheless, resolved to carry it through, I bought a ticket for a train due to leave for Oakland that afternoon and made certain that the agent would remember me by starting an argument with him over the amount of change he returned from a fifty-dollar bill. There was not much paper money on the Pacific Coast then and that incident alone was sufficient to accomplish my end. He remembered me as going towards Oakland.

Returning to the bank shortly after noontime, I made sure the cashier was absent. At the assistant's window I proffered a counter check and my deposit check and explained that I had an opportunity to buy a machine for an even thousand dollars and though I regretted lowering my account by that amount so soon, I should undoubtedly build it up rapidly.

She took the check, made an entry in the deposit book and was about to give me the money without comment when another clerk approached to confer in a whisper with her. The assistant hesitated.

"Was this deposit by check?" she inquired.

"Why, yes—how else? It came by mail to me this morning. Mr.—" naming the cashier, "knows of the sale of my other machine—that's why he gave me the deposit book."

I stared wide-eyed at her as though to imply that she was in error even to ask me such a question.

"But I believe there is a stop order against that check—"

"I don't know anything about stop orders—but if you mean that the check isn't good—" I interrupted her, paused, then continued: "Why, I've known the man who drew it for years. If I had half his money, I could buy this bank." The frown left my face and I smiled. The implication was that she exhibited a woeful, backwoods mentality even to doubt that this check would be other than valid and honored. It is difficult to convey in type the subtle impression that the proper suggestions make—but she was less severe in her attitude and, positive that I had scored, I risked another, final suggestion: "If you are unwilling to cash it—well, I'll return later and take it up with Mr.—"

What person of lesser rank does not aspire to his immediate superior's position? She waved aside my offer to wait by asking in what denomination I would have the bills!

Possessing almost eighteen hundred dollars, I hired a machine to take me to Bakersfield. The cashier would phone to San Francisco, ascertain that the check was worthless and after the police had been notified, they would learn from the ticket-agent that I had taken a train north. I was comfortable and safe in Los Angeles that night.

Although I was anxious to rejoin Red, I had heard so much of Hot Springs, Arkansas, as a meeting-place for thieves, that I decided to spend a few days there before continuing on to Chicago and Milwaukee....

CHAPTER 8

[I]

The fluttery old lady standing in the aisle exhibited her too prominent teeth in a hideously Puritan smile. I was about to deal another hand and continue with our whist game when she extended a tract and admonished the four of us to read and be saved ere our souls were damned by the colored pasteboards. Over the rumble of the car wheels my partner, a buxom matron whose acquaintance I had made on the train, raised her voice: "Oh, take it and get rid of the little busybody." I did—both.

A few moments later I was again preparing to deal when another voice and presence intruded from the aisle. This was a tall and angular man, who would have resembled Abe Lincoln but for his Simon Legree moustache.

"It is a high misdemeanor to play kyards in the state of Texas, suh. It is my duty to arrest you. I am a county officer and a complaint has been lodged by Mrs. Whithers, the lady who will appear against you."

At the next stop, in company with the officer, I left my train acquaintances and proceeded to the county bastille. The Christian lady of the tracts followed. The day was Friday and the hour not yet noon. The legal formalities having been observed, I was taken to court and arraigned before a dumpy and malevolent individual who was addressed as Your Honor. In the sweltering heat of his Star-chamber he appeared to my hostile gaze as a swollen idol about to burst.

I admitted my offence, pleaded my ignorance of the law and asked for a minimum fine because I was *en route* from Los Angeles to Hot Springs and eager to continue my journey. The dear little soul who had lodged the charge fluttered to His Honor's dais. A whispered monologue ensued. "She's president of the Sisters of the White Crusade," someone enlightened me. "They're cleaning up gambling just now." The sister turned from the judge and flashed a triumphant look at me. His Honor mopped his bald dome, clenched his gums together, hitched up one strap of his galluses and glared at me. Then, in the same tone as the old maid used in saying: "If I had my teeth, I'd bite you!" he made his pronouncement:

"You have flagrantly violated the law of this state. Ignorance of the law is no excuse. Although warned several times, you persisted in your gaming until stopped by an officer of the law. That you are not a resident citizen aggravates rather than minimizes your offence. It is the judgment of this court that you be s-s-s—" his lack of teeth now suddenly betrayed him and to cover his confusion he shouted: "Ninety days on the road gang, hard labor! I'll make an example of you, young fellow! Take him away, sheriff."

Over my protests I was escorted urgently, effectively, to the cell-tier. My attempts to reach an attorney, my storming at the injustice of my predicament, my raving in the blinding madness that possessed me, resulted in my being thrown—actually thrown—into a cell. The resident bedbugs must have chortled as the door clanged shut. The floor was slimy and there arose a stench that almost strangled me. Pounding on the iron door with my fists brought an answer; a bucket of water was sluiced through the two slits in the door. Later I subsided from exhaustion.

I had been some twenty hours in that crypt when the door was opened.

"Come out here, dude!"

Staggering and slipping over the scum, I gained the light and stood blinking stupidly. Two men confronted me: one a duplicate of the Simon Legree of the train, but with eyes that seemed chiseled from dirty, flecked ice; the other a vicious-looking, cross-eyed man who snarled from between thin, straight lips. His words fell as though he bit them off and spat them out.

"Here he is, captain. Thinks he's a tough *hombre.*"

The captain flicked one finger in the direction of the stairs. "Git goin'. Tougher they are, the better I like 'em."

I walked to the floor above and was handcuffed to an enormous Negro. Another chain-gang guard stooped to shackle our legs together. He 'lowed to the captain that we wuz set. Another flick of the finger and the raucous instruction to git goin' from Legree started us towards the street door. My companion, from past acquaintance with our impedimenta, had developed a long stride. His first step upset me and only by clinging to him did I save myself from a fall. A passing attorney, struck by the apparition of a Hart, Schaffner and Marx suit in such surroundings, paused beside me. Quickly I sketched my plight and implored his aid. He Wrote my name and opposite it: "Camp Number 4, Chain-Gang."

Driving a topless flivver, with his henchman seated beside him, the captain cast an occasional backward glance at the Negro and me in the back seat. Heat-waves rolled up from the road to spread over the fields. But the current of air produced by the car's jouncing was a relief to me after the enervating sweltering of the previous night. My hands were grimy. In the dazzling light my clothing presented a revolting appearance. The Negro wrinkled his nose and moved as far from me as the shackles would permit.

Ten miles passed while I remained sunk in my misery. Then the big black waxed loquacious: "Suah is a mighty fine capt'n at this camp." He had raised his voice to ensure its carrying to the occupants of the front seat.

"You've been there before?" I asked, listlessly.

"Suah has. Oncet fo' gittin' drunk—an' this time fo' one dollah an' costs." He regarded the captain mournfully.

"One dollar and costs? What crime is that?"

"It's lak thisaway: ah ain't got no dollah, an' costs is fo'-teen dollahs mo'—an' 'at's why I'se gwine out heah." He spread a huge, calloused paw, palm upward, as if the gesture offered an explanation.

Eventually I got it straightened out. He had been arrested for being drunk a second time, fined one dollar and ordered to pay the heavy court-costs. Lacking the necessary fifteen dollars, he had been ordered to the chain-gang to work it out at the rate of fifty cents a day. "I'se a workin'-man, too," he added. "An' ah takes mah money home ever' pay-day. But now ah don't know if mah ole woman'll pay me out or not. . . . Wished ah did."

[II]

The car turned from the highway, followed a dirt road for several miles and again turned, lifting clouds of dust from a deeply rutted lane through fields. Then, abruptly, it rattled from any semblance of traveled road, crossed some packed gravel and shivered to a stop near a large and dirt-streaked oblong tent.

A solitary officer was seated on a chair, tilted back against a shrub near the tent. It was a Saturday afternoon and I wondered at the absence of signs of life about the camp. To my left was another, smaller tent, half boarded up and noticeably cleaner. A swaybacked covered wagon, with three steps spilling from its rear exit, vomited two Negroes. As they approached our car, I saw that they were clad in faded, torn overalls. They bowed and grinned to the officers.

"Gittin' out!" snapped the captain to us. Awkwardly we descended from the machine. Tossing a key to one of the fawning blacks, who bent to unlock the leg-shackles, the captain produced commitment papers from his inside pocket and in the dialogue that followed I was introduced to humor as it is practiced "in Texas, down by the Trinity River."

"What are you out here for, nigger?"

"I'se out heah fo' gittin' drunk," my companion replied.

"You're just a God-damned liar. You're out here to work." Then, as though belched from a shotgun: "Ain'tcha, nigger?"

"Yes, sah, captain, I'se a good worker, too."

"Better you are. What's your name, nigger?"

"William Jackson, sah."

"No, it's not William Jackson!" snarled the captain. "It's Grasshopper—an' when I call you, you wanna jump!"

"Yes, sah, capt'n!"

The Negro who had released the shackles returned the key to Simon Legree. The other officer vanished into the smaller tent. Legree glanced at my commitment paper and elected to make a speech in the drawling accents of the ignorant Southerner:

"Now, you're out here to serve your time. I didn't send for you—but git this straight: I'm the captain—an' you take orders from me. You want to get everything out of your head but one thing, an' that's *work!* If you got any notion you ain't, I'll change it for you—quick. There's only one way you can get along with me, an' that's to work—hard! An' we don't have no trouble with you bullies out here. There ain't no trouble out here—except what I make—savvy?"

I nodded.

"Git goin' to that tent"—indicating the long, dirty one With the officer near one end—"an' remember I'm boss here."

The guard at the entrance rose slowly from his position and took a step backwards. A long, ugly revolver was suspended from his belt. He seemed cast in the same mold as the captain. The Negro beside me lifted the tent-flap. I started to go in with him when I was assailed by a frightful, sickening odor. Blinking my eyes, I jerked back and heard the ominous click of a revolver being cocked. "Git in there an' take them clo's off!" came raucously from the guard.

The reason for the deserted appearance of the camp was made evident as I began to discern what was within. A long logging-chain extended from a sturdy mesquite-bush outside the tent and came through the wall. Branching from it inside, like legs on a centipede, were other, smaller chains and to the ends of them were welded huge leg-irons.

These leg-irons, I observed quickly, were locked about the ankles of forty men. Each man was lying on his side, facing me. Their faces held the look of expectancy common to dogs long confined. Their hair and beards ran riot. Their clothing was ragged and filthy. While I stood swaying in the opening, I was shoved violently forward and fell almost over the feet of the nearest man: a bearded Negro who had shriveled until every joint of his body seemed swollen.

My handcuffs removed, I disrobed to my underwear and was thrown a blue shirt without buttons or collar and with one sleeve torn to shreds and an enormous pair of torn and patched overalls. Putting the overalls on, I almost slid through one leg of them. Then came two shoes. One was size twelve, heavily hobnailed and scarred from hard usage; the other was half as large, but with the forward half cut away above the sole, enabling me to wear it like a sandal. I was permitted to retain my hat—a light-weight panama. Holding the overalls bundled up so that I should not trip on their long ends, I shambled over legs and chains to a designated place between what at first appeared to be a filthy St. Bernard dog and a black cocker-spaniel, but which, on closer inspection, proved to be two men. The guard followed me and instructed me to lie down upon my back and hold up one foot. I complied and he clamped a leg-iron about my ankle. Then he returned to his post outside.

[III]

The jail I had left paled into insignificance beside this. Sweltering in that tent were men who had not shaved or bathed decently for months. An open half-barrel, forming a leaky latrine, dominated the center of the floor. Sweat poured from the wretched bodies of the men and putrid morsels of food added to the stench. Under my head was a small roll of blankets. For a moment I was on the verge of fainting; then two vicious bites on my hot, moist neck stung me to action and I slapped at my attackers. I scored fifty out of a possible hundred; my hand came away with a dull red smear on one finger. As I turned to look for more vermin, my chain rattled.

"All right," came a drawl from outside the tent, "if you don't quit that movin' around, I'll come in there and give you somethin' to move 'round about!"

"Better take it easy," cautioned a voice from the Bernard on my left.

Looking closely into the tangled shock of hair that almost covered his face, I discerned a pair of blue eyes. The cords in his neck, where it joined his torso, were taut as he held his face close enough to whisper: "He'll shoot you in a minute ef you make any noise."

I remained outwardly silent, but writhed in an inward turmoil. For several minutes I fought a losing fight against the vermin. . . . I had not eaten since the previous morning. The rough and filthy boards of the floor became more irksome with each passing moment. Perhaps a quarter of an hour passed. Then I sought relief in a subdued conversation with the Bernard.

"How long have you been here?" I asked him.

"Five months—six months—I've lost track." He was peering over my shoulder, watching the tent-flap for the first sign of the guard. In response to other questions I learned that he had been sentenced for stealing a pair of shoes from a store and had been given the limit of eleven months and twenty-nine days. He had tried to escape shortly after arriving and exhibited a withered arm as a tribute to the guard's marksmanship and his own failure to "make the brush."

Still watching the flap, he commented on the other men. A Negro opposite me on the chain had been out to the gang three times. I looked at him and saw a short, gorilla-like body surmounted by a head that seemed to be composed of fuzz and two enormous white eyeballs. His mouth was opened and the teeth were yellowed and broken. He had bare feet, with torn and claw-like nails marking the toe-ends. He was whispering to a young white boy beside him. The white boy exhibited a mane of curly hair that had been long neglected and his chin was marked by a sparse, virgin beard. His face was darkly tanned. The bronze color extended in a large V down his chest. He was naked to his waist and in contrast to the burly black he appeared like a consumptive. The Bernard informed me that the lad had taken an automobile for a joyride and was doing ninety days.

Soon I noticed that a subdued air of expectancy hung over the various men, particularly the blacks. Then the flap was thrown open. The two Negroes I had first seen materialized and my informant ceased talking. The first Negro had a box suspended before him by means of a strap over one shoulder. From this he took a tin pie-plate and a spoon and handed them to the first man in the line. He then proceeded down the length of the tent, repeating the process. The other Negro followed, carrying a bucket. He ladled out to each man about half a pint of cold canned tomatoes. The first Negro reappeared with another box and distributed a piece of stale corn-pone and two heavy, hard, horribly uneatable biscuits to each man.

The plate given to me had a streak of dirty black scum about its upper edge. The spoon was indented with teeth-marks and its handle was broken off, leaving about an inch with which to maneuver it. There was no salt offered and the tomatoes were flecked with rust from the bottom of the pan.

I might have imagined that I was hungry, the moment before, but the desire to eat had now left me. Narrowly I averted an enforced trip to the open latrine. The Bernard lapped up his ration with an avidity almost ghoulish. Greedily he snatched my proffered plate. The other men sopped up with the biscuits the last remaining drops of juice in their pans, Some even tilted the tins and licked the bottoms in their ravenous attempts to fill their stomachs. Feverish eyes followed the smallest of fallen crumbs; eager fingers pursued and captured the particles of bread. My Bernard combed his beard with his fingers and inspected the nails in his search for a last morsel of food.

The Negroes reappeared and collected the pans and spoons, counting them into the same box, whence they could be again distributed—from all indications, without being washed. Lassitude was reflected in the relaxed attitudes of the men. I reclined on one elbow and offered a prayer that my last-minute effort at the jail to get a lawyer would soon show results. I tried to visualize a night spent in the tent—and shuddered.

"Do you stay here all day?" I asked the Bernard.

"Haw, this is a treat. Usually we work till 'bout four o'clock on Saturday. But the captain was in town, so we rested since noon. Ain't seen that gravel-pit yet, have you?" He leered at my negative nod, then continued: "It's right over back of the corral. An' no preacher can ever scare me about hell no more—I've lived in a sure-nuff hell down there. No shade, no water to drink—nothin'—'cept loading gravel-wagons and diggin' gravel. An' them guards set in the shade of a bush up 'bout the rim of the hole and throw rocks at you when you don't work fast enough to suit 'em. But you're lucky you got here today—we don't work till Monday now—'cept for cleanin' up a bit this afternoon."

"Pipe down!" rolled stentoriously from the opened flap. The guard strode to the first man, flicked a finger as though calling a dog and the prostrate man raised his manacled leg. The guard fitted a key to the lock and after releasing him dropped the leg to the floor. The next man raised his leg and called a number. The guard selected a key and repeated the operation. Upon reaching me he paused, as I remained motionless. "Gittin' it up!" he commanded. I raised my leg. "What the hell's the matter with you? When I say: 'Gittin' it up,' you raise it an' call your number!"

"Number?" I was bewildered. Then a flash of anger swept over me and I considered the notion of wresting his gun from him. Seeming to anticipate some such action, he placed his heavy boot on my stomach. With considerable heat he repeated my question: "Number? Yes, number! What'd I tell you yore number was when you come in?"

"You didn't tell me anything about a number," I asserted.

"Like hell I didn't!" His pressure upon my midriff increased. "Think you're tough, eh? Well, bully, I'll take some o' that outa you!" He threw most of his weight on the foot pressing me down. I twisted suddenly and almost upset him. With catlike agility he recovered his balance and whipped his gun from the holster. Before I could turn back or attempt to rise, he had swung the butt of the gun effectively upon my jaw. Stepping back a pace, he called to another guard: "Jes' watch this!"

"This" consisted of implanting his shoe several times in the small of my back. Then, resuming his pose with one foot upon my stomach, he repeated his original question. "What's you-all sayin' yore number is?" Bearing down with his weight, he repeated, monotonously: "Yore number is—yore number is—yore number is—eighteen! Ain't it? Eighteen's what I said. Now—what's yore number?"

"Eighteen!" I gasped.

"Why in hell didn't you say so? Now, what's yore number when I ask?"

"Eighteen," I responded.

"An' don't fergit the 'capt'n' what goes with it. Stick yore hoof up here, Eighteen, an' I'll turn you loose." He unlocked my leg and flicked his finger towards the tent entrance. "Git goin'!"

The Bernard joined me a minute later. "We'll pick up all the chips and trash and sorta clean up, now. Best if we start near the captain's tent, an' do a good job—'cause he likes it thataway."

[IV]

Other men emerged from the tent under the watchful eyes of the guards—five in number—and were set to work raking the ground, removing wheels from gravel-wagons to grease the axles, or currying the horses in the small corral. I was experiencing considerable difficulty in holding up my overalls, as long use had worn away the original shoulder-straps and the single strand of frayed rope replacing them was inadequate. Stopping to make them secure with a bit of wire the Bernard handed me, I was commanded by one of the guards to drop it and told that if I again tried to smuggle wire into the tent, he'd blow the top of my head off. I wasn't going to be picking any locks while he had anything to say about it.

The sun caused little heat-spirals to whirl from the dust about me, to dance maddeningly before my eyes. My throat was parched. Twice I stumbled and the reflection from a piece of tin patching—one side of the cook-wagon—dazzled me almost to the point of insanity. A forge heat rose around me like a blast from a furnace. I toyed with the idea of refusing to work and while debating between lying in the tent and weaving about in the sun, I broached my notion to the Bernard.

"Refuse to work!" He was astounded. "Why, you can't. There ain't no such thing as refusing to work. They'll beat you to death!"

I scorned his evident terror. Having never been beaten to death, I did not believe that I should be now. But just as I reached a point beyond which I could force myself no further and was prepared to make my declaration of independence, the work ceased and I was herded with the others into the tent.

After the hour in the open air, the close interior was doubly foul and repulsive. Lying in my accustomed place, I turned my face so that it was nestled in the crook of my arm and regretted that I had lost the opportunity of being beaten to death—or at least to unconsciousness, for that at any rate would have made me oblivious of the hideous, gagging stench that stifled me.

A muttered "Git it!" roused me and raising my head, I saw the two Negroes who acted as chef and waiter carry a wash-tub half filled with water and set it beside the latrine. The Bernard shook me and whispered: "Peel off yore clothes, an' git ready. We're in the next bunch."

"For what?" I queried, indifferent to what torture was about to be inflicted upon the next bunch.

"To take a bath."

Stark naked, six men clustered about the tub, blacks and whites. Each one stuck one foot into the water and splashed what he could of it up his legs. Cupping his hands, I saw the Negro who had come with me scoop some water from the tub and spread it over his face and neck. Another attempted to follow suit, but the guard called from the shade of the bush outside the tent: "All right—gittin' back!"

The men melted away from about the tub and fought for space with which to dry themselves on a huge towel composed of flour-sacks sewed together in a crazy-patchwork fashion. Rising with the second group, I halted near the edge of the tub and was instantly hedged away from getting one foot within the charmed circle. I did not regret it. I saw a piece of yellow lye soap passed from hand to hand. Some of the more energetic worked up a lather on their legs.

To wash was a herculean feat. One foot was put into the tub, water was splashed to the thighs and the first foot was withdrawn and the other quickly substituted. Soap was smeared wherever water had moistened the skin. If a candidate for a bath shifted awkwardly when he removed the first foot, he lost his position and was crowded out. About two minutes was allotted by the guard for each group to complete its ablutions. By the time the second bunch had backed from the tub in obedience to the guard's order, the water was filthy and floated a dirty, yellow, abominable froth.

The Bernard returned io his place beside me and removed the lather upon his limbs with the remnants of his underwear. The last six men had to content themselves with wetting their feet and hands. Their toweling was a futile gesture. The patchwork of flour-sacks had been twisted until it began to resemble a thick, loosely woven rope.

"Git set!" called the guard and immediately started his round of locking the men into the leg-shackles. Opposite me he paused. I held my leg up and called: "Number eighteen." He paid no heed to me. Tired from the strain of my unnatural position, I allowed the leg to fall. Instantly he snarled: "Gittin' it up!" I raised it. Again he appeared oblivious of it. Lowering my leg after a minute had elapsed was the signal for another snarl: "Gittin' it up!" Once more I raised it and called out my number. "Sure it's eighteen?" he snapped. I nodded and he fumbled with his keys, as though in futile search of the proper one. My back ached, my eyes burned, the downrush of blood seemed about to split my head asunder and in a reckless mood, engendered by my physical misery, I allowed the leg to fall and closed my eyes.

[V]

The Bernard was shaking my shoulder. I forced my eyelids open a fraction of an inch. The gloomy quarter-light betokened evening. A Negro was distributing pans and cups. Indifferent as to whether or not I received a share, I dozed off once more. I was startled from my coma when the pan and cup rattled to the floor close to my face. Pushing them from me, the Bernard shook me. "Git yore food. Don't miss nuthin'."

The second Negro poured another half-pint of cold tomatoes into the pan and a moment later my cup was filled with some brackish liquid. Parched from thirst and my long fast, I attempted to swallow a mouthful. My throat was grateful for the moisture. In small sips I managed to down half the coffee, tea, burnt bread, or whatever the brew was.

Silence reigned after the pans were collected. The two score men lay or squatted upon the floor and in the darkness which seemed to creep up from the filthy boards, I sensed a gathering of thoughts. No one spoke in words, but the exchanged looks shouted volumes. The white lad and the big Negro, lying side by side, seemed to carry on a conversation with their eyes. The eyes of other men seemed the only indication that they were alive. At long intervals a chain would clink faintly and the strident voice of the guard would pierce the tent-flap with a malicious warning: "Cut down that noise!"

Peering along the row of forms, I saw eyes catch and reflect the small beam of light that struck down from a bull's-eye lantern suspended near the exit. Like the orbs of jungle beasts, those eyes showed through their matted coverings of long hair.

"Git 'em down," said the guard. Chains clanked, forms stirred, the rolls of blankets that served as pillows were unrolled to form pallets. Taking my cue from the Bernard, I turned on my side and arranged my ragged blanket and piece of sacking so that I might recline. Immediately I was enswathed with the revolting odor of sweat. The sack was sewed over the blanket to form a sort of pocket. Taking off my shoes and overalls, I crawled into this from the bottom. For a moment I held the idea of losing myself in sleep, but instantly hundreds of bedbugs and other vermin attacked me. So I crawled from the shroud and passed the next half-hour in useless endeavors to rid myself of them. That bed was one device by which the Lord neglected to try Job's soul!

"Sing a bit, capt'n?" a plaintive Negro voice inquired.

Silence from the throne. I could hear the breathing of the man awaiting the answer. Over the whining of numberless mosquitoes I heard several dampen their lips with their tongues. Perhaps ten minutes passed. Then, in a drawl that was heavy with condescension and venom: "All right—sing, you black bastards."

I conceded victory to the bedbugs and lapsed flat upon my back, moving only when the iron about my ankle bit too insistently into the flesh.

In mournful, dirgelike tone came the first Negro's plaint. "There is trouble—there is trouble—O Lawd, there is trouble on the deep blue sea." Other voices joined. The Negroes sat and swayed in rhythm to the long-drawn-out "Trouble—trouble—trouble—there ain't nullin' but trouble fo' me-e-e!" Over and over they repeated the verses. "Trouble" was lengthened until it filled a full minute in the singing. A full, warm baritone boomed out. It was surprising in its rich quality:

Yondah comes ole Bud Russell
With his transfer-chain—
He's gwine to take us
Back to the pen again. . . .

Then the chorus "Let the Midnight Special shine down its ever-lovin' light on me"

"That Bud Russell," said the Bernard to me, "is the man that's been takin' men to jail for twenty years. Never uses no gun. Just chains 'em on a long chain. Gathers 'em from all the counties and delivers 'em at the pen—thirty—fifty—sixty at a time. Ain't never lost a man, neither. Them niggers sure sing 'em 'bout that man. They just shiver an' shake when they even hears he's comin'."

The singing was cut on a refrain as though a knife had severed the throats of the singers. From the guard had come a rancorous growl. It contained no word that I could decipher, but its effect was instantaneous. After that the least sound from the guard—a shifting of his position upon his chair, the clearing of his throat, the scraping of a match to light his pipe—brought the men to attitudes of tensed expectancy. Their actions were like those of a condemned man who awaits the first audible indication that those who are about to accompany him on his last, fatal walk are approaching. I lay in a half-waking, half-drowsy state. I could neither sleep nor remain awake. Between slapping or scratching and turning on the hard bed I passed another hour. Then from the far end of the tomb came a hesitant request: "Gittin' up, please, captain?"

[VI]

An unconscionably long time passed. I imagined the guard had dozed off to sleep and had not heard the question. The man rose and in the dim light I saw him stand erect. The movement caused his chains to shatter the stillness. The flap was jerked open and in stepped the guard with his revolver ready for use. The man dropped whimperingly to the floor. "You black —— —" snarled the guard. He strode to the shivering figure, administered several vicious kicks and heaped hideous imprecations upon the unfortunate.

The tent was again quiet. The same voice made the same request. The guard ignored it. Renewing his supplication, the man whined: "Please, capt'n, gittin' up to the barr'l, sir?"

The demands of nature, so evident in the man's plea, became insistent; in desperation he turned upon his side. Then the guard drawled: "Git it."

Several times, as I drifted in my semi-delirium, the same scene was enacted.

A discordant and nerve-wracking din brought me to consciousness early on Sunday morning. Someone was beating upon a steel triangle on the tent. The voice of the captain (all the guards seemed to be of that rank, something like a Mexican army, with nothing lower than a general) informed us of the hour and purpose of the noise:

> *"Raise 'em high, bullies,*
> *An' leap on the rode!*
> *It ain't quite daylight,*
> *But it's fo' o'clock!"*

Blankets were rolled up. The pans were passed. Syrup distributed. There was a large fire blazing between our tent and the cook-wagon. Its red light filtered through the canvas and gave us the aspects of lost souls in an antechamber of Hades. Grotesque figures were shadowed on the tent-walls and sloping roof. Moans and groans and sighs of hopelessness interspersed the desultory conversations within. Calls and servile laughter reached me from the officers and the two Negro trusties about the fire.

"Yas, suh, capt'n," was uttered with a monotonous regularity. We were permitted to rest our heads on the blanket rolls, or drift into sleep. But after daylight any man who seemed to be sleeping too soundly was roused and tormented by the guards. Their only pastime lay in plaguing the prisoners.

Noon came and passed with no offering of food. No opportunity was offered for washing. At four o'clock more syrup and some half-cooked rice were thrown into the pans. Then night and a repetition of the preceding evening. The Negroes sang; men clanked their chains to the latrine. I had been in the tent thirty hours and not once had the barrel been removed.

Made desperate by the thought of another night's confinement, I tried to have one of the captains telephone to Dallas and engage a lawyer for me. Refused that, I asked permission to buy some tobacco. Approximately three hundred dollars had been taken from me at the time of my arrest and put in care of the officers who had brought me to the camp. After considerable bickering I was informed that "fo' ten dollahs I might git yo' some." I signed an order on a page torn from the guard's note-book and two hours later I was handed about two ounces of some stringy tobacco labelled "Nigger Hair." In texture and smoking quality it had been appropriately named. Ravenously beseeching me to give them some of it, the men created such a commotion that the guard threatened to shoot blindly into the tent. In silence I distributed the Nigger Hair and resigned myself to what the morning would bring.

When the guard approached me after breakfast, I informed him that I was ill and in need of a doctor's services—immediately. I reasoned that if I could gain the ear of one of the medical profession, I could establish contact with the outside world. The injustice of my sentence rankled. I considered the idea of annoying the guard into shooting me in the leg. If I was not too seriously wounded, I should not regret the pain. Anything was better than a continuance of the horrors of the tent.

With the thought of the work in the gravel-pit goading me I refused the Bernard's advice and maintained that I was sick. The guard threatened me; then: "'Low the capt'n'll tend to you-all when he comes." The others left the tent and amid a confusion of orders and dull thuds which sounded suspiciously like pick-handles struck on shoulders, they marched away.

My ankle was raw where the iron had rubbed away the skin. The gathering flies prevented me from sleeping. The day was warm with that close, oppressive heat which bespeaks a Texas sun. Wagons crunched from the pit and rumbled down the road.

About eleven o'clock two Negroes entered, carrying Grasshopper. He was sun-struck and they dumped him on the floor with callous indifference. The captain who had brought us both to camp entered a moment later. He had been absent from the camp until that minute and upon seeing his two most recent charges within the tent he paused; in all my years of jail experience I have never seen so malevolent an expression as that upon the face of this guard. Bending only long enough to secure the shackle about Grasshopper's leg, he straightened up and surveyed me. "Sick?" He spat out the word. "I'll learn you how to be real sick!"

Grasshopper stirred and Legree turned to him. The Negro's eyes blinked and he made an effort to raise himself, then relaxed on his side. Legree shouted to one of the trusties, who brought in answer a pick-handle. The captain accepted it and the trusty vanished.

"Play sick on me, will you? I'll show you what being sick is!" Again Grasshopper strove to rise. He seemed to recognize the captain and sought to forestall the impending beating by struggling to his knees. He weaved from side to side, his eyes wide in terror. His lips moved, but no words came; his head jerked about as though he essayed to swallow some obstacle lodged in his throat. A creature about to be made a victim and immolated.

The captain, his face distorted by rage, wielded the pick-handle like a bludgeon. As the Negro groveled and moaned for mercy, Legree's frenzy mounted. It attained its zenith when a particularly vicious blow crashed against the black's skull and blood gushed from his nostrils and mouth. Swinging the club idly, Legree regarded the form of the inert Negro, then spat tobacco juice upon him. Still retaining the crimson weapon, the captain strode to where I lay. "Still too sick to work, bully?"

I sensed that he had appeased for the moment his murderous lust.

"Yes—I want to see a doctor."

He regarded me silently, as though considering some inward problem. He glanced at the battered Negro, then drawled: "Well, all right. County doctor will be here 'bout noon. That nigger is sun-struck—savvy? He fell down and a gravel-wagon run over him 'fore we could carry him to this tent. Git that straight—he's sun-struck!" He took a few steps towards the tent-flap, then wheeled about. "Bully, you *bettah* be sick when that doctor tells me 'bout you!"

[VII]

I *was* sick when the doctor examined me. Had he investigated under my arm-pits, he would have found a piece of the yellow soap concealed in each of them.

It was necessary to take the yet unconscious Negro to a hospital. Chained to him, I reached the county jail. There I at last got a lawyer and he appealed from the sentence imposed upon me. The Superior Court set an appeal bond of five hundred dollars. Some friend of the attorney's posted the bond—in consideration of two hundred of my dollars.

Two months later, in the calm and sedate city of Chicago, I learned through the medium of a letter from the attorney that the sentence had been set aside and a fine of twenty-five dollars imposed. . . .

CHAPTER 9

[I]

I discarded all thought of Hot Springs and went to Chicago. On the train an incident occurred, the aftermath of which caused me to fear all cameras—particularly those operated by amateur hands. At a small station a weary-looking young woman came to occupy the seat opposite me. In her arms she carried a baby. The youngster, probably eight to ten months old, was a fat, jolly little fellow and despite the heat in the car he preserved an unusually good humor. But the girl appeared to be laboring under an unusual strain. The weight of the child was burdensome and I felt sorry for her. I had the porter bring a few extra pillows for the baby and amused myself with playing with him, while the young woman closed her eyes for a short nap.

Later she told me that her husband had enlisted in the army to make the world safe for democracy and that she was returning to her mother's home to await his return. A great many people were then enthusiastic with war fever, but to me it was a senseless thing—leaving a young wife and baby, who obviously needed care and attention, to go away, intent upon killing as many strange men as possible, before meeting ultimate death.

The eating-houses that blight the trail of the railroad necessitated leaving the car at each station. The rush of patrons to the food-counter during the twenty minutes allowed by the train's stop was so swift that the young woman was forced to wait until the first lot had finished eating before she could find a place. I observed this the first noon. That evening I volunteered to secure a seat for her. She followed and I held the baby while she ate.

The next day at noon we had stopped at a station and had finished our meal. A few minutes remained before the train's departure. Standing in the shade of a car, I was holding the baby and conversing with the young woman. A common acquaintance, a pop-eyed, over-ripe woman with a camera, approached. Others were near us and she suggested a group picture. I stood behind some passengers and concealed my face. The woman operating the camera was one of that organizing type of ladies who attempt to dominate any gathering into which they can intrude. Imagining that the young woman with the baby and I bore some mysterious relationship to each other, she conceived the bright idea of surreptitiously taking our pictures, alone. With the aid of confederates she arranged to have the group part from us, to leave us standing together. I had meanwhile half turned from the camera-fiend and was again in conversation with the young woman. Someone calling to the baby attracted my attention and as I turned, the camera clicked! Laughter from the stout lady and embarrassment on the part of the little mother. The baby alone seemed not to mind. Effusively the stout woman offered to send the pictures to us at any address I would suggest. She smirked and intimated her belief that there was some connection other than the accidental one of train-friendship. Rather than express my opinion of the busy-body, I humored her and gave a fictitious address. I dismissed the affair until it was later brought to my attention forcefully.

[II]

"Have you got a registration card?" Red asked after our first exchange of greeting. I had wired and he had met me at the depot.

"No. Why should I? I'm young enough so I don't have to be drafted."

"You don't look it and they're pinching every guy that looks like he's of age. It don't make any difference to a guy that's not stealing, but, being a hook, you can't even stand an investigation. Come on up to Milwaukee and I'll get you a phony card. They ain't as hostile up there—in fact, some Socialists are playing the duck completely on the draft and no one seems to care much, yet. I got a furnished house up there and I'm supposed to be a salesman for a tobacco company. The broad and I are married now. I claimed exemption on account of her and three kids. Of course we ain't got no brats—but if they want to see some, I know where I can borrow some. There's a poor family lives near us and they got about a dozen. I made friends with them and the old lady is glad to get rid of as many as I want to take care of. You know what?—the best friend a thief has is someone like that old lady. She ain't got nothing and has a tough time feeding all them kids and I've give her things for 'em once in a while. She'd lie for me or hide me from the bulls any time I needed her help."

Red's lips were not so severely drawn as when I had last seen him, but his eye still retained the same ability to grow large and show a wicked gleam. I attributed his unusual garrulity to a state of being worried; I held the idea that marriage involved some strange change in a man's make-up.

On the electric train, bound for Milwaukee, Red looked about him to assure himself that there was no one within hearing distance, then said: "Say! why didn't you send word to Dan or me after you was clouted in that house prowl? All we knew was that the papers said you lost an argument with some guy and he beat you up and had you pinched. When we sent a shyster up to the can to see you, you was gone to Oakland. We would have done what we could for you, but we figured your old man was squaring it."

I explained what had happened: my escape and my recent check-cashing operations.

"Did you meet a little guy up at the school named Buddy"

"Sure—I've known him all my life," I said, "but how did you know him?"

"Right after you and I had that trouble with Fred and I moved to Frisco, Buddy used to come up to a hang-out and sell papers. There was a lot of thieves and hookers hanging out there and he got to sticking around. I kinda took a liking to him, but he was too damned small: too much of a mark to take any place to do stealing. I was going up to visit him and help him lam from the school after he fell—but you know how it is: first one thing and another."

Informed that Buddy was about to be released, Red said: "I'm going to send some dough to him and have him come to Dan's place and get a letter. We can use him here. I like him—he's a square little guy."

Instantly Red became a closer friend to me. His praise of Buddy found response in my heart. Together we sent two hundred dollars to Buddy—but he was not paroled for another six months. The school authorities, enraged at my escape and believing that Buddy had in some mysterious fashion played a part, decided to hold him another half-year.

I told Red I was wedded to the check-cashing idea. It offered easier money and there was a considerable thrill in inducing people to buy paper that possessed only a moral value.

"You and your thrills!" he snorted. "Why can't you look at this stealing as a business"

"Business . . . ? Well, it isn't such a bad idea at that."

"Of course it ain't," he said. "I'm going to introduce you to some guys that are making real money. It's like this: we don't do any stealing in Milwaukee at all. I live here, but we go out of the state to work. We are 'working over machines.' We buy a wrecked car, recent model and take the plates and numbers off it. We get the bill of sale, the registration slip and all that; then we destroy what we can't sell of the car. With the numbers and paper we register the car in Wisconsin. Just get a license for it and have it listed as being at some house we rent. Then the car that was destroyed in—say, Detroit—is really alive and legal in Wisconsin. Only, we ain't got no car—yet. But after the car is registered, on paper in the state, for a month or two, we then clout another car in Chi and run it up here and work it over. See?"

"Almost—but how work it over?"

"A regular machine-shop. We cut the lugs off the engine, which has the numbers on them and with an acetylene outfit we cut the part of the chassis out that has numbers on it. Then we weld them into the stolen heap to replace its right numbers— and we have a car that has factory numbers on its engine and frame. And the car is registered for over a month before the stolen car is missed. Savvy?"

"Sure—but if you buy a wrecked car, there isn't much margin of profit in duplicating it, is there?" I could not see the deal in its entirety.

"Think so?" Red said. "Listen to this: we take an enclosed—" (naming a high-priced car) "and strip it. Then we saturate it with gasoline and put it on the tracks of a fast train. Just before the engine gets to it we touch a match to the car and beat it. Say! you ought to see the result! We can buy the wreck from the insurance company for as little as five hundred dollars—and when we duplicate it with a new car, it sells for almost five thousand. Not *much* profit! And there's other wrecks we can buy, too. When a garage burns down, we rush for the owner and by bidding a few dollars higher than the others who want it for the junk, we usually get it. Insurance-adjusters will give us 'heaps' because we pay fifty or a hundred dollars more than they could get otherwise."

"It listens interesting," I conceded, "but it seems to me there's a lot of labor attached to it."

"Well, there is—in a way. But you got this advantage: you can 'turn' about three cars a month and they will give you about eight or ten thousand clear. And that's more than a lot of thieves get for their end when they take chances of being killed in robbing a bank. Also, if you *should* happen to get pinched on suspicion, you can get a small bond set and not have to stay in jail. And there's about a hundred angles to fight the case before a jury, too. You see, the 'heap' is actually stolen in another state, but is registered in this one *month* before it's reported missing in the other state. And the owner has to come up here to prosecute, so they can extradite you. Usually he's a business man and if you stall with your hearings, he gets tired and leaves. After a car is changed, it's hard as hell to identify it and the local authorities don't care much because it's a 'beef' from out of the state. They got enough trouble of their own without trying to help other states. That's the way they look at it. If they ever make a law against taking machines from one state to another, it will make it a little tougher—but until then, we're all set."

The basement of Red's "furnished house" proved to be a high-ceilinged place that had been converted into a machine-shop. Two cars were undergoing a change of identities. The body of one sat upon two trestles. The engine rested upon another. As we entered, a boy in greasy overalls was busy with an acetylene torch on the chassis of the dissembled car. He turned off the flow of gas and removed his goggles.

"Meet Al," said Red. "He's the oldest of the kids from that family I told you about. He was working in a garage and I promoted him."

Al was about sixteen. He grinned as he grasped my hand. "Better'n workin' for any guy I ever met," he said. "This is sure a keen way to make dough."

"See how it is?" Red pointed to the magnificent enclosed car that he indicated was ready for sale. "Look it over and see if you can tell it's been changed."

I examined the car. The engine numbers had been welded into the block in such a manner as to baffle any effort to locate the weld. The channel on the frame was smooth as glass. Red explained that it had been milled over, then repainted.

The next day Red rented another furnished house in a different part of the city. His wife moved into it. They inserted an advertisement in the paper, saying that a widow was forced to sell her expensive car. Two days later the finished car was sold and they returned to the original house.

I saw the possibilities and joined forces with Red. He introduced me to six or eight men—some in garages, others in private houses—who were following the same "business." All had friends in other states who watched for opportunities to buy burned or badly wrecked cars. Some of the cars that were stolen for them were procured by youngsters who would steal the model required and deliver it at some agreed destination for as little as one hundred dollars.

Investing a thousand dollars in two wrecks in Chicago, I turned them over for a net profit of four thousand dollars. Red's wife, Vera, posed as a widow forced to dispose of her car. But Red was afraid that she would become too well known to hunters of car bargains and he suggested that I get a girl to do that part of the work for me. Vera was a curious mixture and showed her intelligence when Red made the suggestion.

"What you want," she said to me, "is some girl that hasn't got any family to keep tabs on her. I think I know one who'd fit into the part. Of course you'll have to live in the same house and pose as man and wife—but that won't make any difference to her. Do you want me to write her?"

The prospect was attractive. But my experiences with Peggy had instilled a distrust of women as partners. If I could get a girl like Vera—fine! But I preferred, at that time, to have only passing contacts with women, like those I had enjoyed prior to being sent to the school. They played a part, but not that of a confidante. I was considering the problem, silently.

Vera misinterpreted my hesitation. "You don't have to get married. Not right at first—but you probably would, after a while. It's the only right way to live. I've been a thousand times happier since Red and I were married."

We were seated about the dinner-table and she leaned over to touch Red's hand. He grinned. I mused on the incongruity of her logic. Happier since they had conformed to a legal requirement. Happier in his profession of automobile-thief because he had stood before a justice of the peace and mumbled a semi-religious formula. . . .

"No," I answered her, after a bit more reflection. "No, I think I have a better way. Send for your friend. I'd be glad of her company and all that—but I've another idea how to sell cars."

During the month past I had considered the selling-problem and concluded that a small agency was the proper thing for disposal of the cars. By opening a place and displaying a few cars at a time, I felt sure I could move them rapidly enough to more than offset the expense of rental and help. Within the week I had secured a small store near the Wisconsin Hotel and by taking a ten-year lease on it I was permitted to remodel the front to make a display of one car in each window. By specializing in flashy advertising and using a brilliant color display scheme within the store during the evenings, I soon established a trade that enabled me to sell cars, on a percentage basis, for many of the other thieves. I hired a stenographer to prepare form-letters, engaged a youngster who liked to work around machines to dust and polish them and became a man of business.

Vera and Red, her girl friend and I shared one house. Vera was against Red's continuing to steal cars. She wanted him to make enough money to buy an apartment house and live entirely within the law. She had perhaps found the germ of that idea in her belated observance of the marriage vows. Red was not against the plan, but he had a great many friends who needed help. Some of the boys who stole the cars would get arrested. Red would supply money for their lawyers and hire witnesses; in one instance I recall he posted three thousand dollars for an appeal bond, allowed the boy to run away to California and forfeited the bond after the higher courts had ruled against him. But Vera became insistent about his automobile-stealing. He treated her pleas lightly and it was that which first gave her the feminine idea that she was not completely understood by her husband.

Then in a manner common to thieves a slight misunderstanding arose between us. Red and I worked together in perfect harmony. In business we were ideally mated in our peculiar profession, but socially we were a bore to each other. In an effort to patch this up we went into northern Wisconsin for two weeks and, with the girls, camped near a lake. Other thieves joined us—with their girls. The camp was rather secluded and an old couple cooked for us. Most of our time was spent in drinking or fishing. A few of the men and girls were determined to carry their profession up there with them. They would sit in a shelter erected over the central enclosure formed by the tents and argue the merits of various means of stealing. Infrequently, natives from a farm a mile or so away would visit—and then it was the delight of some of the girls to see who could shock the visitor the most. Smart cracks, lewd actions and embarrassing invitations were made for the discomfiture of the caller. The continual drinking became a swinish affair. There was a reckless disregard of incurring suspicion. And for a bunch of young people to be bathing nude and drinking from bottles resting in a row-boat was not a scene calculated to build up any respect from the farmers. I talked this over with Red. Not because I was not enjoying the Rabelaisian atmosphere, but because I feared the result of talk of our revels—particularly when all patriots were supposed to forget that they had natural desires and think only of saving their country from the Huns. Instead of patching up the rift between us, that outing widened it.

The girl and I returned to Milwaukee. We rented a splendid house for ourselves—the residence of a former judge! I had left an acquaintance in charge of the salesroom during my absence. He had done little besides invite suspicion from the police. He had a prospective customer who wanted a certain make of car. Just then I had an identity for such a car registered in the state. The only thing remaining was to steal a car and work it over. Al, who was still in Red's basement, agreed to do a rush job for me. But to get the car would mean leaving the city for a few days and with the police making daily calls to inspect the cars offered for sale I was loath to leave. I wanted to be at the store if anything developed that I could forestall.

Leaving the store the next afternoon, I met Red, who had had a fight at the camp over some drunken insult to Vera. They had just arrived in town. I told him what I needed in the way of a car and he suggested that we get one in town. This was contrary to all rules we had agreed to follow in our business.

"Aw, I think it'll be all right," said Red, thereby introducing to me the thief's classic remark. . . .

We stood beside a large enclosed car. The keys were in the switch. The space in front of the car was clear—there would be no difficulty encountered in leaving the curb. About a hundred feet from where we stood, a police officer directed traffic. The main stream of automobiles was on the street where we stood. There were office buildings bordering it and stores on the sidewalks, from either of which the owner of the car might come any instant.

"I believe I can make it," I said to Red. "Just wait a moment until I try that door from the other side, so I can enter at the driver's seat."

Always quick of action, Red had one hand on the doorhandle as I was speaking.

"Watch the copper," he said. "If the owner shows, bust him on the chip and swing on the running-board. I'll snatch you away."

He opened the door and slid behind the wheel. I glanced at the officer and saw him leave his post. He was not aware that a car was about to be stolen—there had been a lull in traffic and he was coming into the shade to cool himself. Red switched on the ignition and I heard the starter growl. Darting a look about me to make certain no one was paying us undue attention, I saw two men start from the opposite side of the street. One of them was hatless. They were trying to reach us, but passing cars delayed their progress. The starter was growling. Red worked the levers on the car frantically. Plainly he was baffled for a reason to explain the car's refusal to start. The officer walked leisurely down towards us, glancing idly into the windows as he passed them. We *had* to steal the car now to ensure our getting away safely! There was no other way. The angry snarling of the starter-teeth bespoke Red's anxiety. The men were almost to the middle of the street and one of them waved his hands as though to attract the attention of the officer. Quickly I ducked my head into the car. "Get out! Come on!"

He slid from the car and joined me on the sidewalk. Rapidly we walked eight or ten strides to an alley that cut through, to the opposite street. Turning into it, we ran. I expected to hear a shot and began to watch behind me. I nearly collided with a truck that was making a delivery at the rear entrance of a store. Red preceded me by a few feet as we gained the sidewalk at the alley's terminus. I caught a glimpse of the officer entering the other end. To our left was a garage—into this we dashed. The manager of that place had been talking to a customer in front of his store, but standing in such a position as to witness our race down the length of the alley. I had spent the greater part of my endurance in the fast sprint. The pounding of my heart forced the blood against my brain so swiftly that I was blind for a moment. In my next lucid moment I saw Red dashing through the rear doorway, the garage-owner in pursuit with a gun levelled at Red's fleeing form. It was but a jump to the man from where I stood. I could not remain inactive, although he had passed me without thinking that I too had run through the alley. I leaped to his side and struck down upon the gun as he fired. Red disappeared into the cross-alley and the man turned to fight me. The policeman rushed in from the street. He covered me with his gun and I was forced to submit to a swift punch as retaliation from the garage-owner. I was immediately handcuffed. I protested that I was but an innocent bystander and that I had assaulted the man with the gun only because I had thought he was trying to murder someone. It was not much of an excuse, but I was as indignant as I could possibly pretend.

The policeman argued with me, while the other man retrieved his gun and darted after Red. I nearly succeeded in convincing the officer that he was making a grave mistake in arresting me. I offered to accompany him to the station, there to prove to him that I was a reputable citizen. He asked to see my registration card. Perceiving the date, he informed me that I should have had my classification card by then. I was not aware of the change in the draft rules until that moment. At his suggestion we walked away from the gathering crowd, through the rear of the garage and as we emerged—Red came loping up the alley! He had run in a figure eight! The garage-man was following him and shouting—his gun had been emptied of cartridges.

Red was fagged out—his face almost white—and he submitted to arrest at the point of a gun. A call to police headquarters resulted in a machine's arriving shortly with three detectives. They asked our names. I grew indignant again and asserted that I would prosecute the whole town for my false arrest. The officer could say only that he had arrested us—he had not seen any part of the attempt. The owner of the car was not present and the garage-owner had disappeared to repair a broken nose. He had tried to stop Red after uselessly expending his cartridges and Red had convinced him of the error in his effort. The detectives looked solemn and sought to question Red, but he was reticent. We were taken to Central Station.

Separated immediately after we arrived there, we were plied with questions by the officers; but after a few hours they gave it up. I insisted that I was of a prominent family living up-state and refused to reveal my identity except for the name on the registration card. In disgust for my attitude they locked me up in the "drunk cage." And Milwaukee at that time had a notoriously foul drunk cage—especially in hot weather.

Late that evening a detective took me into the outer offices. I had several hundred dollars to my credit and his attitude informed me at once of the reason for his interest.

"Listen, I'm not going to spend much time talking to you. But get this straight." He seated himself upon a chair opposite mine and leaned over the back of it. "You are in a tough state—savvy? You may make some of these officers believe that this is your first arrest. But me—I *know better!*" He puffed on his cigar a moment to allow time for his words to register. "In this state it takes only about three days to give you all the hearings the law allows and then put you in prison. You've been in the reform school and you've been in other jails—ain'tcha?" He exploded the question.

"I want to see an attorney—and I'll see that you apologize for this," I countered, for I felt certain that he only surmised my past. "Just because I'm trying to save my family from the disgrace of a false arrest, you are taking an unfair advantage of me. And what's more—"

"What's more is this!" he interrupted. "You're going to sleep in Waupon before the week's out, unless—"

"Unless what?" I had been planning to offer him some money with which to secure an attorney and his opening seemed to be in harmony with my thoughts.

"Unless you come clean and tell us where you got all them cars you got down at that store." He smiled, triumphant. "Didn't think I knew you, did you?"

No, I didn't! But more than ever I required an attorney. Since he knew I was in business and knew the location, it became exigent that I secure my release before he or other officers dug too deeply into the affairs of the business. I was not certain just what had been done with two particular cars while I was away—and I was more than anxious to post a bond and regain my freedom. I had almost twelve thousand dollars tied up in cars and my immediate cash was low.

An hour later he found that he could get no satisfaction from the repetition of unanswered questions and resorted to the ancient police-trick of telling me he had learned all about me from Red. That wasn't even a good guess and I dismissed it without consideration. He locked me up for the rest of the night.

Alone in the cell, I tried to take some sane view of the position I was in and in the very rapidity with which my thoughts spun about I was confused. I was wanted at the school. Several cities in California would be glad to see me—and head me towards prison—and I had a number of cars linked to me. That the cars would undoubtedly stand up under inspection seemed a small consolation. It was but a matter of elimination to find some charge to place against me, in addition to the afternoon's attempted theft. Two resolves I made that night I have never forgotten. The first was, not to attempt straightening out the great number of charges it was possible to place against me during the first few hours of an arrest; rather, I found it wise to wait until the interest in the case waned and then to fight the remainder of the charges. Secondly, one is never tried by the arresting officers and it is best never to attempt an alibi until after an attorney has been consulted. For what may loom large and insurmountable in the darkness of the cell on the first night often crumbles to dust under the light of day-examination.

I was allowed to phone an attorney the following morning. He accompanied me to court. There a bond of ten thousand dollars was set. I talked with Red for a few minutes and he said he would arrange the bonds. For some reason his bond was only half as large as mine. The case was continued for a week. That afternoon I was released.

The girl was frantic, near to hysterics, from reading the highly embellished and misleading accounts in the papers of the uncovering of a gigantic "auto-thief ring." It has always given me a passing moment of amusement when I have read of auto-rings since then.

From Red I borrowed a thousand dollars. The fee of the bonding company took that. The girl wanted to leave the city—she feared arrest. I gave her half the money I had and went to the store. It was closed and a policeman stood before it. I was informed that it was closed "for investigation." To my attorney's office I dashed. He made the necessary court gesture. Then the police placed a specific charge of theft involving one of the cars in the store. They produced a man who said he could identify the car. Again I had to borrow money—and yet could not get possession of the other cars to sell them. I posted another bond and was released two days later, to be rearrested by the federal authorities "for investigation." To the federal commissioner I talked with all the earnestness I could command. I said that I was willing—yea, anxious—to enlist in the army—but I must be allowed time to straighten up my affairs. He considered the matter a week and allowed me to go free, but I was to remain in the city and report to him once a week. With this arrangement I felt free to commence liquidating some of the assets that were tied up. But the courts granted continuances to the police in the matter of releasing the cars that had not been identified and rushed my trial on the attempted grand larceny charge. The result was that Red and I were brought to trial about three weeks after our arrest. But we had not been idle. In the few days I had been free I had perfected a defense. This is the refutation that answered the apparently clean-cut case against us:

The State had established that we had been near the car; that Red had sat in it. That I had spoken to him and then he had left the car and together we raced down the alley. That was, seemingly, enough to send us to prison.

I took the stand in our defense and explained that I had just bought a car, the exact duplicate of the one we were charged with attempting to steal. My car was parked fifty feet farther down the street. Red had met me at a tire-store, about half a block away and we had bought some tires for my car. I had been unable to park before the store because of the heavy traffic and hence Red had volunteered to go for my car and drive it around the block to the tire-shop. He had left the store with that purpose. I was talking with the salesman after his departure and suddenly remembered that my car was locked. Red was just entering the wrong car when I caught sight of him. I had hastened to him and explained the error.

The salesman from the store corroborated this perjury. (More expense.) The garage-owner had gone on a trip to Chicago the morning the case was called and the State was unable to produce him. (More expense.) The car-owner had admitted that Red left his car of his own will and without appearing to be alarmed. To offset the policeman's testimony we relied upon our attorney's summing-up to the jury. The officer had not actually seen us running—he could testify only that he had seen us at the farther end of the alley.

Red did not take the witness-stand. While I was under cross-examination, I managed to impress upon the jury the fact that I was being prevented from enlisting in the army only because of the false charges against me. We were found not guilty. But I was directed to come to court the following day to face the other charges.

The main witness in that case probably owned the car in question before it had been worked over. I have a belief that some kid had turned it over to one of the men I was selling it for, with the statement that it had come from out of the state, while in reality they had stolen it in Milwaukee. But I produced a factory expert who testified that the numbers were all in order. (This was before the present practice of concealing numbers had been employed by various manufacturers.) The owner could do nothing but reiterate that he knew how it felt to sit in that car and that he was positive a certain light stain on a part of the upholstery had been on his car. My attorney made the statement appear ridiculous; again I was acquitted. Immediately we instituted suit for recovery of the car from the police garage—and won!

[III]

I was about thirty-five hundred dollars in debt. Red's cash was low and yet I could not secure the release of the cars in stock at the store. Also, the federal authorities were intimating that I had better show some classification on a card soon or they would revoke my parole from the commissioner's office....

Vera's belief that Red did not fully appreciate her was growing. She nagged him constantly. She wanted him to quit and leave the city with her. I was in his house often in the days that followed. In fact, I was always either in court, my attorney's offices, or Red's home. Vera threatened to kill herself if Red did not leave with her. He offered to send her to St. Paul until we could dispose of our interest—but she *would* stay where she knew how much chance he was taking, rather than go away to be prey to her imagination. She just had to have something to worry about—and Red supplied it.

She and I were waiting for Red to come home. It was about eight o'clock and he had not been home for dinner. She was as nearly hysterical as a woman can be without screaming. She pulled at a pillow on the lounge until she had torn it to shreds. I walked about. We knew of no reason why Red should not have been home several hours before. Standing by a window, I watched the few passers-by on the street. They were mostly couples—young couples theatre-bound or out for a walk, or on their way to another house, where they would be welcomed. I wanted to join them. Or, better, I wished to slip from under the load of troubles harassing me. While I felt a certain egotistical pleasure in having outwitted the efforts of the police to hold me in jail, I yet suffered from a constant longing for some of the happiness that I was ever expecting, as due to me. I found a queer diversion in imagining myself walking beside some girl, going to another home, being received by friends who would not be asking about the "angles" employed to avoid being jailed. The incessant talk among thieves and their girls had developed a desire within me for a change of atmosphere. And still I was bound to Milwaukee until we could realize enough to get out of debt.

I turned from the window and Vera spoke quietly: "He just *has* to come before another hour or I'll go crazy—I can't stand this." There was nothing dramatic in her voice. She made the statement so calmly and nonchalantly that the words seemed to send a chill through the room. There was an ominous note of finality in them. She had mounted to the heights of anxiety and there concluded that she must have relief from the constant strain. Though she had stolen often herself and had taken chances many times with Red while engaged in some theft, she yet retained some saving quality that would not allow her to enter completely into the life. Whether the mere marriage ceremony had released that quality I can only guess, but I know that she more and more desired to have her man with her—that she might not be constantly worried by the fear of receiving a phone call from an attorney, telling her that Red was in jail. I thought her rather selfish, at that moment. As I saw it, Red was taking chances daily for her. He was risking long years in prison to gain for her the home she had so often pictured to him. I could not fully understand how mere uncertainty could be a determining factor in their lives.

Again she grew restless. Her calm determination deserted her and she plucked the shredded pillow-case with increasing nervousness. As her eyes met mine, I saw that they were wide and she blinked rapidly. I tried to calm her—despite the fact that I was fighting a battle to retain my own composure—and I succeeded only in adding fuel to the flame rising within her.

"It's not worth it!" she exclaimed. "All the money in the world isn't worth this worry."

"It'll be all right," I offered. "He'll be home soon. Probably he's only busy and—"

"Oh, you don't understand!" She stood erect and crossed to the window. "It isn't only now—it's always! Can you imagine what it means to have the one you love better than life away from your side?"

I thought I could and again I assured her that he would come soon.

"Yes," she said with an odd catch of her breath, "yes, I believe he will. But in the morning he'll be gone again—for the whole day, maybe half the night. And then this awful worry! When he's here, everything's all right, but when I'm alone—oh, I can't explain it! Please! Please! Make him stop! Won't you, please? Ask him to stop and let's all go away! You don't know how much it would mean to me, away from here. Please, make him stop, won't you?"

She was rapidly losing every vestige of control.

"Of course I will," I assured her. "There's no reason why you and he can't take a train out of town tonight. I'll talk with him, Vera—but sit down and don't be worrying so much. It'll be all right."

"If it only *would* be all right!" She returned to the lounge and, grabbing the torn pillow, shook it as though to vent her excitement in physical exertion. "I've heard that so often: 'It'll be all right.' It's a thieves' phrase that gets on my nerves. I can't stand it! I can't stand this—I've got to do something!"

At the ringing of the door-bell she uttered a sharp cry. "That's not him! I know his ring—oh, what has happened?"

Racing to the door, I peered through the glass and saw Al. A moment later he was telling me that Red had sent him and that I was to make sure that there was nothing in the basement which would incriminate us. The officers had told his attorney that they knew where they could locate some evidence against us and Red wanted to be certain there was nothing at home. Al left, remarking that Red would be home in about half an hour.

Hastily I inspected the basement. It had been cleaned of even the grease on the floor. I was positive of this before I entered, but, taking no chances of what might have been put into it within the past two days, I inspected it in every corner and possible hiding-place. There was nothing.

Returning to the room to tell Vera that Red was all right, I found her lying with her face buried in a pillow, her toes beating a tattoo on the end of the lounge. Her body quivered as though in the toils of some tremendous convulsion. I touched her shoulder and she turned a face so distorted with weeping that I was startled.

"I can't s-s-stand this any longer," she sobbed, "you don't know—Oh, he doesn't love me or he wouldn't treat me this way!"

Again she pounded the pillows. I tried to reason with her. She pushed me away. "Oh, leave me alone. Leave me alo-o-o-one," and she was weeping in hysteria.

Afraid of what she might do, I remained at her side. She had extinguished the lights within the room. A shaft of light from the adjacent hallway cut sharply into the darkness and illuminated her form. I stood so that the glare from it would not strike her eyes as she twisted and wriggled about. An anguish so deep, so profound, seemed to possess her that she ceased to be herself. She became a symbol of all thieves' girls, of all the women who have lived, loved and worried with thieves theirs has always been the part of worry.

Her frantic struggling had mounted until it approached the point where it must break, either in great comedy or great tragedy. I was holding her in a futile attempt to induce a return of sanity. Then Red entered. He had opened the door so quietly that I was unaware of his presence until his form shut out a portion of the hall light.

"What the hell's the matter?" He approached and I caught the odor of whisky.

"She's worried," I explained. "She wants you to quit the racket and—"

Vera sat erect. Red dropped to her side. They were facing the light. Her lips were distorted and her hair hung before her eyes. Encircling her with one arm, Red brushed back the locks from her forehead.

"What's it you want?" he asked thickly.

"O-o-o-oh!" She tried to free herself from him.

Together they stood up. Red's eyes were hostile, uncomprehending.

Disengaging herself, she faced him. "I can't stand this! I can't stand this! You've got to quit now—or—" she strove desperately for some control of her mounting voice and failed—"or I'll kill myself!"

"Say!" Red spoke sharply. "Cut that out—what do you think this is? Think I'm going to duck just because you have a fit?"

"Don't! Don't!" She shrank from him as though he had struck her. "Don't talk like that, Red. You don't love me—oh! I'm better dead."

"Aw, Vera—you know I can't quit now. Come on—be a regular fellow. Have a drink and you'll feel better." Red was less angry then, but his irritation was evident. He bent over her and attempted to kiss her. She interposed her hand so suddenly that it seemed like a slap on his face.

"Oh, I'm better dead! I can't go on!" She almost shouted it.

Stung by the unexpected slap, Red jerked himself from her. "Stop talking like that! Stop saying you're better dead. What in the name of Christ is the matter with you? Ain't I giving you all I can?"

"Ple-e-ease, promise me you'll stop stealing."

"Sure—when there ain't nothing more to steal," Red snorted.

"Oh, if I had a gun, I'd kill myself!"

Angrily Red snatched a revolver from his pocket. Believing that she would cease to be hysterical if he offered the means for her self-destruction, he held the gun before her. "Here's a rod—blow your brains out if you want to—or else shut up and have a drink."

With a movement so quick I could scarce believe it had occurred, she caught the revolver from his hand, inserted the muzzle into her mouth and pulled the trigger. The muffled report smote my reason like a hammer. The glass from a shattered picture on the wall tinkled to the floor as she collapsed on the lounge. . . .

[IV]

It was four o'clock in the morning. I counted the strokes of a church bell near by. There had been a lull in the grilling and the vibrations of those measured beats stole into the room as phantom reminders of a life I had lived centuries ago. Relentlessly the detectives had sought to force a confession, that Red or I had killed Vera. But I had repeated the explanation "She killed herself" numberless times. It ran through my mind like some crazy chant. The accusations provoked from the detectives came like blasts from a furnace door.

"She killed herself," I intoned, slumping further into the chair around which stood my inquisitors.

"You killed her!" "You murdered her!" "You almost blew her head off so she couldn't snitch about your auto deals!" "Come clean—your partner has!" "Yeh, he told us that you did it—" "Said you shot her while he was trying to stop it!" "How about it?"

Monotonously I mumbled the words: "She killed herself."

"You're a liar and you know it! If we hadn't got there when we did, you'd both been gone. Better come clean and save your own neck—your partner's going to dump you!"

An occasional cuff alongside my head emphasized the demands. . . . During the lull the same detective who had before accused me of being in the reform school entered the room.

"How the hell did it happen that this guy wasn't fingerprinted when he was down here before?" he shouted to the six men about me.

"Damned if I know, lieutenant," one replied. "Must have missed him—making bond, I guess."

"That's the hell of those bonds," said the lieutenant. "These guys get out before we can get a line on them. I want his record. If he's been 'mugged' before, we'd've had the return on him from Leavenworth by now." (Leavenworth was the National Bureau of Identification.)

Belligerently he stood in front of me. "But we don't need any record to hang this murder on you." Then turning to one of his men: "Has he said anything?" The man shook his head negatively. The lieutenant beckoned him aside and they held a whispered conference. A few minutes later I was taken to the central photograph department, finger-printed, photographed and measured. Then I was locked in a dark cell.

Sleep was impossible. My brain would not allow me a moment's rest. I sat upon the rough bench and immediately rose to begin pacing the narrow cell restlessly. Three steps forward, turn, three steps, turn—over and again I covered that tiny distance. More than ever before in my life I wanted to walk, rapidly. Swing along and in the exercise to relieve the pressure of my tumultuous thoughts. Vera dead! Dead! As on the occasion of Ed's death, I could not reconcile the reality with the way I wanted things to be. I had witnessed it, her suicide, stood paralyzed and stunned while Red knelt and gathered her in his arms, to murmur broken terms of endearment in her deaf ears. I watched as his gaze left her face and encountered mine and I sensed that I had looked into those eyes to behold a soul slowly dying. Horror—self-accusation—and an imminent madness. Even as the police had entered, bent on their search for evidence, he had remained upon the floor, babbling incoherently. They had forced him to relinquish his embrace, yet he continued to stare fixedly upon her, even as they questioned him. His body seemed to have lost the power of movement. He swayed when they shook him, but he stood with wide, unseeing eyes when they released him.

Three steps, turn—three steps, turn—for hours I had paced. It must be past noon, I reasoned. The door of the cell opened and I was led to a room where I found my attorney. He was smiling!

"Been treating you rough?" he asked and indicated a chair.

"That doesn't make any difference—how is Red? What have they done to him?" The light of the room hurt my eyes and the walls seemed incredibly distant from where I sat.

"Oh, he's all right—if he don't go crazy." The attorney leaned closer. "I'm afraid he has, already. I couldn't get a word out of him. He just sat where you are and stared. Tell me, was he really married?"

"Certainly."

"Well, that's all. I just wanted to tell you that there will be only a coroner's investigation. I had a hunch the police were going out there last night and I arrived a few minutes after they brought you downtown. There was a district attorney there—friend of mine—he was getting the evidence and all that. We found a sort of diary the girl had been keeping. She'd been writing of taking her life for almost a year—did you know that?"

"No. Only the last month or so." I had a glimpse of Vera brooding silently through a year and finally beginning to give tongue to her terror. What a pair of blind fools Red and I had been! That Vera, a girl who had been loyal through many soul-trying experiences, could actually speak of wanting to stop stealing should have been enough to show us that she had mentally made the resolve many, many times. I was musing on the number of internal battles she had waged before admitting her fears to Red and the attorney spoke:

"Yes, the diary is what will save you;—both of you. You can thank her for writing it—when you meet her." He was no longer smiling. His face had become solemnly serious as he assumed the pedantic mien of a minister.

"I don't know what happened there. The papers have a jumbled report; claim that you and Red say she killed herself, but you have more than an earthly court to face."

"Say!" The door banged open. The lieutenant advanced towards me, a paper in his hand. "Say! You told me you was never in a reform school—you're just naturally a bald-faced liar! Look!"

He held a circular before my eyes. Upon it was a reproduction of the two photographs made by the Berkeley police. Below it a number of arrests were listed, with a statement of my escape from the school and the request to hold me for any of three California cities.

The lieutenant stormed over my untruthfulness. Exasperated at being recognized, I flung at him: "What do you expect me to do—help you put me in jail? That picture isn't mine!"

I ducked his punch and told him he could finish any conversation he wanted with my attorney. The attorney asked the lieutenant to leave us together.

"That's a fine mess," he said after the door had been closed. "Is it you?"

"Well," he rubbed his hands together. "Well, that will mean a fight against extradition. At least you can prove your age—the federal court won't bother you now," he concluded.

Fight against extradition, I thought. More money. Red was not allowed to talk to me—from whom could I borrow enough to pay the attorney? I asked him, with a view to offering a note. He should allow me credit now, inasmuch as I had spent many hundreds with him.

"No. I'll tell you how it is," he replied to my question. "In this game you must pay as you go along. Now, as long as you're fighting cases in the state, I would carry you up to several thousand. But an extradition fight is different. If you lose—well, how should I get my money?"

"I'd make it up to you," I affirmed, "Just at present I'm all tied up with some machines—" I caught myself. "You'll get the money—just make a fight to win."

He rose to my suggestion about the machines. Seeking further information, trying to find the location of the cars, his renewed interest—all these pointed out the certainty that I should have my priceless attorney to fight for me.

[IV]

Two weeks later an officer arrived from Chico, California. The charge upon which they would attempt to extradite me was not one of recent date; rather, one of forgery that I had committed during the year preceding my commitment to the school! The erroneous newspaper-reports—that I had murdered Vera—had echoed throughout that state and penetrated to the small town of Chico. . . .

Red had been released after the hearing, which had exonerated him. He enlisted in the army. When it was arranged through the attorney for Red and me to talk before he left, Red said: "I'm not giving a damn about cars or anything." He had recovered part of his control, but he was short in his answers. "I've give the 'mouthpiece' all I could get for the 'heaps'—and I've sent Dan's aunt about a thousand. If you 'spring' on this rap here, wire her for it. If they ditch you—well, you'll meet Dan. . ."

We shook hands. "If it breaks against me," I said, "come out and say hello when you get back from France."

"I ain't figuring on coming back." And he was gone. . . .

The attorney left that night to stay a few days at the capital, to fight demands of the California officer. The following morning the lieutenant had me brought before him.

"You aren't going to California!" he said.

I noticed a stranger beside him. The man was of the same type as the Berkeley police chief: intelligence and a direct, penetrating gaze.

"Ever see this?" He extended the *Detective, a* police magazine. On the front page was a snapshot. Observing it closely, I discerned the features of the girl and baby I had met on the train *en route* to Chicago. I was holding the baby. The camera must have possessed an unusually fine lens, for my features were unmistakable. We had been in the shade of the car and the bright sun had been reflected much the same as in a studio. Above the picture was the caption:

"KIDNAPPERS!"

The relief I experienced in seeing myself listed as wanted for a crime of which I was innocent was so great that I wanted to cry aloud. I laughed; then my curiosity overcame me. Who was the girl? Whose child had been kidnapped? Where had it happened and when?

My questions were treated as the final mark of my criminal traits.

The stranger informed me that it was to no avail to disclaim knowledge of the affair. The girl had been employed by a wealthy family in Texas. The family had been disrupted through internal discord. The father had secured the baby through an order of the court there. His wife had entered into some scheme with the nurse-girl and persuaded her to kidnap the youngster. My photograph with her was undeniable—he knew! He knew, he insisted. He was the special agent for the railroad and his *wife* had made the picture. They had recognized the resemblance of the girl to the pictures of her published in the papers. Then when my picture had been printed in connection with the Milwaukee affair, he was positive—and had come from Chicago to clinch the identification.

I asked to see my attorney. They laughingly said he could be of no use to me. Then the lieutenant shot a question out that startled me: "Why didn't you and the girl meet the baby's mother as you had agreed?"

This was all news to me. There had evidently been a counterplot and, although this may assume the air of melodrama in the telling, it is all a matter of police record. Later I learned that the baby was restored to its parents, but in the interval the girl had sought by several crude methods to extort money from each of them.

I rather regretted that I had not the address of the girl. She had acted her part without a flaw. . . . But I learned to regard all cameras, when they pointed in my direction, as "evil eyes." . . .

CHAPTER 10

[I]

The Overland Limited had left Chicago. I was seated in the dining-car. The gentleman in gray, seated at my left, handed me the menu. After glancing at its offerings I had indicated several items to the waiter when my attention was distracted by the arrival, at the opposite side of the foursome table, of a bright-eyed little woman escorting a lovely girl. I started! Miss Maxwell, the teacher who had attempted to instill some knowledge into me, at grammar-school.

Our recognition was mutual. "This is indeed a surprise!" She introduced the girl as her niece. I murmured some conventional banality.

"Lila, this young man was one of the pupils I had in my class when I was teaching school in California." She smiled at me. Lila nodded and glanced through the window at the darkening landscape.

The waiter returned to take our orders. The gentleman on my left completed his order. Across the white of silver and sparkle of glass I studied the girl. Lila, her scarf thrown back from her shoulders in concession to the evening's warmth, held the card delicately. With exquisite grace she indicated her desires. The slender fingers seemed to meet the isinglass covering of the printed list with a touch that was almost a caress. Her black, lustrous hair, worn in a long bob, was caught at one side and held imprisoned by a jeweled barrette. Suddenly she raised her eyes from their downward gaze and I felt myself falling into the warm brown depths of them. For a long moment we sat thus. . . .

The waiter departed. The gentleman in gray on my left cleared his throat as if to speak, glanced at me, then relaxed slightly into his chair, still observing me.

"Where have you been for the past three—no, four years?" asked Miss Maxwell.

"Traveling. I was away from home for two years—in the Orient," I answered.

"Oh, yes, I did hear that. My, how you have changed! Lila, you should have seen him before he became so pale. He was nearly as ruddy as you are. . . ."

I flushed and looked to the window on my right. The reflection of the car's interior was on the inside surface of the pane. Lila's face and dark eyes appeared thereon.

A plate was set before me. Other plates followed. I swallowed some ice-water, gratefully. In an attempt to reach a sauce-bottle, I tipped over a water-decanter. Miss Maxwell laughed, lightly. The waiter attended to the results of my nervousness. Lila continued to peer through the window. From the corner of my eye I caught streaks of yellow lights against the purple darkness. As a station was passed, a brief brilliance flashed from without.

"He was always bashful," Miss Maxwell said. "I could never get him to speak before the class—not even to recite his lessons. And he hasn't outgrown that bashfulness yet."

The gentleman at my left stirred sugar into his coffee. I could feel his gaze upon me. I conveyed some food to my mouth. The rumble of the wheels rose to intermingle with the noise I believed to be caused by the mastication of food. My ears knew a great roaring, as though a dynamo were whirling within them. My hand trembled violently.

"Are you going far?" Miss Maxwell asked.

"To San Francisco." I replied.

Lila exchanged a quick glance with me. I could do no more than look the smallest fraction of an instant into her eyes.

"Lila and I are going only to Kansas City. I wish we were going the rest of the way. There's so much I want to ask you about. But you must write to me. You will, won't you?"

Again I darted a glance at Lila. "Yes," I agreed, "I'll write you."

The waiter cleared away our dishes. He deposited before us some chilled desserts. I wet my lips with some pinkish stuff, replaced the spoon and looked out of the window.

The gentleman stirred, peering at my rejected dessert. He ordered the waiter to bring another cup of coffee. Miss Maxwell and Lila were studying the delicacies offered by the card. Suddenly the heated air of the car seemed cold to me. The roaring within my ears increased. The gentleman was again stirring sugar into his coffee. My eyes closed for a moment and I experienced the dizzy sensation common to climbers of great heights. With my head tilted back and fearing to fall, I opened my eyes. Lila was regarding me intently. I attempted to smile and failed—miserably. . . .

A slip of paper was presented on a silver plate. The gentleman had finished his coffee. He took the paper, inspecting it closely. His brow wrinkled. He added the figures with a stub pencil produced from his vest-pocket.

"We shan't retire for another hour," said Miss Maxwell. "Will you come back and visit with us?"

Lila added her invitation. I sought to shut off the whirling within my ears—it seemed about to burn through and sear my sanity. I swallowed and tried to answer, but my tongue and throat were dry. The gentleman placed a bill on the tray, laying it carefully over the slip of paper. He looked at me with a direct gaze. I managed to find voice and say: "I'll be glad to visit with you."

"Of course you will," Miss Maxwell encouraged me. "And we'll be glad to have your company. We're in the second car to the rear."

The waiter stood beside my table. He counted the silver change into the hand of the gentleman in gray on my left. The chill of the car increased. My head seemed about to burst asunder. I caught the edge of the table with my fingers and looked wildly about me. Lila's wide, startled eyes sought mine. The gentleman on my left turned to me. From his coat-pocket he extracted a pair of handcuffs and adjusted them about my wrists. In a state of despair that numbed me I rose and preceded him from the diner.

I had lost my fight against extradition and was in the company of Mr. "Teddie" Peck, city marshal of Chico, California.

Our berths were made up when we returned to our car. After I had disrobed, he directed me to climb into the upper berth. He then secured a "swing around" handcuff on my left wrist, pushed the long chain attached to it between the berth and the side wall of the car and fastened the end of the chain to his leg in the lower berth. After assuring himself that I was preparing to sleep, he entered his lower berth and extinguished the light.

Alone, with that shiny chain, like a glistening snake crawling from the edge of the blankets to close its steel jaws on my wrist, I pondered far into the night. The involved affairs in Milwaukee fell from me as mist dissolves before the sun. I had lived through them—I was not going to relive them. I was headed towards the Pacific Coast, but over two thousand miles must be covered before I arrived. For a time, in Milwaukee, I had been discouraged and the mood of depression returned if I allowed myself to dwell on the situation for a moment.

The rush and rumble of the car wheels excited me. The long stops at stations, intershot with their half-heard noises and the movement of some passenger down the length of the aisle, all increased the excitement. I meditated: "I am going to California and probably to prison." But the words were without force. It seemed that I but spoke a part in a play. Prison! Why, I had been there—and with the recollection of the impression it had made, I resolved *not* to arrive with Mr. Peck. Examining the handcuff, I found that I could slip it down until it was against my knuckles. Wetting the skin, I tried to force it over them, but the tension grew too great and I feared a broken hand. Then I lay on my back, placed the cuffed wrist between my feet and sought to wrench it off by kicking violently against it. Blood oozed from the bruised skin, but the cuff remained. The hand started to swell and it required several minutes of frantic effort to get the cuff back to its original position. I had just straightened out on the berth when Peck's head showed between the curtains. Feigning sleep, I observed him and noted with satisfaction that he appeared to be convinced of my safety.

He was about fifty years old, of unusual size and the lines of his face, in that light, bespoke the gentleman who pays frequent homage to Bacchus. Ah, an idea! I was in splendid physical condition. To lose the sleep of one night would entail no great hardship—on me. But I would annoy Peck and watch the results next day. Perhaps he might fall asleep and I could extract his gun from its holster, bulking large on his hip. . . . Until the car awoke to morning life, I had Peck getting up to inspect his chain every half-hour. I would rattle it, twist and turn in the berth, then, when he arose to inquire the cause of my disturbance, I would insist that I was sick and had to go to the dressing-room.

My reform-school training came in excellently that morning. I was shaving with a safety razor. The blade was a stiff-backed one. I recalled two boys at the school who had severed the heavy screening over the window with just such an implement. I managed to secrete two of the blades; then I dozed through the day and derived considerable amusement from the lassitude that hung over Peck. He did not dare to sleep for fear of losing me— and having to pay his expenses for the round trip out of his own pocket.

I looked closely at the chain from the cuff that night and then folded the links so that I could hold the sixth one in my left hand and work the razor blade across the inside of the link. It was hard work. If I deviated from a straight, short stroke with the blade, a small chip would show in the cutting edge. But I gradually cut a tiny nick in the link. Whenever I imagined that Peck was dozing, I would rattle the chain, then rest from my labors while he rose and inspected me. After he returned to his berth, I again worked.

The next morning he took the cuff from my wrist, held the chain taut and looked casually over it for any marks. Since the cut was inside the link, the adjoining link covered the mark. We were both tired during the next two days. I slept a few hours each day. From Ogden, Utah, he sent a telegram to California announcing our arrival at noon of the following day.

I intended to free myself and leave the train at Reno. But the chain was tougher than I had anticipated. Feverishly I sawed with the blade, but as we came into the city, the steel yet held against my efforts. I dozed during the long wait there and was aroused only when the train started again. I was an hour ahead of Peck in sleep. I worked through the night and about one o'clock, as I held the chain to the light, I observed that the cut was almost completed. Wrapping the links so that I could twist them, I exerted all my strength on the chain—and it snapped. That tiny sharp sound, rising above the mingled noises of the car, was one of the sweetest notes I've ever heard.

I dressed and secured the dangling links of chain to my arm with a torn strip from my tie. While swinging from the berth, I bumped my elbow on the rail between the upper and lower berths. For an instant I stood with the sound of the thump ringing in my ears like a note of lost hopes. Watching the curtains sway, I expected to see Peck shove a gun through them and to hear a command to undress and return to the upper berth, but he was sleeping the sleep of the just. Noisily he informed me that thoughts of my flight were not disturbing him. I got my shoes from beneath the berth. In looking for my overcoat I discovered that the Negro porter was sleeping with his head against it. . . .

We were coasting down the grade into Truckee. I noted that I could not climb out of the window of the smoking-room in the sleeper and went forward, into another car. Someone came from the car that I had just left and, before he could note it, I had darted into the ladies' dressing-room. The curious change of atmosphere, from the car interior to the room wherein I stood, was one I was not prepared to combat. It was almost aggressive. In a flash I recalled the dressing-rooms of theatres. I thought of Peggy and Tiny and that old fraud Sir James. Trying the window convinced me that it would not budge. There was a hairbrush near by. I grasped it to use as a pry and managed to force the window open. The cold, chill air of the high mountains rushed in. It was like an elixir to me. I strained until I had the window lifted far enough to permit me to pass through it, taking no chance of leaving from a platform and having an employee discover my escape soon enough to give an alarm.

Peering from the window, I could discern only the vague shapes of trees close at hand. The shrill sound of the train's whistle drifted back to me. Its headlight cut sharply into the night as it swung around a long curve. My ears were tingling and my eyes watery, yet I continued to gulp the air in great lungfuls. I had almost forgotten Peck, I was so occupied with the beauty of the night elements. There was an insistent knocking on the locked door. I was in a panic. To leave the train in that wilderness was to invite almost certain starvation. To climb those mountains would take a full day. With the difficulties of my cross-country hike from the school still fresh in my mind, I shuddered at thought of such a necessity. But the knocking increased. I recall thinking how much more imperative and ominous the rapping of irate fingers was than a shouted command. The very formlessness of the disturbance imparts a mysterious power to it.

With difficulty I climbed through the window and lowered myself until I was hanging by my hands, facing the car side. To my left was the rail near the car-steps. Straining towards it with one hand, I succeeded in grasping it and securing a foothold on the lower car-step. Swiftly, nervously, I swung to it and crouched in the small space under the door platform. This recalled to mind the first time I had attempted to beat a train—with Buddy. But the cramped position and the insistent cold soon forced me to conclude that I must leave the train before I became unduly chilled—possibly to fall and be severely injured.

The train coasted along the side of a mountain river, its winding course indicating that it was yet high in the Sierra Nevadas. Then a few lights glowed in a widening of the narrow valley. The air-brakes were brought into play. As the cars slackened their speed, I swung off and raced along for fifty feet or more before I could recover sufficient balance to permit me to stop. Truckee sprawled along the sides of the river. The station was illuminated and over the main street, behind it, a few lights danced across the darkness of the mountain-side. A string of small houses and shacks followed the river's bank, dwindling away into the distance. Two men came from one of the houses. The light of a lantern and their uniforms marked them as railroad employees. I darted into a hiding-place and waited until they had passed. The train had stopped at the station. There was little activity, the greatest part of it centering about the engine. Seen at night, with the reflection from the furnaces making silhouettes of the engineer and the fireman, it impressed me as a great rapacious beast, snorting and growling its impatience over the delay. I felt a kindred feeling—the sooner it left, the easier I should breathe.

Cautiously I made my way towards the end of the train. A white bridge showed near by. As I started across the bridge, an employee left the train and came towards me. Throwing all restraint to the gods of chance, I raced from him. The other side of the town offered a rutty street, its houses even dingier than those facing on the main street. A dog barked as I passed the front of one ramshackle place. A light gleamed from another. Reaching the end of the road, I sought shelter among the trees. And there, scanning the town, again I knew the folly of fleeing from imaginary pursuers. The employee had turned in at the lighted house. The dog had ceased to bark. It was past four o'clock. I did some exercising to ward off the cold, wishing impatiently that the train would leave the station.

The engine continued to snort and to throw small sparks into darkness. The chain on my arm and wrist rattled faintly. Vulcan working over his forge, I mused, watching the sparks cough upwards. But I had to keep moving; there was little inducement to idle dreaming. Probably an hour later, while I walked about a circle among the trees, the train whistled and growled its way from the station.

The relief of knowing that my escape had not been detected at that point was so great that I found myself almost ravenously hungry. With the dying down of the thrill of the leap and race from the train, I began to think of lesser desires. Skirting the station, I made my way to an all-night saloon and entered through the rear door. A long counter at that end was given over to the preparation of food. The warmth of a great stove was pleasant after the hour in the open. A few men stirred uneasily as they slept on chairs near the stove. Watching closely for any sign of unusual interest, I ordered a large steak and, while waiting for it to be cooked, drank a few mouthfuls of coffee. The waiter-cook, in a greasy blue shirt and dirty apron, appeared indifferent to my presence.

With the steak before me, I cut into it, but was unable to swallow even a single mouthful at first. I was still going at top speed and had been unaware of it. A few trainmen entered the front door. They seated themselves and ordered meals, without glancing at me. Reassured, I paid my bill, then sought some rest by slumping into a chair and tilting it against the wall. I reasoned that I could get a train going back to Reno—from there into Oregon and, eventually, back to Chicago. The more I sought to curb myself, to remain quiet, the greater grew my restlessness. I was unable to sit without fidgeting and shortly I left the saloon. I knew, from a time-table I had secured on the train, that I had to wait until six o'clock for my coveted train to arrive. There were only two ways to leave Truckee—and I didn't propose to continue on towards Sacramento, thence to Chico.

Leaving the town, I climbed a road that led into the mountains. The sky was growing lighter. Before I had reached the top of the first rise, daylight was flooding the valley below me. As I plodded steadily upwards, the trees grew thinner. Glancing up suddenly, a tremendous flash burst before my eyes. I dropped to the ground, expecting to feel the impact of a bullet. Then my ears ceased ringing, affected as they had been by the light air of the mountains and I realized that there had been no report accompanying the flash. Trembling violently, I looked up to find that a cleared space in the trees had permitted the sun to strike me full between the eyes.

The relief to my senses was marked. I reveled in the sun, laughed at my foolish imagination. Since my escape every thought had been filled with specters. When a shadow had been unusually dark, I had peopled it with lurking officers. If a light wind stirred a few leaves, I heard posses charging towards me. And the first bright light was a pistol flash. . . .

Returning to the town, I sought the porch of a hotel, with an open view of the station, about a hundred yards away. A train had just come and gone, but, although headed the way that I wanted to go, it was not the train I desired. For a few moments I sat quietly, trying to assume the appearance of a casual guest. There was no one on the porch at that hour, but several men were about the station. I watched the various passengers as they appeared. Scanning the men as individuals, I started from my seat as my eyes caught the unmistakable form of Teddy Peck! He was standing half turned from me. By his side lay my suitcase—under one arm my overcoat. My visions of him a hundred miles away, speeding farther, were blasted!

Later I learned that he had become aware of my escape just as the train was leaving Truckee. Running the length of the cars in his union suit, he had made a futile search. Leaving the train at Summit, a small station twenty miles from Truckee, he had caught a local to Truckee and was waiting to entrain for Reno. He believed, as I reasoned he would, that I had escaped in Nevada.

To put the hotel building as a screen between us was the work of a moment. I walked to the end of the main street. A sign over an ancient livery stable boasted garage facilities. I intended to hire a machine, to change my route to the original one I should have traveled had I not escaped. As I approached the doorway, a powerful cut-down, with two young men in dusty coveralls seated in it, came throbbing into the street. They stopped the car at my request. I quickly learned that they had been on a vacation trip through the desert country and were returning to San Francisco. Explaining that I had to be in Sacramento at the Capitol Building before noon, I asked them if they would take me there for twenty-five dollars. I was resolved to offer the full eighty dollars I possessed if the first inducement was not large enough. They were glad to have a chance to lighten the expense of the trip. Donning a sweater and a pair of goggles, I slipped in between them and sat low in the seat as we passed the station.

I had some difficulty in keeping my arm from rubbing against the chap who was driving and, try as I might, I could not prevent the chain from rattling a bit. After we had traveled fifty miles in the cramped positions that my crowding entailed, they stopped to stretch.

The taller chap, a bushy-eyebrowed, slow-speaking fellow, with a twinkle in his eye, grinned at me. "What's the matter with your arm?"

"Hurt it—have to handle it with care."

"Yes, it's a good thing to always handle arms with care," he replied cryptically.

His partner, pausing long enough in his swinging of arms and legs to balance himself, added: "Always with care. That's us. Right side up and with care!"

"What was that guy in the garage telling us about some sheriff on the train?" asked the first chap.

"Said the sheriff was his uncle and had lost a prisoner somewhere back in Nevada."

Well, I reasoned to myself, they know who I am, but there isn't a thing I can do except to trust to their good nature. My evident lack of interest in their conversation brought from the taller one: "Well, let's get going and deliver our passenger—right side up, with care!"

And they did. There was no further reference to prisoners during the trip.

I ate dinner in Sacramento, washed some of the dirt from my face and took a stage to Stockton. Another stage brought me to East Oakland early in the evening. Leaving the auto, I entered a hardware-store and purchased several files. Crossing to San Francisco was an ordeal—electric cars, then the boat. Through it all, I feared that I should meet someone who knew me and that would be fatal.

I selected a seat on the glass-enclosed upper deck, reasoning that I was in less danger of detection than if I remained on the lower deck, reserved for smoking. A discarded magazine lay at my side. I lifted it and attempted to appear interested in it. The print blurred as I scanned the pages. I kept my left hand, with the cuff on it, inserted in my pocket, but imagined that a part of it was showing. The desire to look down and to reassure myself that I was mistaken became so insistent that I had to adjust my position to curb the desire. An elderly woman, seated at the other end of the long seat nearest to the outside of the boat, was looking intently at me. I flashed a casual glance at her and simulated interest in the magazine. A few minutes later a man came down the aisle and turned into the opening where I sat. I could *feel* his gaze upon me. As he passed, his walk indicated that he was looking over his shoulder and, by some premonition, I knew that I had been recognized. He joined the woman. From the corner of an eye I saw them confer. There was not a doubt that I was the object of their discussion. With a positive and startling knowledge I was made aware of this. For the longest five minutes of my life, while the boat neared San Francisco and the air about me became overpowering, I restrained myself from looking directly at them. I knew that they must entertain some doubt, however small, of my identity, or they would have taken some action at once. Then it occurred to me that they might be sitting in their attitude of strained quietude because they feared to pass the narrow space between me and the opposite seat. As long as they remained seated, I would do likewise. But the drawing power of their constant staring was more than I could sustain. I straightened from my slumped position, laid the magazine on the seat and looked full into their faces. They had occupied a seat across from Peck and me on the Overland Limited, all the way from Chicago!

Standing up from the shock of discovery, I was not reassured when I noted their equally amazed countenances. Turning into the aisle, I went towards the stern of the boat. Glancing into a mirror just before I quit the upper deck, I caught sight of my face. It resembled that of a monkey. The skin circling my eyes was white, while that of my face was a violent crimson. The latter had become sunburned during my trip, but the goggles had protected the jail-paled skin from the elements during that wild auto-drive.

Descending to the lower deck, I wormed my way through the crowded cars and trucks and reached the open portion of the deck, while the boat was yet some hundreds of yards from the slip. I was doubly marked then, so I reasoned. To show my face was to invite a second look from even the most disinterested person. And in my mind I was certain that the elderly couple I had left upstairs would now be informing some officer of the ship that I was aboard. There then occurred one of the things which in the telling appear to be odd, but which have been duplicated so often in my life that they seem to me to be but commonplace.

I was dressed in a blue suit. Beyond the rope where passengers were allowed to stand while the boat was crossing the water, there was a uniformed band of probably twenty-five pieces. They had been playing during the crossing and many of the passengers were crowding against the edge of the formation. By dint of much effort and a total disregard of the feelings of others, I made my way through the crowd, to the band group. Seizing an opportunity, I stooped low, crawled under the restraining rope and joined the players. I gradually edged to the farthest portion of the boat—the deck that would touch the pier apron first. A chap with a bass drum smiled as I seated myself so that the drum hid me from view of the passengers. I was just seated when the lights flashed on; the boat was entering the slip. Glancing cautiously over the curved edge of my concealment, I discerned the form of the elderly woman, standing on a large box, with a ship's officer and a husky deck-hand beside her. They were scrutinizing the crowd closely. On the opposite side of the deck I saw her husband, with a similar arrangement of force. They had done as I reasoned they would do, but I was out in front of where they were looking for me. When the boat was secured, I was the first person to leave it. I bounded down the long exit and crossed the tangle of streetcar lines in front of the Ferry Building with a reckless disregard for my physical safety.

Freedom! I was not to go to prison—at least, not just then. But what to do with my freedom? Rather, how to put it to use? Circumstances had brought me back to the very city where I least wished to be. The flare in the papers made my chances of leaving without being detected very slight. The increased interest that was being shown in any young man not in uniform also added to the chance of my being held for investigation, if some patriot decided to inquire into my previous record. Boats to Mexico were being closely watched. Although I knew that police surveillance is not the preventative that the papers lead the public to believe it to be, yet I was baffled to find a way out of the city; one that would enable me to reach some part of the country that was not war-crazy. I pondered over this problem that night as I filed the cuff from my wrist and postponed any decision by falling to sleep while sitting on the edge of the bed.

As long as I lived in cheap rooming-houses and ate meals at different obscure restaurants, I was comparatively safe from apprehension. But a few days of this sharpened my restlessness to a point where it prodded me into making a move. I was also almost broke again. In order to obtain some money I made a few calls at business houses under the pretext of interviewing the managers as to the number of men enlisted from their forces. Stating that I was collecting the statistics for a series of patriotic articles, I had no difficulty in gaining admission to their offices. But the safes were all locked, or the cash drawers had a guardian. Then, in a photograph studio, I was closeted with the manager in his own office, my pencil busy writing some data on the numbers of soldier and sailor pictures he had made within the last two months. Someone called him outside for a few minutes. I ransacked the desk drawers quickly. In one I found a large check-book; three checks to the page and each check attractively printed. I had just ripped several pages from their bindings and stuffed them into my pocket when the manager returned. It was a shivery moment, but he presented a face free from suspicion. Concluding my pretense of interest in his business, I excused myself and left.

Those checks were ideally prepared for my purpose. The manager's name was printed across one end. The firm name flared aggressively across the top of the paper and the bank against which they were drawn was one of the most prominent in San Francisco. With a dozen of these checks filled in for amounts ranging from fifty to one hundred dollars I had little difficulty in disposing of them that afternoon and the following morning. In funds again, I paid a short visit to Dan's aunt and learned that Buddy had not yet been released from the reform school. She gave me the address of a hang-out where I might locate some of Dan's friends. More from a sense of loneliness than from any desire to do further stealing, I sought them in a small hotel near the water front. But they were transit birds. The bartender of the saloon below was of the opinion that they were most of them working in the ship-yards, or in other war activities.

With no definite objective in view, I passed a recruiting sign on the corner. A voice called to me. "Are you going with the rest, buddy?"

A huge square-shouldered marine smiled and tapped the vivid poster beside him. Thereon was a marine in a helmet, bent forward with a bayoneted rifle ready to plunge it into a startled German soldier. The sweep of the lines in the composition all denoted a gloriously mad murderer lunging on, indomitable and unswervable. Certain and swift death for the creature whose breast was about to receive the bayonet. The cashing of those checks had induced a heightened emotional feeling. I responded to the suggestion of the poster. To drop all the specters that were plaguing me and to have definite enemies! Men who were inferior, men who were made but to receive the thrusts of my bayonet. And all this would be mine—if I went "with the rest." To join the marines and put all thought of fear behind me! To lop off at one stroke all the claims of the civil authorities! To "do my bit" for my country and then to come back and be forgiven for the annoyance I had caused the authorities—ah, that was worth while! At that moment I saw the termination of my fruitless plunging towards no set goal and there came to me the vision of myself vindicating all the power of right, helping to make the world safe! Just what it needed to be made safe from was a bit hazy—but, as is so common when one wants to believe an absurdity, I told myself that most people believed that the world needed saving and, for the nonce, I would agree with them.

Two days later I passed my nineteenth birthday in the recruit barracks on Mare Island. There were hundreds of men crowded into the ill-equipped wooden houses and I recall musing that saving us from the rigors of the cold weather might, be a considerable step towards making the rest of the world safe. But, as I swore an oath to murder whomsoever I should be ordered to, I consoled myself with the thought that I was safe from the civil authorities. I was a definitely identified nephew of Uncle Sam and mere police officers could not bother me. I held the idea that a man enlisted in the fighting forces could not be taken from the ranks and placed before a civil court for trial. . . . There were rumors about the camp that we were to be trained within seven weeks and then sent "over there."

About two weeks later, after I had learned the difference between my right and left feet and that a noise sounding like "Rap-pup" meant to bring my rifle to my shoulder in a certain manner, as I was sitting in a tent shared with two other young men, I heard a noise in the company street. Peering between the tent-flaps, I saw the afternoon sunlight on a huge, vicious automatic attached to the leg of an exceedingly efficient marine. Two other marines were with him. From a paper in his hand he read tersely to a shivering recruit who occupied the tent next to ours:

"Private —, you are under arrest! You are wanted by the civil authorities of Los Angeles. Get your blankets—you are going to Eighty-four. Orders of the commandant."

My dream of security vanished! I was no more secure from arrest than if I had been walking the streets of San Francisco. Less so, in fact, for I had been finger-printed and it would be but a matter of a few days until my record would be known. In taking my oath I had sworn that I was not a fugitive. I recalled the dire penalties the administering major had cautioned us we should incur if we failed to reveal our pasts.

I was more than anxious for the company to start for France, Siberia, the North or South pole—anywhere! And when another week passed and there was nothing further said about our leaving soon, my anxiety grew insupportable. Carrying on in a false atmosphere of patriotism where the least disinclination to damn the Huns every few moments labelled one a pro-German and also the expectation of having a noncommissioned officer inform me that I was under arrest, were a strain a bit greater than I could long sustain. Then shore leave was granted.

I bought a one-way ticket from Vallejo. Arriving in San Francisco, I changed into civilian clothes and went to the Canadian recruiting office. I informed the man in charge that I was not certain that this country would get into the war before it was over. I also volunteered the information that I was born near London. He asked me the name of the place and I made a wild guess. It was before channel-swimmers had popularized knowledge of English towns.

"Dover," I asserted and looked as bored as possible.

He laughed and then called to another man who came to us, limping grotesquely. "The lad is an Englishman—from Dover," the first man explained.

The other extended his hand. "Glad to have you with us—we'll ship you to British Columbia by boat next Saturday."

I signed a few papers. The crippled man made the necessary entries concerning the place of my birth. I was directed to report for examination that afternoon.

But Saturday was four days away. To get to Vancouver would be but the work of two days if I paid my own fare and took the train. Donning my uniform, yet carrying the civilian suit in a hand-bag, I crossed the Bay and left Oakland on the Shasta Limited that night.

Although I had a ticket to Seattle, I decided to stop a day or two in Portland. Despite my ramblings, I had managed to keep in touch with various members of the road show and, from the columns of the *Billboard,* I knew that the two girls of the sister-act were playing in Portland that week. A visit to them would form a pleasant break in what had been an all too hectic month. To review some of our old affairs loomed pleasantly attractive. Then, too, I was a soldier and was going to war—and there are certain pleasantries that are accorded such valiant spirits!

Nor was I mistaken in my concept of the role assigned to women by the world war! After the performance the younger sister and I went to a restaurant, where I confided that I was going to Canada to enlist. I entrusted her, in response to her gracious treatment, with the name of my parents and she tearfully assured me that she would make certain that they learned of my great sacrifice in the event that I was killed. Discussing such delightful subjects brought us closer together and we suddenly discovered that we had a great deal in common and that it would be impossible for us to part—impossible, that is, until they had completed their week's engagement at the theatre. Allowing the world to seek its safety as best it could for the few days remaining, I delayed in continuing my crusade. And that was another of the fatal mistakes that I've frequently made.

With my uniform freshly creased and feeling that this part of the globe seemed to prosper, I was strolling along Burnside Street and had stopped to chat with a chance acquaintance. The girls were engaged in their afternoon's performance and I was killing time before going to the theatre. Someone brushed against me. Turning to observe him, I looked into the face of one of the two officers who had arrested me after Ed's murder of the Dago in our Seattle apartment.

"Steady!" he said. "You're under arrest!" He sought to grasp my arm and I tore from him and ran through the traffic.

A street car was leaving from the corner. Swinging up to it, I neglected to pay the conductor and walked rapidly to the front end. A backward glance revealed the officer running after the car and waving his arms wildly. The conductor signaled for a quick stop. I jerked open the front door and jumped to the pavement as the car slowed down. A passing machine missed me narrowly; obeying a primitive impulse, I grabbed at it. Instantly I was knocked from my feet, to regain them and leap up on the running-board of an automobile.

The street behind the car was in an uproar. The driver of the cur turned and looked at me curiously. I advanced towards him and he looked ahead for a moment to observe where he was driving. Shoving the knuckles of my hand between his shoulder blades, I directed him to drive away from there as speedily as he could or have his heart blown out. He straightened and leaned forward. I increased the pressure on his back and then he seemed to be convinced that I held a gun. The car shot forward and swung into the middle of the street. I could feel the driver trembling and his nervousness was not reassuring.

Chancing another backward glance, I discerned the officer on the side of another car in the lead of what appeared to be a fleet of cars, all intent upon my arrest. The driver increased speed and we had traveled the distance of a block before he crashed into a truck that was making a turn from a side street. There was a great screeching of horns and a violent shock, as I leaped clear of the wreckage, only to alight on my side and skid several feet over the car tracks. Before I could rise, it seemed to me that half the population of Portland had collected about me. There was a momentary wave of sympathy for the soldier who had been hurt, but it subsided quickly when the officer arrived and placed me under arrest. He was almost swamped by questions. Indeed, before he could make an intelligent reply, granting that he intended to do so, some imaginative person had shouted that I was a German spy, in an American uniform. For the first and only time in my life I was almost glad to see the uniforms of several of the city's finest officers emerge from the crowd, to save me from being trampled or beaten to death.

At police headquarters a newspaper photographer attempted to take my picture. When I kicked the camera from his hands, I started a small war between myself and the officers. I lost, ignominiously.

"Well, you ought to be glad I come and got you instead of letting them take you down and shoot you for being a deserter," Peck informed me. He had been notified to come up and get me.

"Deserter! What are you talking about? Why, I'm only on a leave of absence and if I hadn't been arrested, I'd have been half-way to France by now." I was indignant. The lack of appreciation that he showed for my patriotic moves since leaving him, rankled.

"What on? The bum checks you cashed in Frisco?"

He knew more than I had anticipated. I ceased talking to him.

On the train he displayed enough chains and locks to hold a battleship in tow. He was taking no chances, he assured me. He had almost had to pay for that Milwaukee trip and he was going to make certain that I arrived in Chico with him this time.

I did.

[II]

My conviction was assured by the local newspapers before I had even been held to answer to the Superior Court. I do not know just what scrambled account of my escapades they presented. But I was a slacker; I was a deserter; I had brutally assaulted a patriotic citizen in Portland, almost killed him; and I had escaped from a reform school as well as having woefully upset the peace of Mr. Teddy Peck, popular marshal of Chico, California.

Before I was transferred from the small city-jail to the county jail in Oroville, the county seat of Butte County, I was made aware of the low regard in which I was held by several old sots who were doing nightly penance for having looked upon the wine when it was red and palatable.

"He's a disgrace to his country," one of them said.

"Yeah. They oughta shoot the likes of him," another amplified.

In the county jail, after I had fought a losing fight against bedbugs and an assortment of other vermin, I started calculating the actions of the jailers. The prisoners were permitted to leave the cage and to sit on the top of the cells during the day. The room was on a level with the street and watching the passing people was a constant incentive to forming plans for escape. At night, about eight o'clock, one jailer came into the room and after the men had entered the cage, locked the outer door and then locked the barred door to the room as he left. Over this last door he closed a solid door and secured it with a huge lock. Thus we could hear anyone before he could gain entrance to the room proper. There were about fifteen prisoners in that part of the jail. Most of them were awaiting their trials. Three of them, however, were federal prisoners, held under a nine months' sentence for evading the draft. They were prone to consider me a fellow spirit and since I anticipated using them in a plan for escaping from the jail, I was careful not to disillusion them.

My chances for avoiding conviction were nil. To begin with, I *was* guilty. Then, too, my various offences against the law had become too well known for me to pick a jury that would not convict me without leaving the jury-box. I was greatly discouraged. It was not the temporary discouragement of being in jail; rather, it was a sickening return of the feeling I had known when I pleaded with my father and the probation officer.

All the uselessness of scampering about the country and, at all too frequent intervals, being arrested was present in my consciousness and I wanted to make the reality of the situation change and conform to the way I really wanted to live. With this in view and the thought that I could transcend the miseries of the reform school and possibly learn something there, I called the district attorney. I would plead guilty if he would recommend that I be returned to the school. I would make what restitution I could to the people who had lost money on checks. He listened, considered the proposal and then agreed.

The morning that I went into court I was elated to know that I was not to be branded a felon and sent to prison. That I had come so close to joining the men in San Quentin was a shock. But I resolved that I would not allow myself to run away from the school again. And, too, the thought that I had made this arrangement with the district attorney and had not called on my father for aid pleased me. I was being independent. I no longer needed to cry out to my folks for aid. I was sufficiently old to take care of myself. With such thoughts I stood before His Honor and entered a plea of guilty. It was a shivery moment! At the instant before I released the word of admission, I had a fearful premonition that I should add a "not" to the plea.

His Honor frowned, cleared his throat, listened to a recital of my record by an assistant district attorney and then, before I could say a word in my own behalf, I was sentenced to from one to fourteen years in prison. It was the first sentence imposed under the then recently enacted indeterminate-sentence law. His Honor made much of the fact that I was the first prisoner sentenced from that county. While I sought to decline the Honor thus conferred upon me and to tell the Court that I had agreed to a plea of guilty only upon a promise to send me to the reform school, the sheriff firmly, but not roughly, led me from the court-room....

For a few hours I raved—inwardly. That I had been tricked did not matter so much as the fact that I had been tricked through placing confidence in the given word of a public official. Wallingford! Your delightful counterpart Sir James—the forerunners of many I've met since then!

But that night, late, I had a consoling idea. The indeterminate-sentence law had been enacted while I was away. My crime of forgery had been committed previously. "No *ex post facto* law or bill of attainder shall ever be passed." From somewhere in my haphazard reading that phrase returned. Ah! I would obtain the code and see just what the legality of my sentence was The second thought was more gratifying. I knew that I could hide outside the cage at lock-up time and while the jailer was securing the door of the cage, I could sneak from one side and gain the doorway that led to the steps down to the sheriff's office and so to the street.

Next morning, while I mulled over the scheme, the sheriff arrived to transfer another prisoner and me to San Quentin. Immediately my hopes went sailing. I crashed from the heights of my air castle and alighted on the cold steel floor. Into my bunk I dove. A high fever possessed me. It was not entirely simulated; the thought of going to prison *that* morning was enough to raise a fever—and it did. The result was that the sheriff took two other men and allowed me to remain "sick in bed."

That evening I did not get the chance that I sought. Two Chinamen were on trial for murder and their case had been given to the jury just at lock-up time. Three deputies brought one of the Chinamen to the cage and locked him in to await the jury's verdict.

Chow Soon and I sat up all that night. He spoke fair English and, for an Oriental, showed more emotion than I had ever believed possible. It proved to me that, regardless of the mixture of blood or the color of it, men from all quarters of the earth are not so vastly different when they are in love. For Chow's worry was his bride of less than a month. The fact that twelve men were in another part of the building debating as to whether he should be hanged or given life imprisonment was incidental. The thought uppermost in his mind—the one to which he recurred throughout the night—was that of his girl-wife—the sweetness of her, the dearness of her, the utter uselessness of life without her. Had Chow been born in this country, I should have imagined that he had been reading popular magazines; but he had been here very few years. His position as officer in a tong, his business and his friends and countless cousins did not seem worthy of thought. Or, if he did think of them, he expressed not a word of those details.

Far into the early morning we sat and talked. Chow rolled cigarettes like small cones, stood them on their wide end and made various designs with the tiny shapes. When he had about fifty of them arranged, I glanced at them and they suddenly resembled the face and outlined hair of a Chinese girl. I am not certain how he accomplished it. Perhaps it was a trick of my imagination. The bailiff came for him soon after breakfast, bringing the news of his conviction and its attendant life sentence.

The three young chaps were willing to aid me in my plan. They did not want to escape with me; they had almost convinced the authorities that an enlistment in the army was the action most desirable and the three of them did not want to risk the chance of being able to go to war! I refrained from commenting on their sudden change of attitude. No doubt it was better to be fighting cooties in a patriotic cause than to be fighting the vermin of that jail in an unpatriotic one.

That night the jailer came in, locked the cage and stood chatting for a moment with the men. I was hiding around the corner just out of his sight. One of the slackers asked for a candle. The jailer, a corpulent, good-natured individual, waddled to the entrance door. I gauged his movements and was immediately behind him as he turned to his left to enter a small storeroom. I was so close that I could have taken the revolver from his hip-pocket. Instead, I turned to the right and raced up a flight of stairs. I heard a chirp of surprise from the fat jailer, but it registered consciously only when I later recalled the incident. Out through the office I ran. Two deputies, relaxed in comfortable chairs, with their feet on the counter-desk, sat still for a second. I reached the door and shoved against it. In the excitement I had the impression that it should open outwards. Everything that was between me and the street should have given way. By the time I had retreated a step and snatched the door inwards, the deputies had their guns out and culled upon me to surrender. The screen door outside swung open as I fell against it. I heard two shots and then volplaned down a flight of stops and hit the concrete sidewalk on my hands and knees.

The jail stood in the middle of a park. A small retaining wall, about waist-high, surrounded this park. I ran round the end of the building and almost flew through the park. I vaulted the wall before I was aware that I had reached it. Another shot added speed to my feet; but, for all that, my head seemed to be yards in front of my feet. I was almost crying with vexation because I could not keep up physically with the distances that I was covering mentally. A group of women and children was gathered at one corner. I ran straight towards them. I reasoned that, with them for a background, the deputies would be less likely to shoot directly at me. Just as I approached the group, I stumbled. The overalls I had on were torn at the knees from my flight down the steps and the last fall tore my kneecaps. Extending my hands to break the fall, I wrenched my left wrist; the skin and flesh of the right hand were cruelly bruised by the sharp rocks of the unpaved street. But the force of my fear carried me up and away I sped.

I darted between two houses. Through an uncurtained window I caught sight of a family gathered about their dinner table. Even the fleeting glance gave me a pang. Some of the tranquility that seemed to be theirs was the state I had sought—and here I was escaping again! Zigzagging for two blocks, through yards and between houses, I paused to rest in the shadow cast by a large barn. The excitement of my run made me believe that anyone I met would be aware of my escape. In the quietness I heard a housewife come to a rear porch. She opened an ice-box, rattled a few dishes, humming softly to herself, blissfully unaware that within sound of her a "desperate escape" lay, envying her the peace in which she worked.

Probably half an hour later I arose and cautiously made my way back towards that part of town which I had so precipitately left. There was a purpose in doing this. It may appear that I was courting trouble; but I had not listened to thieves' talk and been through other escapes without learning something of the workings of official minds. The officers had seen me run in this direction; it was logical that they would hunt in this district for me. But on this side of the town the country was open, the land being cultivated in small ranches. On the other side of town there were mountains and by skirting them I could travel through country that would afford fair protection. Several automobiles went along the next street. I believed them to be filled with people anxious to find me. Turning into the street that passed the county jail, I kept to the opposite sidewalk. There was a crowd gathered near the rear door, the one through which I had so unceremoniously left. Odd how curiosity will draw a group to look at a mere doorway! That a man had run through that door and was now somewhere in the town, gave to the place an attraction. Two youngsters were walking a bit ahead of me. I caught up with them. They smiled to my "hello" and informed me that they were going home. Taking one by each hand, I walked down past the county jail, paused a moment to glance across the street, listened to a comment on the escape and learned that one of the first bullets fired had hit the screen door just at the height of a man's head. I could see it if I cared to go over there. But I was not interested.—I had to get my youngsters home. They clung closer to me after hearing the conversation and were free in their expressions of gladness that they did not have to go home alone "with that bad man about."

I left them at their gate and smiled, despite the pain in my knees and hands, when they scampered with great haste to their doorway.

The mountains edging the valley were cut by a serpentine road. In the full silvery flood of light the moon poured over the scene, I had little difficulty finding my way. A machine throbbed round a curve behind me. There was no time to leap to the other side of the fence. I flung myself face downwards on the ground and rolled to one side. The headlights seemed unusually bright and I cursed myself for my carelessness. Fortunately, the car passed, but so close that I felt certain it would run over me. The sensation I had then was similar to that experienced when one is lying in bed near a railroad track and hears the roar of the approaching engine.

Towards morning I was beside a small stream. I bathed my injuries; the icy water was soothing. Encouraged, I disrobed and refreshed myself. I had no definite city to reach. Without funds, my clothing a torn pair of overalls, a khaki shirt and a battered cloth hat, feeling very tired and hungry, I sought for some sensible thing to do. I tried to retreat from the reality of my position, to laugh at myself, but there were too many perils surrounding me to do any retreating. Yet, I thought, I *can* get away from a lot of imaginary grief and torment if I force myself into the proper mental attitude. The brooding darkness, which followed the waning of the moon, seemed in league with my tumultuous thoughts. Again I started a stumbling course. Sleep was a vain gesture. I caught at it, but it mocked my efforts to capture it. Several times, in concession to the pain of my knees, I rested and tried to doze. Each time I rose more weary than when I had stopped . . .

To me came an admonition of Red's: "Poor people are the best friends a thief can have." I knew a family in indigent circumstances near a little settlement, Brown's Valley. I had spent a week with them several years previous when a stolen machine that I was driving to a prospective sale had broken down near their small farm. I recalled the family as consisting of an elderly woman, a son of almost forty and an ancient grandfather. They had been so keenly appreciative of the money I had left with them to cover my board and room that I was certain I should find a temporary safety with them. Nor was I mistaken. I had just approached the house when the elderly woman greeted me as though I were a son. She remembered me? Indeed she did! And the dear old soul accepted my explanation that I had been rejected from the army and was walking about the country in an effort to cure a slight weakness of my lungs. I *offered* to pay her as soon as I could mail a letter and receive the answer. Her effusive protest that she would consider herself unpatriotic to accept money from one who was trying to get into the army made me feel miserable. The trust and confidence she showed hurt me keenly. She attended my injuries, gave me another pair of overalls and regretted that she could not do more. The "boy" was not present until that evening and when he did come, he accepted me without question.

I remained at that place for approximately two weeks. They were a self-contained family, did not subscribe to the papers; and I probably could have lived with them for years without suspicion's being directed towards me.

Dan's aunt sent me a hundred dollars. She cautioned me in her letter against coming to San Francisco. I had no intention of going there, but the country safe to me was shrinking so rapidly that I could not conceive of any place to go. Yet go I must! As soon as I could walk without limping, the restlessness that had spurred me on for months became so insistent that I had to be traveling.

I watched, from the safety of some brush, the actions of a neighbor who lived about a half-mile from where I was staying. He owned an automobile—a four-cylindered affair, but capable of getting me to the southern border. Having failed in my effort to reach Canada, I was thinking of Mexico, with a stop-over at some intermediate point to replenish my purse.

Two days later I visited the neighbor's house, during his absence, located his check-book, dressed myself in a suit of his clothing and borrowed his automobile. Thus fortified, I drove to Marysville, cashed a forged check at a creamery and started down the highway toward Sacramento. An itinerant laborer asked me for a ride and that being before the days when chance highway acquaintances were prone to murder their benefactors and steal their machines, I picked the man up. It would serve to lessen chances of identification if two men were in the machine.

One of the rear tires, punctured by a bit of glass, brought us to a stop at Lincoln. The garage-man who repaired the damage obligingly cashed a fifty-dollar check for me. Through Sacramento and on over the road to Stockton I piloted the car. I had deposited the man at Sacramento; he was excess baggage and to carry him with me would avail nothing, I reasoned. There were some youngsters coming home from school just outside of Stockton. I stopped and invited them to ride. Their company was a pleasant relief from the strain of driving. In their carefree chatter and happy laughter I found a pleasure which again brought home to me the many delights of life that I was missing. Only to get square with the world once more! Only to be free again from the thought of constant pursuit! To be able to walk about and not have the ever present uncertainty of what the next step would bring! Only to know that I could sleep in a certain bed or a certain house instead of continually finding myself in some lonely jail! . . . But the youngsters laughed, pointed out their homes as we arrived at them and intensified my longing to be freed of all the penalties I had accumulated for myself.

I was alone in the machine; a pair of goggles about my eyes, my cap turned so that the visor was hindmost, my shirtsleeves rolled up and as twisted an expression as I could contrive to hold on my mouth. With that disguise I felt comparatively safe from recognition as I steered the car through Stockton.

Two miles down the highway a speedy machine passed me. Glancing casually into it, I observed five men. Real-estate agents, I thought. They preceded me for a few hundred yards, then slowed down beside a large truck standing on the edge of the road. The men sprang from their machine as I approached. My car was going about thirty miles an hour. Spreading in fan shape in the space left, they displayed guns and revolvers and waved me to stop.

The unexpectedness of their action instilled a thorough disgust with myself. After all I had anticipated and believed I had come safely through, here I was about to be arrested. An utter recklessness and disregard for what might happen superseded the first nausea of disgust. I had stopped the flow of gasoline to the engine, but, with the surcharge of recklessness, I jammed my foot against the throttle and drove into the small space. The highway was built up from marshy land and the sides sloped sharply away. There was a scant six feet between the end of the officers' ear and the edge of the bank. Awakened to sudden life by the quick flow of gasoline, the engine jerked me forward and skidded the side of my car over the bank. I caught a quick flash of an officer's face and sensed that the machine had brushed him in its skid. Risking a glance over my shoulder, I saw him spiral about in mid-air before he landed in the mire of the swamp. He had jumped to save himself and the machine had added just sufficient speed to his leap to throw him off balance.

Glass from the wind-shield shattered down about my hands and cut a deep gash in one thumb. A moment later, the car picking up speed as I sought to out-distance the officers, the glass again showered from the wind-shield. Then I was aware that they were firing at me. I crouched lower in the seat and prayed that the dusk would come quickly. To leave the machine and strike across country, even taking a chance on the marshy character of the land, seemed my only hope of evading them.

Through curves and over bridges I raced like a madman. I took chances that should have wrecked the machine several times. No sane man could have whipped in and out of that road and not have been killed. For that reason the officers were unable to overtake me until we reached a straight stretch of road. They used the reserve power of their car there and soon were alongside me. That I had not fired at them in reply to their first fusillade saved me from being shot. They felt certain that I had no gun—hence they motioned me to slow down or they would crowd me off the road and wreck my car. . . .

It was with a mingled feeling of relief and bitterness that I submitted to arrest.

"You're lucky you aren't dead," one said. "We thought you were rodded up."

"But how did you know who I was?" I asked, my curiosity getting the best of me.

"Funny thing," a rather sharp-appearing individual said; "I was just leaving the identification bureau and happened to see an old circular Teddy Peck sent out for you. Then I saw you on the street. Odd how that happened!"

Through a depressing dusk I drove back to Stockton. Two officers accompanied me and the other machine trailed us.

The next morning I was taken to the identification room and again met the man who had recognized me despite my attempt at disguise. He was young—very young, I thought, for it seemed to me that most police officers were old men. That chap, however, was really the most wide-awake officer I had met with the exception of the Berkeley police chief. He smiled when I mentioned this to him.

"You had best be thinking about your own troubles," he said. "You have several charges against you now. Let me see"; he consulted a paper beside him. "Grand larceny of the machine. Two charges of cashing forged checks. Assault upon that officer you knocked into the mud—oh yes and the jail break at Oroville. Rather a formidable list! What do you think about it?"

"I want to see an attorney," I said.

"The same old song," he remarked—but his eyes smiled and he ceased questioning me.

The sheriff from Oroville and the deputy from whom I had escaped arrived that afternoon.

"Where's Peck's bad boy?" the sheriff called into the cells as the jailer brought him down the tier.

Peck's bad boy! What a roasting I got while that name hung on me! That label was the forerunner of several years of torment concerning that name. From the view-point of newspapers it seemed appropriate, so whenever they had occasion to refer to me, it was as Peck's Bad Boy.

For a while I debated the advisability of wiring to my father, but I decided against it. All the charges against me would not be pressed, I reasoned, especially as the sheriff was anxious to take me back to Oroville and, later, to San Quentin. Two days passed while I lingered in the Stockton jail. But then the charges were gradually dropped. All except the stealing of the automobile. That was filed against me and the owner of the car bitterly assured me that he would prosecute me even though I did the full fourteen years of my former conviction.

CHAPTER 11

[I]

Crossing the broken, dark asphalt in the brightness of the sun gave me the impression of traveling over dead hopes in a mockery of brilliance. Ancient stairs let me down from the prison yard into the gloom of a musty barbershop. Forms moved behind a short row of chairs against one wall. Phantoms in hickory shirts—the white blurred faces registering in my consciousness like Benda masks with lowered eyes.

A khaki-clad guard seated upon a raised bench motioned me to remove my ill-fitting prison coat and to recline in one of the chairs. I stood irresolute, blinking.

"Next!" came a voice surprisingly sharp in such a depressing atmosphere.

One man sat upright while another worked with comb and scissors on the mop of shaggy black hair. The other chairs were vacant. No other customer waited. I climbed on the wooden pallet next to the man whose hair was being cut. He smiled at me. His teeth were even and startlingly prominent. Light from a high, distant window made a small, white, glistening patch upon the somber color of his irises.

A phantom pressed my shoulders back on the hard incline of the chair and I was stretched almost prone, as upon an operating-table. His hands adjusted a prickly cloth about my neck. Some cold soap-froth was applied to my beard. Slowly, evenly, with measured strokes, his hand rubbed the lather until it had half dried. A razor scraped over one cheek and slid off the point of my chin. My head was turned to face the man whose hair was being cut. He smiled again and his lips moved, but I lost the words in the rasping of the razor down my other cheek. My head was turned until I gazed at the ceiling; a hand from the phantom tilted my chin upward. The razor climbed from my neck to my chin, twice. A cold damp towel was drawn across my face.

"'S all," said a voice.

I sat erect. The guard had walked to the front of the shop. I was facing the dark-haired man.

"Quick service," he said.

"Yes," I agreed. "How often can you get your hair cut?"

"Once a month. But you'll get used to it. . . . Is he doing a good job on my hair?"

"Splendid," I lied. The hair on one side was horribly mutilated.

"Have you got long to do?" he asked.

"About fourteen years, I guess."

"Oh, that's too bad! But you can get it cut down." He shivered and the cloth covering his form rippled with the movement. "Don't let that worry you. There's a lot of good guys here. You'll get along all right."

I glanced about and saw that we were the target of all the eyes then raised from the masks; only the guard at the base of the steps seemed indifferent to us.

"How's he doing with the hair-cut now?" the man asked.

"Splendid!"

"That's good. You know what? I've always been particular about my hair-cuts. It adds to a man's appearance. Now, you take some people—they don't seem to mind how they look. But I've got a sort of horror of having hair straggling down my neck. My hair grows so fast that I have a devil of a time keeping it looking right—in here." He smiled again with his mouth, his eyes remaining mirrors of those two white patches from the window.

There was an elaborate snipping of shining scissors and a large portion of the tangled hair fell to the floor. The man regarded it intently.

"Not so close," he cautioned the wielder of the scissors. "If you're not careful, you'll have it so I can't make it part. And I always have the very devil of a time making it lie down after a short cut. Try to feather-edge it from about the ears. But use some judgment."

He lifted his eyes from the fallen hair and rested his gaze upon me as though seeking in my eyes a reflection of the progressing operation. I tried to appear as if I felt that the hair-cutting was making satisfactory progress.

"Do you mind looking at the other side?" he asked. "Just step over and see if it balances on both sides: will you, please?"

I stood before him and made the requested inspection. From that angle his eyes showed free of the patches. There was a curious light of anxiety within them. With my assurance that the work was progressing symmetrically, the light vanished. Quick relief and gratitude succeeded it.

"I can never believe that I grow so much hair in the short time of one month," he said, his teeth exposed in a smile. "It worries me to see so much hair cut off at once. You know, if a man lets his appearance go, he looks like the very devil. And I was thinking I would change the part from the right to the left side. If you change like that every so often, it saves you from growing bald over your forehead. Some people don't know that, but it's so. Try it and see if you don't get good results from it."

The guard returned to his bench. Suddenly he noticed me in conversation with the man.

"Get away from there!" ordered the guard. "If you're shaved, you can go over to the turnkey's office." He jerked his hand towards the stairs.

The sunlight was dazzling after the darkness. With my eyes squinted, I navigated the dark asphalt in a staggering course. In the shade of an awning suspended from the front of the office, I stood for a few moments. A prisoner joined me. He removed his cap and mopped his forehead.

From the black maw of the barber-shop came the man who had been so particular about his hair. The guard followed, a few paces behind. They crossed the yard and disappeared in the shadow of a huge cell building.

The prisoner beside me said: "That guy will have his time in soon. He's a short-timer."

Small wonder that he was particular about his appearance, I thought.

"When is he to be discharged?" I asked.

"Ten o'clock Friday morning."

"He's lucky—wish I had only that long to do," I said.

"I don't," said the prisoner. "He goes out in a pine box...."

[II]

Dan met me the following morning. "Sunday is a keen day to get a slant at the joint," he said. "Tough that you had to make it here, but you sure tried to stay away!"

We were standing under the end of a long shed. The lines of men from the dining-room were filing past us to a certain mark and then breaking out into pairs or small groups. I compared them with my former impression of the prison inmates and found that I had indeed seen the faces of the men through the softening glow of the footlights. There were many vicious faces.

Some of the lines in cheeks and under eyes would have provided much of interest for Greco to paint.

"Come on around back of the cells," Dan said. "I'll show you where the gang hangs out. There's a lot of Hods back there—you'll probably know some of them."

He pronounced the name as though it were "Whods." I had heard of the Frisco Hoodlum gang, but thought they had been broken up by the police. So they had! But in prison they were present and powerful. A considerable amount of the political conniving by which favors were secured for Hods, or their friends, was planned and put into operation in that alley.

Four cell-blocks ended about twenty feet from a wall forming an alley. Against the building was reclining a series of groups. Some gathered about two chess-players seated on the asphalt. Four other men sat on small stools and held a two-foot-square board on their knees while they played dominoes. In the angle formed by iron stairs from the higher tiers, six or eight men and boys were playing dice. One of their number kept watch for the officer at one end of the alley. The blue-gray clothing, the rumpled coats, the grotesquely shaped caps and the large, ill-made shoes gave to the men an appearance of having been gathered from various fields where they had posed as scarecrows. Within a few minutes, however, I began to discern a difference in the clothing. Some wore shirts that were tailored and fitted them snugly, others sported trousers that were sharply pressed and some had shoes from "outside," polished and rubber-heeled. I noted this and wondered about the difference. My own clothing made me feel acutely self-conscious as the men eyed me, glanced at Dan and then returned to their walking or gaming.

Later I learned the significance of their glances. I was in forbidden territory. The Hods controlled the alley. If a stray inmate ventured within some certain well-established but invisible line, he was immediately told to "mope!" Which, being interpreted, is: "Leave this alley and stay out of it; if you don't you'll get your head broken." The tenseness of prison slang and its all-embracing significance doubtless accounts for its constant use.

"His Nobs, the Slim Irishman," said Dan, nodding to a tall thin man, about forty-five. "Remember his caper? Slugged two coppers; his partner was topped."

Slim Irish came over and asked the usual questions. Length of time, tough joint—or did I think so?—why did Red (whom he seemed to know intimately) join the army? Others followed. They all seemed to know me and I wondered about their knowledge. Some of them offered comment on my escapes. All asked if I was supplied with smoking-tobacco. It was like the first meeting with a group of future lodge-members.

"That's all here," said Dan. "Come on and I'll show you the rest of the joint.

"This is the upper yard. It looks like it's going to rain, so we better make the lower yard for a quick gander, then get back and stick near this shed. The rest of the outfit will be under this corner if it starts raining. All of us have a spot here and the dings and odds-and-ends don't get into our spot at any time. Keep 'em in their places. You won't have any trouble. I showed you up to most of the right guys already. The rest of these harmless bums—" he swept his eyes over the milling two thousand men—"well, don't pay any attention to 'em. If they get in your way, bust 'em in the kisser and let 'em fall. But don't look for trouble."

We walked through a crowd just then and I noticed that several of the "dings" made ample room for Dan as he shoved against them to clear a passage for us. We descended some stairs, crossed an alley between two huge buildings and walked through a rotunda to emerge in another yard. Some men were playing handball in a court in one corner; another group crowded about a larger court in the opposite corner.

"Mexes," Dan volunteered. "They're crazy about that game."

One or two men spoke to Dan in passing. "Hozzit?" they flung and continued without waiting for an answer. "'S all right," Dan replied and continued walking. A moment later he guided me to a small picket-fence enclosure. Approximately one hundred Chinamen were playing mah jong. The craze for that game had not then swept the country. It looked exceedingly involved to me. Two other old Chinamen were surrounded by a group of their countrymen.

"Playing Chink chess," explained Dan. "That's the laundry in the building back of them and this place here is Chinatown."

Several guitars and mandolins started to play. I turned to the sound, for the harmony and precision of the players rather surprised me. "That's the Mexican outfit. Mex town is over there." He indicated the handball-players. "There's a big yard below this, but they don't let us go out in it."

I peered through a huge slat-iron gate and saw more walls beyond. At regular intervals guard "shacks" were placed on top of the walls. But it was the size of the place that impressed me. A great sprawling series of yards and red brick buildings. Later, when I had access to the prison records, I read the yearly report of the operation and growth of the prison and the sprawling nature of the place was made plain to me. It was not planned; it grew as the population increased and wherever there was room for a wall or building, there it was built.

From the dull slate-colored sky a dreary drizzle began to fall. A few wisps of fog drifted over one end of the walls; a guard standing on the ground rapped his iron-tipped cane on a water-pipe and the men glanced upwards. Then they slowly formed into a line. Dan hurried me towards the first part of the forming line. Together we walked back through the rotunda, up the stairs and into the upper yard. There, in the shelter of the low shed, we were joined by the men we had met that morning.

The remainder of the day passed under that shed is one of the bleakest memories that I have. The drizzle increased until the yard was sluiced with sheets of rain. Huddled into a pack, so closely pressed together that all we could do was to stand or twist slightly, the minutes lengthened into hours. My feet ached from the irksome shoes. My injured knees pained me as the cold bit sharply into the sores. The odor of cigarettes, the smell of jute—from the clothing of the men who sweated nine hours a day in the jute-mill—and the damp, penetrating staleness peculiar to prisons, all wrapped about me. The conversation was fragmentary and the gist of it was that the guards were no good, the treatment of the prisoners a disgrace, the food rotten and the cells lousy. Adjectives were all profane.

"That guy," someone said, "is a rat." Another echoed the condemnation and added: "So's the fink with him."

"This guy's queer!" "That's guy's wrong!" "There's the guy who testified against Shorty!" Comment was rife. I wondered if there was anyone of whom they could say one good word. In that moment I knew a swift revulsion.

Before I had arrived in prison, I held the romantic idea that prisoners and particularly those in San Quentin, lived in a series of adventures little less exciting than those I had known in the outside world. That they would be banded together into one harmonious whole I never doubted. That they would have plans under way for escaping and probably could show me a way out of the prison and that I should only be forced to wait until I had established connection with Dan and his group—these thoughts were what had enabled me to repress an impulse to fight the sheriff for his gun. I had held the idea of making a desperate battle and either getting killed or regaining my freedom while being transported to prison. But the restraining thought that Dan would be able to show me a way to escape had prevented my putting into action the fantastic thought.

And then in prison I found that the very thieves of whom I had read as being desperate, daring, murderous, were cynical, morose, moody and even squabbling amongst themselves. Two of the domino-players were arguing angrily over the exact count scored. Their voices rasped and grated and they offered insults with each breath they took and expelled. I wondered why they did not fight it out and settle the disagreement.

"They're just a bit off their feed," Dan explained. "A guy gets to boiling up in here and says a lot of guff he don't mean. You get used to it."

That night, in the solitude of a small cell, I lay on the straw-stuffed mattress, listened to the driving rain swishing over the balconies and kept track of the hours through hearing the guards cry out the call: "All's well." I suffered a poignant disillusionment. The thieves I had met were not the romantic characters presented in such vivid word-pictures by the newspapers. Those thieves I had met—and they were reputed the hardest in the prison—ceased to be idols to worship, or mentors from whom to learn something. Instead they crashed into the dust and lay beside my King of the Tramps, my Wallingford mayor and other minor deities of my own creation.

[III]

Giving to prison politics, I was assigned to work in the furniture factory.

Thirty new men were on the "porch." The captain, who was in charge of the men within the walls, came past us and briefly questioned each in turn.

He asked the man next to me: "What do you do for a living on the outside?"

"I'm a blacksmith." The man looked it. "And I'm only here for overdrawing my bank account. If you'd give me a chance at my trade—"

"Mill," said the captain. A convict clerk, his face freshly shaven, his hair neatly trimmed and wearing tailored clothes, checked the name on a list he carried.

"And you?" said the captain.

"I'm a cabinet-maker, sir," I replied, as I had been coached to do.

"Did you work at it outside?"

"That's all I ever did—until I got into this trouble," I said and looked as regretful as I could.

"Well—" the captain hesitated.

"This is the man I was telling you of," said the clerk.

"Well—" the captain spoke slowly and regarded me intently—"well, I guess perhaps—" Suddenly he noticed my hands. "How did you do that?"

I held the skinned hands upwards. "It was an accident. I was working on a—" I was not certain of any machine used in a cabinet-maker's trade and covered my hesitation by blurting out: —"planer! My hand slipped into it."

"We-e-ll, all right," the captain said. The clerk winked to me from behind the captain's back. I caught a gleam of approbation. The part I was told to play had been satisfactorily performed.

To the next man, a small, consumptive-looking individual, the captain gave a passing glance and snorted. The clerk checked the man to the jute-mill. Two of us were assigned to trades that morning. The rest went to the dreaded jute-mill.

I kept my own counsel at my work. A fat old German, a dry-witted swindler, appreciated my predicament as soon as I picked up the first tool on my bench. He asked the foreman to give him a helper and I was transferred to his bench. We were engaged in making office desks, chairs and odd patterns for the iron-molders.

I worked there six months. And I learned a fair amount from the old German. But the work was irksome. I was anxious to be on the move. The outlet I found was in walking up and down the yards when work was over. This solitary pacing earned me the reputation of being constantly "boiled up," and several of the men I met sought to dissuade me from "doing my time so hard." I did not enlighten them that during those walks I was less inclined to think of the prison than when I sat and listened to endless repetitions of scandals. Some of the least miserable moments I knew were during those pacings.

I devoted my evenings to reading. I read rapidly and often as many as six books a week. Of course I did not digest them and often while reading, my mind would slide off the subject and I would find myself planning for the future. Although my eyes continued to follow the printed lines, I would realize with a start that I had turned several pages and could not recall the least portion of what I imagined I had been reading. Then I became interested in some of the courses offered by the University of California. I compared my knowledge of English with the requirements they insisted that an applicant possess and found myself woefully lacking. I signed for a course in Spanish. The few weeks I dallied with that served to jumble my meagre knowledge of English into a mixture that I have never yet succeeded in clarifying.

Through letters I had managed to have the charges that were pending removed from the various district attorneys' offices. All but one charge had been dismissed. One day Dan introduced me to a prison lawyer, Saunders. He was a silver-haired, rosy-faced, jolly little man. I was aware that he was superior to the majority of the men in prison and warmed to him after a few moments of conversation. He had a bad habit of being too willing to entertain his friends. This had led him to prison three times. All of his terms were for a short duration. But immediately upon his release he would start on a round of pleasure and, when his funds were low, he would cash a forged check to keep the festivities in full swing.

I outlined to him the case and the manner in which sentence had been pronounced against me. He considered the problem and, a few days later, delighted me with the information that I was able to secure my release from prison through a writ of habeas corpus. I wanted to be told just that and so accepted it in its entirety. He showed me portions of the State Constitution and gave me law cases to read. He prepared a writ for me. A common friend who worked in the warden's office typed it. With high hopes I mailed the writ to the Appellate Court.

Dan and several of the others were elated. During the days that passed while awaiting a return from the court, I made some ambitious plans. Dan was about to be released. I would wait in San Francisco for him. Then together we would start on a series of robberies that would make us independent. But the same irritant was present in our companionship that had vexed Red and me. Doubtless we could steal together and in harmony; but socially we grated on each other's nerves. Probably twenty men approached me and, so certain were they that I would be released by the court, entrusted me with messages to their friends outside. I wondered why some of them did not write to their friends—for it was easy to have a letter smuggled out—and then I learned that they could not write an intelligible letter. The very men about whom I had woven most of my romantic beliefs were the most illiterate. Even to sign their names, when drawing tooth paste or soap from the prison commissary, was considered so great an effort that many of them had friends make the requisitions. . . .

The Appellate Court granted my application for a writ. It withheld the decision for several days. In the interval a similar case was decided by the Supreme Court. The ruling there was that if a man had been sentenced under the indeterminate-sentence law and his crime had been committed previously to the enactment of the law, that man should be returned to the sentencing court and there given a definite sentence. My hopes burst! But Saunders was positive that we could yet win if I submitted to being returned to the Oroville court and receiving a definite sentence. He insisted that if they re-sentenced me they would lose jurisdiction of the case and that I could then secure release through the federal courts.

When I stood before the judge in Oroville, he asked me if I had anything to say before sentence was pronounced. The sheriff, in bringing me back to court, had assured me that I was going to receive a sentence of at least ten years and probably the limit of fourteen years. I thought of a thousand things that I wanted to say. Conflicting thoughts struggled for expression. Several times I started to speak. The desire to tell him, in all sincerity and yet without any apparent striving to be sincere, that I had undergone a great change within the last eight months—that desire defeated me. During the moment that I stood there, my face flushed and, conscious of the eyes upon me and also of the whispering that was creeping over the court-room, I *did* realize that I had undergone a tremendous change. The thought of further stealing was repugnant. That I had planned to join with Dan rankled as it dragged through my mind. Without any further attempts to make a speech I started to talk, easily and in a modulated voice:

"Your Honor, there are several things that I wish to say before you pronounce sentence upon me. Whether or not I succeed in telling you of them will depend upon your indulgence and patience. I stand before you as a convict. I am nineteen years and six months old. I have been in a reform school and several county jails and I have escaped from them all except the place of my present confinement, San Quentin. The district attorney, the sheriff and the other law officers connected with your court will tell you that I have a bad record. And they speak truly. On paper it is bad! Yet throughout the time that I have been building up that record, I have been wanting to find another outlet for the energy that I was releasing in the wrong direction. At the reform school I held some idea that I could learn a trade. But I worked with a pick and shovel until I sickened of it and ran away. Now, in San Quentin, I have been employed in the furniture factory. I have a fair knowledge of that work. If you can possibly feel that the ends of justice will be served by giving me a minimum sentence and allow me to finish learning that trade, then you will have been the first person who has not told me that I have all the training that I need. So many people, officials, with whom I have come in contact, have insisted that I am qualified to earn my living in any line of endeavor that I choose. But that is not so. In earning capacity I am but a common laborer. Instead of sending me back to that prison for a long term, will you not give me a chance? There is much more I want to say, but the words will not come."

His Honor was listening closely. The district attorney started to his feet, a paper in his hand. Sensing that he was about to read a re-hash of my escapades after I broke from the Oroville jail, I spoke quickly, urgently, to His Honor: "If the Court please, I am ready to receive sentence."

I was standing rigid, every muscle of my body tensed, my mind concentrated on His Honor. With all the will-power I could summon I sought to duplicate the thought-transference that I had seen demonstrated so often in Seattle. And I caught the exact psychological moment.

"It is the judgment of this court," His Honor said, still looking directly into my eyes, "that you be confined in the State Prison at San Quentin for a period—" His eyes flickered as the district attorney sought to interrupt him; then he concluded: "for a period of five years."

I could have shouted my relief! Instead, I glanced at the district attorney and was rewarded with a look of disappointment from him. Five years was *not* a small sentence, but with the possibility of a fourteen-year sentence removed, it looked small indeed.

As His Honor scratched the sentence in a book, I made a motion for appeal. Saunders had given me the proper form and I had memorized it. With a triumphant note, I said to the Court; "At this time I give oral notice of appeal from the judgment of this court. The grounds are that this court has no jurisdiction to sentence me. I was first sentenced under a law that did not exist. Now the court, made aware of its error, seeks to rectify it—at my expense. My contention is that this last sentence is illegal and without effect and that I am held under a judgment that is no judgment in law and therefore violative of my constitutional rights. All legal time for imposing sentence on me elapsed months ago, yet this court has imposed a *second* sentence without vacating the first sentence, a portion of which has been served."

The sudden change in my attitude brought His Honor erect. That I had charged his court with error seemed a personal insult. Although I was perfectly correct in my statement of the case, yet he allowed my notice of appeal to be filed only grudgingly.

[IV]

During the several months ensuing, while the appeal was pending, I occupied myself in a new phase of prison life. Through a friend of the Hods, I was transferred to work in the photograph gallery. It was managed by two convicts. One of them was a fair photographer, the other a combination locksmith and general nuisance. I knew nothing of photography, but the work fascinated me from the first day. The gallery was in a small house, set off *by* itself and we were free from official observation. The study of chemistry, experimenting with pictures and odd poses, dabbling in colored photography and being occupied with a work that I liked did much to save me from growing too despondent. For I had been brought to a full realization of the length of time that I was to live in that prison and the thought was not inspiring. For a time I made plans for escaping, but a young man of my age and appearance would be captured soon if he was not in uniform. I waited for the war to end. The blowing of the whistles on Armistice Day gave me double happiness.

Then my appeal came up for decision. I was told I was lucky that I was not doing the maximum! Again I turned to thoughts of escape, only to discover that I could apply for parole within eight months. Almost two years had slid by while I was occupied with my photographic work and I had not been aware of their passage. I decided to wait and be paroled. All the preceding photographers had made paroles as soon as they had served half their time and I was confident that I should do likewise.

Buddy had come into the prison and was almost ready to leave. He was sentenced to three years and served fourteen months. Many of the boys from the reform school came to San Quentin. I thought of our chasing through life from one institution to another as a very futile way of living. And I was trying to make myself believe that I should do no more stealing.

Talking this over with Buddy one day, I got a rather curious slant on the operation of his mind.

"With my trade learned," I said to him, "I am going to go to work for some photographer, finish my parole and then get my father to loan me enough to start a studio of my own. I know I can make a success of it."

Buddy laughed. "Me too—I got a fine trade. Making jute sacks is a swell thing to teach a guy. But you'll be just like the rest of us. Soon's you get out, you'll meet some of the guys from here, Dan or Red or Irish, or any of the outfit and right away you'll be one of them again. Because you're in a spot here where you don't have to mix up with anyone very much, you get those funny ideas of reforming. But a few drinks, a shot of junk, or a few hours with the bunch—aw, you know how it is."

Eight months later I applied for parole. With high hopes I appeared before the board of prison directors. They considered my case and briefly questioned me and the following day I received a letter from the clerk. I was denied parole.

For days I walked about in a daze. I could not reconcile the reality of the printed word with the bright future I had painted for myself. Instead of being in the outside world and working at an Honorable profession, I was leaving my cell at six in the morning, walking to the mess hall, returning to the gallery, working uninterestedly at routine work, moping and sulking and then lying awake half the night mentally raving against the injustice of my position. I truly believe that if I had been paroled at that time, I should have gone far in the photographic world, for the deeper I had dug into the work, the more it had fascinated me. Following my denial of parole, however, even the smell of the dark-room grew distasteful. I ceased reading anything but the lightest of fiction. All books on chemistry I gave away. The routine work was done, but I experimented no longer. And even with this work I grew careless. I did not care if pictures were not properly developed or if they did not lie long enough in the fixing bath to ensure them a fair degree of permanency. I also violated all the written rules and many that were unwritten, in my efforts to do favors for friends. There was considerable material in the gallery that was useful to my friends. I stole everything I could and moved it out. In the captain's office was a barrel of grain alcohol. Some wise photographer had instilled the belief in the officials' heads that grain alcohol was essential to a photographer. I regularly drew two quarts a week. Not one drop was ever used in the work. All of it went to friends. When sugar became scarce, especially during the rationing of sugar during the war restriction period, I explained to the captain that sugar was an essential to the gallery. Since the war I was forced to work with inferior chemicals, I explained and I needed sugar to keep the developer from souring. . . . He wanted some enlargements made. In all seriousness I explained that I needed the albumen from raw eggs to form a basis upon which to sensitize the paper for the enlargements. I required also several quarts of milk to use for preparing the paper to receive the egg covering. As a result I drew twenty pounds of sugar a week, three dozen eggs a week and four quarts of fresh milk daily. All of which was sent over to the yard.

I was popular. And, being a good-natured chump, I believed that the merely incidental supply of food-stuffs had nothing to do with it. I did not appreciate what a delicacy I was offering so constantly. For I was allowed to go outside the walls and frequently made pictures of the warden's children, their playmates, or parties that were held on the spacious lawns. And each time I went to the warden's house I was royally feted. My old Chinese friend Chow Soon, with whom I had sat up during the night the jury decided his fate, was the cook for the warden. Whenever I entered the kitchen, Chow would shout orders to the six or eight other Chinamen and in a moment a table would be prepared holding more food than I could have eaten in a week.

Then I was caught with a lot of "counterband." The "counterband" consisted of bringing into the walls several dozen cookies, some cake and an assortment of other sweets. I had them all in the carrying case of a large stand camera. The guard on the gate had so often passed me through with only a nod and slight glance that I had become over-confident.

My work was causing complaint from the different departments. They complained that the photographs turned yellow and did not look like the men whom they were supposed to represent. The same complaint had been sung by the different sheriffs' offices throughout the state, but a friend of mine in the warden's office had managed to steal their letters of protest. I was "removed" from the gallery and went to work in the laundry. . . .

All the time I had been in prison, about two years and a half, I had not once sought help from my father. One day in the laundry, while stringing dirty socks on a cord, I decided to write him a letter. I was disgusted with life, as it is lived in prison. The handling of soiled underwear is not calculated to bring colorful dreams.

Two weeks later my father visited me at the prison. It was a Monday. He talked as he always did, mentioning his friends as being my friends and saying that he hoped I had learned my lesson. Did I want to come home?

Did I! Quickly I outlined the work I had accomplished in my studies and was again enthusiastic for entering photography. He left me with the assurance that he would get busy. But I knew that four months must elapse before I could appear before the board for parole.

The following Saturday I was called before the board. I had been ordered on the parole list. This was a special action. Some member of the board had taken this upon himself. But behind it I sensed the hand of my father. I told the board that I had learned photography. I liked the work. I was certain that I could make good at it. One member said that it was not much of a trade. What I needed, he said, was to do some manual labor. I had too much excess energy, so the judge had written and he believed it would be better for me to go up to some logging camp and work. The following Monday I was released and informed that I was paroled to stay out of San Francisco and Oakland.

[V]

It was a bitter pill to swallow. That I had worked over two years at photography and was fully intending to follow it as a life-work and then to be refused the chance to do so, soured me on parole and its restrictions. However, I decided to have a try at keeping my parole.

The Volstead Act had become effective, at least in letter and almost everyone was drinking because liquor was forbidden. I had never cared for intoxicants. My experience with white wine during my youth had acted as a restraint. But with the restrictions the parole had put upon me, I desired some release. Hence, although I was cautioned by the parole officer not to come to San Francisco, but to go to the logging camp as soon as I was released, the first thing I did was to catch a train to connect with the ferries. That night, through a glorious bourbon haze, I saw San Francisco as I had never seen it before. And for the ensuing week I drifted through a series of parties and entertainments, most of them in celebration of my release. I recall now that three Turkish baths entered into that week—and when I did sober up long enough to know where I was, a week had passed.

Various friends had supplied me with money. I had purchased clothing and two suit-cases to hold it. But with realization of my position I decided to go to the woods and look over the work. Perhaps I could manage to have my parole changed after I had worked a few months.

During the train ride to Fort Bragg, on the northern California coast, I tried to remember what had happened in the past week. For a few moments, shortly after leaving Sausalito, I had a glimpse of the prison. Somehow, viewed from that distance, it seemed to have no relation to me. Although I was but a week removed from it, the activities I had known there, the acquaintances I had made there and the misery I had undergone, all these seemed not realities, but lingering torments from a recent bad dream. And I mused over my debauch and the reason for it. The conclusion I arrived at was that I had been so long away from high lights and gay laughter, real food and pleasant friends, that I had tried desperately to make up for the blank two and a half years in the space of a week. I was like a dog let loose from a chain. I had wanted to run and play, indulge myself, satiate myself. And I wondered how many others had experienced the same feelings. . . .

There is a wild, rugged beauty up along the northwestern coast of California that defies description. It has to be felt—absorbed. South from Eureka for two hundred miles the shoreline is broken into a series of sheer drops from redwood cliffs into the Pacific. And again there are stretches of sandy beaches woven about great jagged rocks. Wharves are impossible. All supplies incoming and lumber and other products outgoing, are slung in great slings over cables, often a thousand feet long, which extend out into the ocean to link the boats to the shore. At one place, near a little cable-landing at Westport, there is a unique formation of rocks. There, with silver spray breaking from green water over cavernous rocks, a little semicircular bite has been taken from the shore and the place is filled with sand to form a tiny beach framed with multicolored growths and backed by the straight, gigantic redwoods. It is a place of rare beauty—secluded, for the few families who live at the landing know it only as "the stretch where seaweed piles up." . . . There are bits of flotsam upon the beach: water-smoothed logs, a bit of broken boat and hundreds of tiny shells. One little stump, half buried in the sand, sits so that the arch of an element-torn cave forms a frame for it, giving a vista of the water breaking over the shore beyond.

I repaired to that place the first morning after my arrival at Westport. The logging camp to which I was to report was some five miles farther north. Seating myself on that stump, I relaxed and drank in the perfume of the ocean. The soft swish of the waves as they tumbled in soothing rhythm to flow up to my feet gave me a tranquility I had long sought. But with it there came a longing for company—companionship. To know that beauty and quietness alone was not right. Such places, such moods, are not for me alone, I thought. They are made to be shared. But with whom? The natives of the little village were total strangers to me. I knew that at the logging camp there were other men from the prison, probably twenty of them. But neither of these groups would understand what I was responding to at that moment. Then, from the nights of sleeplessness I had spent in prison, came a hazy picture of the sweetheart I had so often called to me. She was of no definite age and to describe her would be to capture the elusive charm of all that one longs for—and never quite possesses. . . . I was not lonesome in the generally accepted sense of the word. True, I was solitary, but not alone. I had *her.* The indefinable *her* of a hundred hot nights of longing. In fancy she seated herself beside me. I noticed that her head was just high enough to nestle comfortably in my shoulder; and in imagination I encircled her with my arm. Together we rested and watched the ocean in its ceaseless movements. And to me she spoke, so softly and musically that I must learn to her to catch each word.

"This is better than prison. This freedom, this contentment, this tranquility, are they not better than the confinement, the discord, the turmoil of prison life? . . ."

"They are," I answered. "But—"

She spoke quickly: "But what? Are you afraid that this cannot last?"

"I am."

"You need not be. These moments are yours for the taking. You need not seek them. They are with you ever. You must only learn to appreciate them, for with greater understanding of them they come with greater frequency—and they are yours! No one can take them from you. One week ago you left prison and imagined that you were cynical and soured. And for several days you made a petulant childish gesture against the petty restrictions that parole imposed. Now you are sorry you did so. You fear your own appetites and believe that these few moments have been given you only so that they may make you feel miserable when they are taken from you. You need not fear— just learn to let yourself understand how much of happiness you may have if you will only let yourself take it. Now I've lectured you enough. . . . Tell me you're glad I came to you and that you *are* going to make good!"

I turned to face her—then smiled at my fancy. But the last words remained.

"You *are* going to make good!"

[VI]

Ira Thompson, the manager of the woods, was a great hulking, good-natured fellow. He had worked in logging camps for years. Possessed of an unusually fine house for that country, where the architecture favored hastily constructed boxlike houses, he was married to one of the finest women who ever lived. She met me at the door of their home and, in response to my inquiry, directed me to follow a path through the woods to where I could find Mr. Thompson.

"You're a hell of a lookin' lumberjack," he said, after he had read my parole papers.

I flushed my resentment. "Well, you're a hell of a looking manager," I replied.

His large mouth opened in a slow grin. "That makes it even, I guess." He shook my hand and together we laughed. Then he explained his first remark and waved my attempt at apology aside.

"I didn't think you was from the prison," he chuckled. "Most of the boys from there get here about nightfall and they're hungry and have those funny clothes on. You can tell 'em a mile off. Damned shame that they send the boys up that way—everyone knows who they are. But when you come along just now, I thought you was selling something."

"Where are the rest of the fellows?" I asked.

"Up at the mill or in the woods. You'll meet 'em at dinnertime."

"What kind of work do I have to do?"

He cast an appraising glance over me, then drawled: "Well, you're most large enough to do anything, aren't you?"

"Certainly. And I want to make good up here, Mr. Thompson."

"Well, if you don't, you'll be the first man who ever didn't. I've been getting paroled men off and on for several years and lots of them are married and settled down up here now."

"Fine! But how about the other people? Will they know I'm from the prison?" I was rather sensitive on that point.

"Sure! They'll all know it pretty quick. But what the hell do you care about that? It ain't nothing to boast of—but it ain't nothing to be ashamed of, either. If you make good, you can tell 'em all to go to hell."

In overalls and heavy shirt I went to work in the mill. Assigned to a tail-edger, I strained and sweated for ten hours a day. The scream of the huge band sawing through the logs, the rattle of the machinery, the rancorous snarl of the edger-saws as they bit viciously into the slabs, were all as parts of a huge, elementary symphony. There was no compromise between any of the parts. The logs came dripping from the pond, were rolled and turned, then skidded on the carriage, A terrifyingly efficient arm of steel shot from its place of concealment and pecked at the log. The sawyer, with the slightest movement of a control lever, directed the work of this arm. The log was kicked, twisted and soon in proper place for dissection. It was impossible to talk above that noise and signs were exchanged with fingers and hands. Yet I found the activity and dangerous character of the work exciting. After the first few days I became accustomed to the routine and for a month I took a great interest in the edger. Studying the operator, a pallid Swede, I soon learned the proper manner in which to cut boards and estimate the amount of lumber they would produce and how to keep my hands out of the machinery.

Then the Swede was drunk for several days. I operated the machine. Another helper assisted me. I imagined that the Swede's absence was not noticed and was surprised when Thompson informed me that I was to take the job permanently. I sought the Swede and he wanted to fight me for taking his job. I offered it to him. His attitude amused me, for he seemed to feel that a personal hatred existed between us. When he refused to take his job again, I went to Thompson and told him that I was going back to my old work and that he had better re-engage the Swede.

My decision to refuse the other job had come to me while walking to the manager's house. The Swede was a workingman. I was not. And in that there came to me the realization that the whole time I had been working, I had been unconsciously planning for the time when I could leave the woods and get back with Dan, Irish, or some of the thieves I knew. With their presence removed, they again took the form of attractive partners. I recalled the offences they had committed and attributed to them many qualities they could not possibly have possessed. But to take a working-man's job from him—well, it did not seem right. I was not afraid of not getting work and he appeared to believe that that job was the only one that existed.

Mr. Thompson argued with me. He said that I was foolish and I agreed with him. However, the Swede returned to work.

The other men from the prison used to meet in my cabin almost every night. I knew three of them. The others were but faces I had seen in prison. We played cards, shot craps and sought to pass the evening until eleven o'clock. But within a short time some of the same discord that always attends gambling entered our relationships. In a flare of anger I chased the whole crowd out of the cabin one night. That I used a broken bottle to emphasize my orders added fuel to a smoldering fire which yet remained within the Swede. He returned to the cabin soon and answering his invitation, I came out into the moonlight to "fight it out like a man."

The verdict of the onlookers was a draw. I believe I lost. The Swede almost chewed one of my ears off and at another time did a clog-dance on my face. When neither of us could rise, the decision was rendered.

Then some of my friends threw the Swede into the millpond; his friends pulled him out and, returning to the cabin to give me the same treatment, encountered some of the fellows with me. After that the mill did not operate for two days. In the interval Mrs. Thompson patched us all up. She seemed to take a special interest in the men from the prison and brought several of us books to read during those two days. In a short conversation with me she asked why I had not come to call on her husband and her. She had sent invitations to the camp several times, asking different men from the prison to call at her home and someone had neglected to deliver the message. I made inquiries and later discovered that a fellow from the prison had taken it upon himself to discard the notes. He had been one of the favored at the prison—wore tailored clothes and "outside" shoes and enjoyed the privilege of an office job. He was working at a very menial position in the mill, a job on a par with his abilities, yet sought to control the other fellows as he had in prison. Charging him with his deceit, he admitted it and said he was the only one worthy of calling on the manager! I took exception to this and a week later received a letter from the parole office saying that if I did not stop my fighting, I would be returned to prison. Mr. Thompson had not made any report of the free-for-all fight, so I knew that the parole officer referred to my mix-up with the favored one.

The incident is trivial in the telling, but at that time it loomed colossal. I was working hard, ten and often eleven hours a day and on Sundays I would go to the cable-landing and work loading ties on the small coast boats. I was determined to save money and make a showing. But I had such a great amount of mental leisure that I started to brood over the meanness of the underhanded letter to the parole officer. The longer I mulled it over, the more firmly I believed that I was being imposed upon. I knew a great self-sympathy. When I thought of the work I was doing and the effort I was making, the thought of a possible return to prison would come to me and I experienced hours of madness while I planned horrible deaths for the man who had brought it all about. The work was often dirty beyond description. At just those times I would retreat from the filth of it all and plan a death for my antagonist. He was really not worthy of a thought. But, as so often happens when one dwells long on a single subject, I exalted him into a sardonic tormentor. I could not regain my peace of mind unless I removed him. There was reason for discarding thought of him—but I was not reasoning at that time.

Then I received a letter from a friend of mine who had just been released from San Quentin. He was writing for Dan. A common friend of ours had been arrested and needed money. Would I come to San Francisco?

[VII]

The edger screamed its glee as another huge slab was fed into its gaping maw. The rollers, like hideous straight lips, closed in the slab and sucked the raw redwood inward. Water, stained from the juice of the wood, spurted from over the rollers. I thought of a gusher of blood expelled from the nostrils of a gigantic beast. Enclosed by a bedlam of noise, I missed the cadenced sound which usually proclaimed that the machinery of the mill was whirling in harmony. Glancing at the sawyer, I discerned a strained look on his face. His eyes encountered mine, then shifted quickly. Other men were looking about them, as though subconsciously disturbed. They, too, seemed to await an unusual occurrence. Then it happened!

I did not actually hear the whistle of the huge forty-foot saw as it broke from its fragile casing; I was only aware that it had done so when I saw the Swede working near the edger make a quick movement with his hands. The same instant I saw him bend double from the impact of a tremendous blow. The saw had swirled through the air and severed his body in two parts. He was opening and closing his mouth when I reached him. One shining ten-foot length of the saw lay near him and with one hand he was pushing against it, the muscles of his arm working jerkily. I wondered then, despite my narrow escape—for the remainder of the saw had passed over my head—at the fighting instinct that made even the muscles of a man follow his last living thought. The emergency whistle blew long and shrilly. The machinery slowed—and in the ensuing silence I heard water running over the dam from the mill-pond.

A man's life gone in a moment! He had fought for his job; he had stood in daily risk of his life and yet he had fought for that risk. The mill-wright rushed another saw into operation at once. Later he explained to me that if he had allowed the men an hour to think over the accident, they would have been in a frame of mind that would prevent them from working. And I remembered that. If he could rush them into their respective positions before they did any thinking of their own volition, he could retain them as employees. But if they had a single thought of their own bidding, he would have to recruit a new crew for the mill.

The letter from the city had come two days later. I was working in a state of extreme nervousness. The often-pictured death of my antagonist was not so vivid, but I was growing more and more restless. Then came the thought: your own friends have appealed to you for aid and you are not going to them! Suppose that you were in jail and needed help. Would they hesitate to come to you? Would they take hours to arrive at a decision? I could believe only that they would rush to my aid. With that thought, that partial decision made, other similar thoughts were released. It was a dangerous position I worked in. Was it worth while continuing to accept the risk and also the chance that in an impulsive moment I should call down on me the wrath of the parole officer? I did not have to seek far for justification of my desire to leave the woods. My single regret was the loss of the freshness, the freedom, the fragrance and beauty of the nights in the open. But I assured myself that I would make up for them in the lights and color of the city. Then, too, there were other contacts that I had not known for months. . .

In San Francisco I went to the parole officer and explained that a man had been killed on the job that I was asked to fill. He was fully informed of the nature of some jobs that paroled men are asked to work at, he said. But he advised me against staying in San Francisco. I produced an employment blank and explained that I would have work before the week was out and he agreed to allow me to stay. One remark he made at our parting is worthy of recording. "You've got a bigger job on your hands making good here than you had in the woods. But stay out of jail! Don't imagine that you can be putting out ten or fifteen dollars for a dinner and dance with some skirt and yet make both ends meet on a salary."

The impression I retained of him was of a gruff, sincere, middle-aged man who was acting in a similar capacity to that of a school-teacher. He was anxious to have his charges make good at their work and conduct, but he held no illusions about the rowdy natures that prison had instilled into his "pupils."

"If you *have* to take a drink, take it! But don't get sloppy drunk at some known bootleg joint, be arrested and then expect me to get you out of jail. And if you can't get along at your work, tell me about it. Don't go galloping off to some other state. They all come back." He waved me from his office—and I was ready to meet Dan.

[VIII]

I obtained a job with an ice-cream company. It would stand investigation from the parole office and if anyone called for me, the foreman agreed to say that I was out on one of the trucks making a delivery. The biggest advantage I had there was the fact that I did not even have to appear to punch a clock. For the sake of appearances I worked part of one day.

I learned from Dan of his adventures and heard more news of thieves than I had heard for almost a year. I had saved several hundred dollars while working at the mill and, curiously, was loath to spend it in the reckless fashion in which I had spent stolen money at other times. The money I had now represented hard labor. I could almost see the parts of the hours I had worked for each fifty-cent piece that I laid on a tobacconist's counter.

Red had returned from France and, in the manner of thieves, had been located by Dan. Vera's death had driven him into the army desirous of being killed. He had instead been decorated for bravery! Buddy also was in town. Dan laughed when I asked about our friend in jail. "Christ sake," he said, "I thought you knew about that. Any time you get a letter about a friend, sick, or in the can—well, it means that we're forming an outfit to root!"

CHAPTER 12

[I]

I stood at my apartment window, watching the midnight theatre crowds in the street below. Buddy and Red were due in a few minutes. Dan was lolling on the bed, his hat set back from his forehead. His face, when I turned to him, was screwed up to keep the smoke from a cigarette out of his eyes. He was about forty, conservatively dressed at the moment and was occupying himself with tracing on the bed-cover a design of the floor plan of a bank we were preparing to rob.

I was not greatly attracted by the prospect of robbing a bank in such proximity to my home town and yet reasoned that it would entail no unusual risk. This risk was to be avoided by entering the building with the first employee; then, with our faces covered, capturing the others as they entered. This would preclude the possibility of some clerk's mentally registering our features and later identifying us. It was a progressive innovation. With the risk of identification removed, there was nothing to fear. We knew that clerks were trained, even schooled, to the realization that their lives were worth more than the loss of the insured money.

"That dough is ours already, Ernie," said Dan. He tossed the cigarette aside. I watched the humorous wrinkles gather at the corners of his pleasant, dark eyes. There was an easy confidence expressed in his indication of the floor plan on the bed. "I've cased it, on and off for a month. The main guy with the screws to the vault gets there about eight-thirty. There's about fifteen clerks and broads to take charge of, but we can get 'em as they come in. The only chance of a rank is pushing in with that first guy. But we'll brace him between us just as he gets to the door."

"Bracing him between us," would be easy with Dan. He had commenced with stealing pocket-books and graduated logically into the "industry" after his prison term.

I had not seen Buddy for two years. But I knew that he was using morphine, that he was living with a girl who had quit a friend of mine after his conviction and that he had been stealing successfully from banks during the time since I had seen him last. His mixture of morphine and business did not impress me as sensible. I expressed something of this to Dan.

"Aw, he's all right on a caper. I tell the damn little fool that using so much stuff will make a bum out of him, but Billie—that twist he's with—got him hooked. The stuff's all right if you use judgment, but when you get hoggish it gets you—makes you harmless."

"Don't worry," I told him, electing to use his style of speech, "I never took a shot in my life. But I don't like the idea of rooting with a guy that's using it—"

"That's a lot of guff!" Dan said, sharply. "I take a geezer once in a while myself. It never hurt me—but you gotta use judgment."

Apparently he was right. He had not been arrested since leaving prison, although at the present time the police and operatives for various insurance companies were anxious to interview him. He evaded them by remaining away from bootleg joints—"scatters"—which were the meeting-places of known thieves. The lengthening interval made it constantly more improbable that he would he identified by witnesses of any of the several robberies in which the police believed he had participated. I had touched on a matter of professional pride and with his open resentment, I refrained from further comment.

The door-bell rang and answering it, I found Buddy waiting. Red stood behind him, several feet farther down the hall, one hand in his overcoat-pocket. A significant attitude; it was his first visit to my apartment. Dan had arranged with them to come here, but despite his assurance that it was safe, Red was exercising the primary rule of caution: be suspicious at all times.

"Well, for Christ's sake—Ernie!" Buddy extended his hand. There was no indication of the drug-user in the firmness of his grasp. His face was a trifle paler than when I had seen him last and he looked more than four years older. The blue eyes under light brows expressed genuine gladness. "We didn't expect to find you here. . . . You know Red, don't you?"

"Sure. Come on in." I turned to the taciturn Irishman. He was more than six feet tall and his overcoat caused him to seem gigantic. Buddy, undersized, seemed a child beside him. A quick lift of his chin. "How's it?" Red said, shortly. Although we shook hands, there was no mention of our past escapades. They had been lived through—and buried.

Buddy removed his muffler and hat, throwing them upon the bed. Dan nodded to the new-comers and poured drinks. "I didn't know you were going against this racket," Buddy said to me. "When did you turn out?"

The question rankled. "What's the difference?" It was as though he questioned my ability to hold up my end. Buddy, Red and Dan had worked together several times and knew each other's prowess. I was, so far as Buddy was concerned, an unknown quality.

Dan cleared his throat. I remember being present at a political dinner and hearing the speaker of the evening make just such a sound before beginning his talk.

"Well, here's the way it lays. The jug is over across the Bay. Take the seven o'clock ferry over in the morning. I'll meet you at Sixteenth and Lindol Streets. You bring that heap over, Buddy—it's running all right, ain't it? . . . Good. I don't want to lose any time out here, because the old woman and me are going back to St. Paul and spend the summer up on the lakes. So don't miss—make it over there, sure!"

"That heap is kinda hot," Buddy offered. "It's been stolen over three months ago now—but we used it while you was away, huh, Red?"

Red stood silent, listening to Dan. Apparently these elementary details bored him. He nodded. "It's cold enough now and there's square plates on it." Hands deep in his pockets, he gazed at his shoes.

Dan reflected a moment. His face wore the quasi-profound look of an executive desirous of impressing his audience. "Better drive it around the Bay. There's always city dicks at the ferries on this side." He creased the bed-covers again. "Here's the way the jug is laid out. There's four cages that are 'Receiving'—and the counter makes an L like this. As fast as we catch 'em coming in, all we got to do is lay 'em down so no one can see 'em from the street." He explained further that "keeping 'em from touching off a bug"—that is, preventing any clerk from pressing an alarm button—and getting the money in all possible haste would be about everything we need do. He and I were to enter first, Red was to follow, Buddy remaining at the wheel of the car. There was nothing complicated about the proposed action.

Red did not seem greatly impressed. "I want to take a look at it myself," he said slowly. He at once became the "man hard to sell" of our conference.

"Look!" exploded Dan and I saw black anger flash from his eyes. "You can see at a glance what it is when we get there. It's a cinch and it will go eighty or ninety grand, maybe more." He stood up from the bed.

"We ought to take at least one gander before making it," Buddy temporized. "How about the traffic-cop and making a get-away?"

Dan spoke with heat and flung his words at them. He said there was no traffic officer within two blocks of the bank; that he and Mae—his girl—had an apartment where we could go after the robbery, to divide the money; that an electric train, one of the locals from the ferry, passed in front of the bank at eight o'clock and the noise and confusion of the train stopping at the corner station would be in our favor, adding that the first clerk arrived at eight o'clock regularly.

"That's all right—but I won't go against anything until I look It over." Red continued to gaze at his shoes. There was nothing of antagonism in his answer: he stated a fact as another might have said: "It is contrary to my policy."

"Do you think I'd run you into anything I didn't know was right?" Dan was simulating a fine frenzy. "I know what I'm talking about—"

Some of the disgust I had known at the political dinner, after listening to much wrangling, returned. "Not so loud," I interrupted.

"To hell with that," he said, but lowered his voice. "If you guys don't want to work, what in hell did you come up here for? Here I put in *my* time and *my* dough to get this set right and now you want to waste a lot of it looking it over. That's the trouble with a lotta you guys. You want to spend all your life casing some spot instead of working. Just because you get over for a big piece of change when you *do* root, you don't want to do nothing—till you're broke again." He snatched a tumbler up and filled it half-way with whisky.

Silence hung heavy within the room. Buddy was regarding his cigarette; Red had not raised his eyes during the tirade; Dan drained the glass and flung it to the floor. I looked from one to the other, waiting. Dan picked up his overcoat from the end of the bed. Extracting a heavy automatic from one pocket, he transferred it to a holster under his arm. Jamming his hat upon his head, he thrust one arm into his coat as though preparing to leave the apartment. Suddenly he stopped. In this abrupt halt a powerful tension was generated. I could feel it drawing me like a terrifically charged electric cable. I was aware that the smoke from a cigarette that I held between my fingers climbed upwards and opened into a wavering, gray parasol. Thought was suspended within me; I stared and breathed softly through parted lips, nervously dry. I have known many such situations since then; they seem to constitute a ceremonial observance. From the "It's easy, we can make it" stage of egotistical confidence a plan usually develops, by violent dissension, or fruitful monosyllables—as though following a formality to be seriously observed and requisite to the validity of the ultimate agreement.

"Well—how about it?" Dan looked from Red to Buddy and then swept his eyes past me. His coat half-hung over one shoulder. "Do we root—or are you going to dog it?"

Red stiffened. The eye with the cast flashed quick viciousness. He was in profile to me and I saw the muscles of his jaw tighten, making a tiny, white bulge on his highly colored cheek. Buddy eyed him narrowly, nervously, seeking an indication of what position he should take. Plainly he awaited a sign that would decide his actions. He shoved his hands into his pockets. "Aw, it'll be all right, I guess," Red said, half defiantly. His lip curled as though he sneered at some doubt still lingering in his mind.

"Sure, we can make it. What's the difference?" said Buddy; "it'll be all right."

"You both got short rods, haven't you?" asked Dan. "Good! Bring 'em with you. I got a couple rifles and a shotgun that we can put in the heap in case we get a tail. But there's not much chance of that. Come on, take another drink and I'll see you in the morning—*sure.*"

We drank.

"Let's get started, Ernie," Dan said to me. "You better come over and flop with Mae and me tonight. Got to get out, fellows. If I miss that last boat over, the old woman will think I'm cheating on her. So long."

"So long," they chorused. We left them in possession of my apartment for the evening.

Together we gained the street and buttoned our coats against the chill, damp fog. We boarded a street car and rode on separate seats to the Ferry Building. Keeping Dan in sight, I followed him on the boat and to the deck reserved for smoking. As the boat throbbed and churned its way over the water, I reflected on the laying out of a robbery that would startle the entire Pacific Coast.

But really there had not been much actual planning, I realized. It seemed childish to scheme and talk. We knew what to do. There was a bank on the other side of the Bay that we could rob of perhaps a hundred thousand dollars. Should we rob it together? That was the extent of our reasoning. Nothing of right or wrong entered into our calculations. Any aversion I might have entertained, in the dim, remote past, to such proceedings had been sublimated and found its outlet in past justifications of similar actions.

A robbery that would startle the whole Coast—had I thought it that? No; I was wrong. There had been a time when it would have made a sensation, but not now. Should a murder occur during its consummation, it might live in public interest for a week. Otherwise it would be only a one-day flash. The public would read of it idly. One man might remark to another that bandits had stolen fifty thousand dollars yesterday, but he would employ the same tone as that in which he mentioned a severe rain-storm—then sigh and think of the installments due on his radio. Others would merely glance over the headlines, mentally commenting: "Another robbery" and then turn to the comic strips.

But to me, running over the details and possibilities, it was all very real and very important. Vividly real. So concentrated on it was I, indeed, that when a man walked in front of me, I started, imagining that the thoughts of tomorrow were showing on my face. I looked about as the passengers scattered over the boat. None of them was paying any attention to me.

But I tossed and turned on the davenport all that night. I executed the robbery a score of times—always with variations. I was standing near the entrance, watching the first clerk approach. Straining to move, I felt a terrifying, encroaching paralysis. Rooted to the sidewalk, I could not budge. . . . Then, waking in the semi-darkness, I would shiver off the nightmare.

Again, torrential rain descended in front of the bank. A blue-uniformed figure appeared and I tugged at my reluctant gun. The blinding dazzlement of worlds exploding filled my eyes, their detonations blasting my eardrums. Then a lull—and a muddy, hatless, blue form lay in the gutter. Red blood gushed from a gap in what a moment before had been a living forehead. It mingled with the swirling, dirty water to half conceal the blue in a crimson shroud. Horror jerked me up through layers of unreality to the consciousness of my warm bed and coverings. Nausea gripped me suddenly. Again I lay quiet and the tiny noises—the felt disturbances—assailed me. If I opened my eyes, they fled, like fish frightened away from a sudden light. With my eyes closed they came from their scattered retreats and renewed their torments. If only these things were tangible, I thought, if only I could fight them! If I could come to grips with them! If I could only banish them!

"I can't stand this much longer," flashed before me, as though captioned on a screen. It was effaced a bit later by the thought that I *was* superior to these delusions.

Then I laughed, softly, quietly, trying to reassure myself as men have always done in the darkness of their bedchambers and caves. But the very intensity I used in fighting against the specters inverted itself, combined with them, returning enleagued to mock me. Then time collapsed into one dimension and I slid down into tumultuous blackness, pregnant with monstrosities of rapine, robbery and murder.

[II]

Dan, dressed, called me at six-thirty in the morning. It was unnecessary to awaken me. He sat near while I pulled on my clothes. Mae appeared for a brief moment, holding a wrapper about her as she passed through the room to the kitchenette.

"Hell of a note!" she tossed over her shoulder, "this gettin' me up in the middle of the night.... But it's worth it, I guess."

"I don't like this having someone else know my business," I whispered to Dan and nodded towards the kitchen.

He grinned. "If half the guys on our racket were as close-mouthed as Mae, there'd be less use for jails. Of course, it's a cinch she knows you're a hook, or you wouldn't be with me. What's the odds? It'll be all right. Anyway, she's going to drive the Ford coupé to meet us for a switch of machines after we work."

This last, coming as it did on the tail of my restless night, dragged in another uneasiness. A girl's participating in a robbery to which I was a party was a new consideration. But I knew it was becoming prevalent in the fraternity, so rather than risk being classified as old-fashioned I said nothing more about it.

After breakfast we left the apartment and, with Mae driving, arrived at Sixteenth and Lindol Streets about seven-thirty. The bank was ten or twelve blocks distant. The corner was deserted; Buddy and Red had not arrived. Restlessly we drove a few blocks towards the heart of town; returning, we found the corner still unoccupied.

Dan looked at his watch. "Christ almighty! Twenty to eight now!" Angrily he pushed his foot against the rifles and shotgun on the floor. Crowded together in the small compartment, we were uncomfortable and Mae snarled at him to "take it easy!"

He turned his head to look back at the cross-streets and his movement pressed my revolver into my ribs. "Sit still!" I growled. My developing nervousness was irritating me. "Looking around that way will mark us," I said.

"Don't be telling me what to do!" His voice was bitter, acrid. His eyes were puffy and the lids heavy for want of sleep. Realizing suddenly that he, too, was under the same strain and pressure, I remained silent. Again he twisted about. "What ails those guys? Here it is time to be getting down to the spot and—"

It occurred to me that they might have gone to the bank to look it over before coming to the appointed corner. When I communicated this thought to Dan, he directed Mae to "make it snappy and get down there." It was as though we—she and I—were to blame for the non-appearance of Buddy and Red. He remonstrated with Mae and she evinced her exasperation by jerking the wheel for an abrupt turn and jamming the throttle.

I took a last look at the corner. "There's a Cad parking there now. It may be Buddy," I offered. My words went unheeded. The three of us were possessed by an ugly mood. I was disgusted— not with the thought of the robbery, but with the way it was going. Snarling and growling, irritated and angry, it would not have required much more friction to cause us to begin fighting among ourselves. The thought of the revolvers we carried; the other guns on the floor and the risk we incurred in driving about with them; and the meagre chance we should have of avoiding arrest, except by shooting our way clear if an officer interposed—all these things combined to make the little, enclosed cab hot and stuffy with a penetrating heat. I lowered a side window as we paused in the heavier traffic of Twelfth Street and was surprised to find sweat on my face and hands.

Mae speeded the car up between crossings and, once in Seventh Street, guided the wheels in the street-car tracks as she drove past the bank. It was in the middle of the block.

"See," said Dan, as we approached it, "the curtains are up and no one can see in from the street. Ain't it a gift?" he smiled with his eyes for a fleeting instant, then the look of anxiety returned. We scanned the street, but saw none who even resembled Buddy or Red. Several Cadillacs passed, but they were not carrying the men we sought. I was trying to watch both sides of the street simultaneously and for the moment I failed to notice the look Dan was giving me. I turned suddenly to meet a glare of scorn and disgust. He showed me the face of his watch—it was ten minutes to eight o'clock.

"A *fine* pair of suckers they are!" His words were mordant. "If I had another heap here, I'd go up against it this way—just the two of us. . . . What say? Shall we give it a whirl? Maybe we can clout a heap and get back in time. Dash up by the high school in Twelfth Street, Mae! We might connect there. . . . It's getting late—hurry up! Step on it! Step on it! Christ, this is business!"

"Business?" said Mae, with heavy sarcasm; "business—sure it is! You're like a couple of brats going out for the first time—no organization—nothing!"

I have never had much difficulty in stealing an automobile. Usually the high-priced, closed cars are left unlocked and are easy to steal. The smaller cars receive more careful attention, probably because they represent more to their owners. Near the school was an assortment of Fords and Dodges and a sprinkling of Buicks, Hudsons and Studebakers. But there were people entering or leaving the cars, for this was a favorite place for business employees to park. So there was too much chance of detection—and there were chains, or wheel-spikes, on most of the cars.

"Nothing here," I said. "Follow that car. Perhaps it will park—the driver seems to be hunting a place now." I indicated an expensive, eight-cylinder machine.

The driver pushed it through the traffic past the City Hall. Dan and I had our handkerchiefs out and were industriously wiping our noses for the time it took to travel the block. The danger of recognition was great here and I shivered, visualizing the slaughter that would result if some officer saw us and decided to investigate our machine. Dan was cursing heatedly through his handkerchief.

"Get out of here—let the machine go to hell! Get off this street. I'm getting crazy to let myself be bummin' around like this. What the hell did you want to come up here for, Mae? You know I'm hot, here in town—and we're right in front of the police station."

The accomplished Mae realized the seriousness of our position and refrained from comment. Deftly she extricated the car from a threatening box in traffic and turned towards Sixteenth Street at the first chance. I breathed easier then. That the robbery was not to be made that morning was evident and by unvoiced consent we rode several blocks in silence. Approaching Lindol Street, I saw Buddy and a girl seated in a car, looking anxiously about the street. We drew alongside them.

"Where you been?" demanded Dan.

"Right here." Buddy was hollow-eyed. "I left over there about four o'clock and drove around the Bay and up here as soon as possible. It ain't too late now. Let's get started. Where's Red?"

Dan's face was livid. Leaning across me, he said in a hoarse whisper: "Red! He was supposed to come with you! Hell, yes—of course it's too late! And we can't stop here. You, Billie," addressing the girl with Buddy, "get in here with Mae, Come on, Ernie, we'll change over so we can talk." The transfer was made. "Tail us about half a block behind," Dan instructed Mae and we drove off.

There followed a general discussion of all our faults. Buddy and Dan stormed at each other. Occasionally I cut in, attempting to stem the useless upbraiding. I was soundly cursed and retaliated.

The nervous energy generated to carry us through the robbery was being expended in venting our spleen on each other. The hatred and meanness that should have gone into the actual operation of the business was being wasted. I felt as if I had just recovered from a protracted drunk and my head ached painfully. For a while we rode in a sort of armed truce. The remarks we had made there would, in normal circumstances, have caused a fight or at least an exchange of blows; but they did not actually register within our consciousness. They constituted a sort of release of the emotional heightening the restless night had instilled and were accepted as an integral part of our association.

Chagrin and disappointment and a curious relief, were mingled in my own reaction and I wondered if Dan and Buddy were experiencing the same sensations. Evidently not, for Dan turned to where I was seated and said: "There's another jug I know of—out on San Pablo Avenue—smaller, only a branch. Want to take a gander at it? We're here now—we might as well get something. God damn that red-head! Why in hell didn't he show up?"

The question was purely academic. Neither of us offered an immediate answer. But I awoke with renewed interest. Dan had discarded his anger.

"Suits me," I replied at length. "How about you, Bud?" It was a compromise, this taking a smaller place, but I needed the money and with Buddy's affirmative nod the car started out the avenue.

[III]

The branch bank occupied a corner. Large plate-glass windows gave an almost unobstructed new of its interior from the street. A bad feature: a traffic officer was located in the middle of the cross-streets a scant fifty feet away. There were lights within and several clerks moving about. But it was not yet nine o'clock, so the doors were not open to the public. I left the machine and waited until the girls came up. I gave them instructions and they parked about half a block farther up the avenue. Sauntering casually to the entrance, I paused a moment to survey the counters and open vault. Its shiny steel mouth yawned wide. I watched a clerk come out with a large, locked tray, which he took to his cage and opened. Busily engaged in sorting bills into their respective sections of an open drawer, he paid no attention to me. Affecting an indifferent attitude, I turned my back to the bank and lit a cigarette, puffed on it for a minute or so and then turned about again and saw another clerk engaged upon a similar task.

My heart was beating rapidly and I was having difficulty inhaling the smoke from my cigarette. The roof of my mouth was suddenly hot and dry. My eyes watered and my throat tingled. A man and woman standing near by—apparently waiting for a car—looked at me; hastily I applied a handkerchief to my face and coughed. I was trying to forestall their seeing my face, to recall it later, after they had read of the robbery. I turned from them and continued down the street.

At a drug-store on the next corner I drank a soft drink and took a grip on myself. I was feeling an approaching loneliness. With Dan and Buddy I had fine confidence, but, standing by myself, at that instant I knew the sensation of being alone in a crowd. There was considerable bustle and activity on the corner. Several street cars passed. I returned to the bank, secure in the belief that the couple I had observed would be gone.

I paused to glance over the furnishings of the bank once more. A man brushed against me and instinctively my left arm contracted on the revolver, slung up under it. He excused himself and as he looked into my face, his eyes seemed to open a trifle with surprise. At once I felt a shock at having betrayed my thoughts! Although I tried to restrain myself, I peered over my shoulder after he had taken several steps and was alarmed when he, too, turned to look directly at me. Little incidents: the couple, this man; but they were magnified out of all proportion. I walked to the other window of the bank and stood between an elderly woman and a man rending a paper. From time to time the man glanced up at passing cars. The old lady was indifferently clad and fidgeted about. I ventured a side glance at her and discovered that she was covertly watching me. She stirred and I noticed that a pompon on her breast trembled. The nervous movement transferred itself and I leaned hard against the glass to repress a quick shiver. She spoke to me—some question about the time. I started, then made an elaborate movement to extract my watch. . . . She thanked me, it seemed, in a queer manner.

I essayed a yawn to cover my growing confusion, but it died at birth as I looked to the middle of the street. The traffic officer, with one hand raised, was obviously staring at me. I was but one of a group of several and it is highly improbable that he was aware of my existence, but at that moment I stood alone, naked.

Pivoting on my heel, I walked swiftly down the avenue. Two blocks away I joined Dan and Buddy at the car. "How's she look?" queried Dan.

"All right, far as I can see." I gave the answer expected, but I wanted to say that I thought we should be crazy to go any further with it. Something restrained me, for in the brief interval of my walk some of my confidence had returned. It was as though I, a solitary Assassin, returned to the citadel of Hassan and a fanatical devotion flowed out and inspired me.

"Stick with Buddy a moment—I'll take a flash myself." Dan left us. Buddy was leaning back in the seat, but there was a strained attempt to counterfeit ease in his attitude. I recognized it and felt easier in my own mind. The cheer of misery, I guess.

The motor was running, quietly, smoothly, with the gearshift lever enmeshed; he held the clutch out with one foot, ready for an instantaneous start. Buddy observed my interest in the arrangement and forced a grin. "Have to be set to go any second in a hot heap. Can't tell who might show up. These cruising bulls in cars sneak up on you if you give them half a chance. It wasn't so bad when they was all in uniform, but they dress like business men now, an' you got to watch."

I lit another cigarette and began to watch each passing machine, imagining that the next one would be filled with cruising bulls. None came, however and I was glad when Dan returned.

"It's all right," he said after he had entered the machine and we were out in the noise of the traffic. "That counter ends at the avenue window and there's a small swinging gate there. You" (to me) "can step over it easy. That will bring all the clerics at the money-drawers in line with you. Cover them with your rod and hold it close to you, so it can't be seen from the street. Just motion 'em back—give 'em their orders and don't worry about 'em doing anything. Just keep 'em away from the alarms. If they hit one and start the big buzzer over the door going, there'll be a lot of battle for us. So be sure an' keep 'em away. Clean the drawers as you come to each cage. Just throw the dough on the counter and then brush it all off into the bag in one sweep. That'll be best, 'cause if you try to put in each grab as you get it, you'll be there all morning."

I listened attentively. Socrates expounding to his pupils had never a more fascinated hearer.

"You take the other end, Buddy. Come in at that other door and vault through the second paying window. Kick the big fat geezer there in the face if you have to—but he'll take his orders same as anyone else. Just one flash of the rod and then come over and swamp him. Surprise 'em. That's the stuff that builds fortunes—surprise. We're in and over and on 'em before they get a chance to squawk."

"How much do you think she'll go for?" Buddy was ahead of Dan in his planning.

"Can't tell. There's a big spike on the vault. Them iron gates are hell—but we might catch it open. It oughta give up twenty—maybe thirty grand." Dan reflected a moment before adding: "But it'll be summer dough, anyway, I wanta get away from this coast."

"You want me to go in first and wait for you—is that right?" I asked. "I take that big bag and wait at one of the check-writing counters until you and Buddy are in?"

"Bag—hell!" Dan snorted. "That's the worst rank in the world nowadays. If you started into a jug with a leather that size, you'd get shot before you got to the counter. There's a couple of canvas sacks back in the car with the broads. Jesus Christ! I forgot about them. Turn this heap around and we'll office them to follow us again. We gotta get the long rods from that car."

Dan jerked his head to the girls as we passed and Mae steered out from the curb and followed us. We drove out towards the foot-hills and in a thinly built-up district the transfer of weapons was effected. The girls were instructed to go to a certain corner about fifteen blocks from the bank, to wait for us. It was a few minutes past ten o'clock when we parted.

A hundred yards from the bank Buddy slowed down. Some last-minute details. "Just walk down there and stall a minute," Dan said. "I'll get out right after you and follow. Soon's you get the heap parked, Buddy—come right in. Then we're all right. I'll keep the customers in. But make it snappy. Speed! That's the main idea. This is a fast clout. You ain't got more than a minute after you start and you got to make every second count. If only that bull don't rank us!"

"If he does—it's just too bad for him," said Buddy.

The canvas sack—a two-foot-square affair—made a slight bulge. It made me appear like a woman enceinte.

The noise of the traffic; the harsh growl of a machine getting under way; the form of a scantily clad girl as she minced by me, her thighs showing full against her dress at each step; a child tugging at a long chain attached to a bulldog; the acrid smell of burnt gasoline; hurrying figures in bright or dark colors; a shaft of sunlight slashing across the sidewalk just at the bank entrance—all these intermingled and I felt as though I were a stranger from another planet. They seemed, to my heightened imagination at that time, foreign, utterly apart. They bore no relation to me or my errand.

Before entering the bank I recalled the precautions I had intended to take towards lessening the chance of later identification. An infinitesimal instant I hesitated; but I had drifted so far that retreat was impossible. The force of my present position stilled my fears and I crossed the Rubicon.

[IV]

The floor seemed suddenly softened, as though I were treading on a billowy substance. I endeavored to make my feet take a normal stride and they mocked me by lifting themselves as though inflated. With an effort I gained the side counter. With a temporary gratitude, like that of a saved sinner, I placed my hand firmly on the cold glass top. I had not yet ventured a glance at the cages or clients of the bank. I had been fully occupied in reaching this haven.

A stout woman at my elbow was scratching a pen across a check. She raised large, fishy eyes to me and for a fleeting second I caught my own reflection in them. Sharply outlined by the strong light from the window at my back, I saw my head and shoulders in silhouette. Suspicion written plainly on her face, she dropped her eyes to the task before her and edged slightly away from me. I reached for a blank check and pretended to write, watching from the tail of my eye for Buddy or Dan. The small swinging gate through which I was to pass was but a step from where I stood.

The band of my hat grew suddenly tight. It seemed to restrict the flow of blood, congesting it at my temples. I raised a hand to touch my cheek-bone and my fingers came away as though burned by the contact. I tried to swallow and my tongue clove to my palate. I coughed nervously and the woman beside me started as though I had stabbed her with a pin. My cheeks felt hot and I knew they were livid. . . . The constriction about my forehead increased. All this occurred in less than sixty seconds. The check before me was hopelessly blotched—ink stained my finger-tips. I crumpled it.

Then, fearing that some of the writing might be decipherable, I shoved the paper into my pocket.

The woman turned to the paying cage nearest me. The teller looked past her in my direction and I clenched my teeth to strangle another cough.

"Stand fast everybody! Don't move!" Sharp and ominous the command cut through my consciousness. They were in the bank—and I had missed them! I scanned the row of startled clerks, to see Buddy behind the counter. Dan was near the main door, a vicious black gun in his hand. I took a step and almost fell. My foot had gone to sleep while I had stood at the counter Limping to the swinging door, I entered. Again that sensation of walking on billows of fluff. "Stand back!" I ordered the teller who was about to cash the fat woman's check. I caught a quick, alarmed look from him as he stepped back from the counter. The woman peered intently through the wicket, then slid from my sight. "Lay down—don't touch anything," I said in what I intended to be a harsh voice.

Two other clerks and one woman employee, farther along the counter, acted as though operated by a mechanism. They were prone on the tiles before I had extracted half the contents of the small compartments of the first drawer. Nervousness—the suspense—left me. A soothing calm followed. It seemed logical and natural to be lifting currency from a drawer. That this was the peak of a bank robbery never entered my mind. I was simply transferring bills from one position to another while a dozen people stood across the counter from me. I didn't actually look at them, but the impression I got was of a group on a motion-picture screen, suddenly frozen into unusual and awkward poses.

Through this I was propelled by a will greater than my own. There was nothing of conscious volition in my actions and I knew a curious division of myself. It seemed that I stood at one side and watched, dispassionately, while a chap who resembled a business-college student engaged himself in a practical study of banking. It was all impersonal, as if I witnessed it enacted upon a stage. I was an observing spectator—but with no greatly absorbing interest. The action was flat, common place; there was nothing dramatic about it. It seemed to me that everyone connected with it was unnecessarily serious and concerned. Everyone appeared to attach an importance to it beyond its worth. There came to me for one brief moment a hint of perverse amusement: if they—those grotesquely frozen figures—could have known the turmoil raging within me a few seconds ago!

My gun was still in its holster. In my haste to get started I had neglected to draw it out. But it was not needed. The clerks had seen the other two. The manner in which Buddy displayed his gave it a commanding personality. With both hands free I soon had one drawer emptied and moved rapidly to the next. There the bills were stacked higher and the jumble of yellow and green currency piled up steadily into a long, uneven mound on the polished black wood of the counter. Working with all the possible speed and precision I could command at the moment, I heard Dan growl: "Don't move or I'll blow your guts out! Do as you're told—you'll be all right."

Then I was aware that we had been working in a silence almost heavy. It seemed to press down on me. The noises from the street came as from another world. One of the men on the floor stirred. Buddy flashed a glance and covered him with his gun. I had my sack out now and was stuffing bills into it in a glorious fan of color. Buddy held his sack in his left hand and was sweeping the money from the counter with his gun and right hand.

From the door came Dan's cadenced voice. "Make it snappy. Make it snappy. No rank yet. Everything's going fine. Don't miss anything." Then suddenly he snarled: "Come on in!" and I saw him capture a citizen who had started to enter the bank and, seeing the situation, had attempted to escape. "Come in, you—!" Dan was almost touching him when the man obeyed. "Stand over there and be quiet!"

"All set, Bill," I called to Dan. I was finished and started for the end of the counter.

"She's still quiet," said Dan tersely, endeavoring to keep an eye on the center of the cross-streets and watch both doors at the same time. "Try that chip. See if it's sloughed. Make it snappy! Christ! There goes that bastard!" A man had dashed out the door farthest from Dan. "Out! Out!" Dan cried. It was an unnecessary order. I leaped to the counter and cased out through the wicket. Narrowly I avoided stepping on the face of the fat woman who had dropped from my sight. She lay in a faint near the baseboard.

At the door I slung the sack under my coat and pulled my gun out, ready for action. A squat, duck-like man with a red, bulging neck was entering. I poked the steel barrel into his belly and he stepped aside. His mouth dropped open.

"Take it on the natural," came from Dan. He was still covering the people in the bank. "Don't run and rank yourself—the fuzz don't know what's doin' yet."

Crossing the sidewalk, I was surprised to find Buddy at the wheel of our car. He had made more speed than I had thought was possible. On the floor in the rear of the car his bag lay gaping, money spilled from it. I flung down my bag beside it and looked for the traffic officer. He was still directing traffic. A gathering circle of people were about a prostrate man near the other door of the bank. Some idea of the rapidity with which all this occurred is shown in this incident: the man had left the bank, crossed to the curb and stumbled, yet before he could regain his feet, we had left the counter and were in the machine.

With a jerk the car lunged forward. Dan was standing on the running-board. We passed within ten feet of the policeman. Our guns were ready, but he paid no heed to us. The dash to the next intersection was made in a few seconds. "We're ranked," Dan said and bent to lift a rifle in preparation for the chase that was forming.

I looked back and saw a bluecoat on the side of a car coming rapidly after us. Buddy steered through a stream of cross-traffic just then and I lost sight of the pursuing car for the interval of half a block. Then it shot out of the current and raced along over the intervening distance. Our car was picking up and from the excited actions of those in the machines we passed I could sense the narrow escapes from clashes that Buddy was guiding us through.

The machine following us seemed to gain slightly on us in the third block and then—without a word of warning—Buddy skidded our car, which was then traveling nearly fifty miles an hour. For several yards we broadsided to the corner. He pressed down on the throttle, the reserve power picked us out of the skid and he made a perfect turn down a side street. Then he raced the car until we seemed to be flying.

A swift thrill and exhilaration entered my blood. I wanted to cry out with some insane frenzy that flowed through me. A fragment of Shelley came to my mind:

The joy, the triumph, the delight, the madness!
The boundless, overflowing, bursting gladness.
The vaporous exultation not to be confined! . . .

It coursed from my head to my feet and I knew a tingling that purged me of all the restraints the morning's preparation had imposed. The following car could not make the sharp turn and I did not see it again. Still driving with reckless speed, Buddy brought us to where the girls awaited us.

We changed cars. Dan and I crammed the spilled money back into the sacks and with the guns held under our coats we all crowded into the coupé. We were wedged against each other; my head bobbed against the roof. Dan laughed when Mae asked: "Clean? No battle?"

"Sure! Everybody was on their good behavior," he chuckled.

"Too bad that guy got out." Buddy spoke from the depths of the car. "Couldn't you have stopped him?"

"Had to throw a slug or let him out," Dan explained, "and we was too near through to start blasting."

[V]

Once in the apartment, the money was dumped on the bed and Dan, Buddy and I began sorting it into bills of the same denomination. The burnt money—bills that had been defaced or pasted together—was thrown upon the floor. The girls got those bills. Later they would pass them one at a time. The danger of marked money was too great for a known thief to hazard carrying it about.

There was a changed attitude in that apartment then. The bitterness and irritation that had filled it in the morning, to follow us on our trip to the first bank, was gone. There had come instead a jovial good-fellowship. Dan smiled pleasantly and, with his eyes lighted from the emotions of the robbery and the swift dash, he was handsome.

Buddy worked methodically, commenting on the actions of various clerks and customers. "What a kick!" he said to me. "That fat broad that keeled over when you captured the first guy! She'll have something to tell her Tuesday sewing-circle about. The bold, bad bandits!" He tossed a package of bills over to the larger denominations.

"Hey, Mae, don't be snatching that dough—it's not spoiled! You twist, lay off this dough on the bed!" Mae had been fingering the various piles of money and surreptitiously slipping bills to the floor to mingle with the burnt money.

Soon we had it counted into three piles. There it was on the white spread. We had divided it evenly. For an instant a revulsion swept over me: the sight of the money seemed vulgar I was not entertaining any aversion to accepting my portion, but as it lay there heaped up, it seemed to have lost some of its dignity: it didn't represent anything. At least, nothing of the value that I felt I had, somewhere, inadvertently lost. I was descending from the heights of a transcendental emotional orgy—and I was becoming a philosopher! . . . Some latent germ of a youthfully implanted Puritanism struggled to the surface, bleared my vision and made the jumbled currency appear immoral. I wiped the traitorous bacillus from my eyes, strangled it and called up visions of voluptuous delights.

"Take any bunch that suits you," Dan said. Buddy scooped together one pile. I took another and straightened it out into a package that I could wrap with paper and carry under my arm. "Nineteen grand, eight hundred," Dan announced. "That makes—let me see—well, it's over six and a half each. Not so bad."

"Not so bad," conceded Buddy, "but if you hadn't let that guy get away, we could have weeded the chip and got over worth while." He was still regretting the escape of the customer, which had prevented us from rifling the vault.

"What the hell's the difference?" snorted Dan, good-naturedly. "You'll never make six grand any easier." Then turning to me: "Leaving?"

"Yes, I'm going to get out of town before it gets too hot."

"Going to stay on the Coast? No? Well, listen. If you leave, show up around Murphy's—the Irish Jew's—in St. Paul in about six weeks and we can join up with an outfit that's going down-state to root. Just drop in there—it's a jewelry-store—and tell him you're a friend of mine. He'll send you out to us. Mae and I are going to do a bit of simple life at the lakes."

With arrangements concluded for taking part in another robbery, two-thirds of the way across the continent and with the proceeds from the one just accomplished safely wrapped in a package under my arm, I left the apartment and boarded an electric train that connected with the ferries. An hour later, as I left the boat on the opposite shore, I purchased a newspaper. In the seclusion of my apartment I read the report of the robbery.

One paragraph arrested my attention. ". . . The robbery was evidently well planned, for the bandits worked with speed and seemed familiar with the interior of the bank. One of the clerks is certain that he has seen the tallest of the trio loitering about the bank several times during the past week. . . . Chief of Police Dolan has put every available man on the case and the capture of the bandits is hourly expected. All avenues of escape are closely guarded and all rooming-houses and hotels are being combed."

I stood at my apartment window and gazed down on the noontime crowds in the street. The last eighteen hours had encompassed an epic. The single high point visible to me in looking back over the affair was Buddy's remark: "The bold, bad bandits!"

EPILOGUE

Two years later Dan and I walked wearily from the rock-quarry to the upper yard of the prison. He had arrived the preceding day; I had been there six months. He was directly in front of me as we climbed the long stairs in line with several hundred other convicts. The heat from the granite slabs arose and scorched our faces. The large and grotesquely shaped "mule breakfasts" covering our heads gave no protection from the forge heat welling up about us as we ascended the inferno of those stairs. The usual order was reversed: Dante descended—we climbed—into hell. For within the close, hot, narrow confinement of our vermin-infested cell the temperature was several degrees hotter than in the yards. This because the massive stone block absorbed and held the terrific rays of the sun. The interior of the whitewashed cell was like a steam-room of a Turkish bath.

Dispiritedly we stripped to the waist, discarded our shoes and dropped on our respective bunks—listless and too exhausted even to wash our faces or wet our lips with the tepid water from a bucket near the black, narrow door.

Dan spoke gaspingly. "Get hotter 'n this?"

"I guess so. Summer's just starting." I was lying on my back, my eyes half closed, grotesqueries of the superheated air dancing between me and the low ceiling.

"Christ," Dan breathed—it was almost a supplication. "Red's lucky—missin' this."

"Uh huh," I agreed and closed my eyes tight to keep out the stinging seepage of perspiration from my forehead.

"Yeah," continued Dan, "he's better dead."

"Dead!" I sat up and faced him. "How—? I didn't know that!"

"You should've—aw, I forgot you don't get the scandal sheets. He tried to take Buddy from the bulls while they was bringing him back from bein' sentenced for killing that flat-foot. In the battle he got slugged—twice. He died last week—just look at what he's missin'." Dan raised himself on one elbow and attempted to roll a cigarette. His moist hands spoiled the paper and he twisted it a bit, letting the flakes of tobacco filter through his fingers and drift to the floor. A man's life snuffed out—a few bits of tobacco descending to mingle with the dirt on the sack-rug. . . . He brushed the remainder from the palm of his hand.

"I knew Buddy was up here in the condemned cells, but that's news about Red—" I stopped as a long-drawn-out, insane cry shattered the sultry stillness of the corridor.

Our eyes met. Again and again the cry shuddered through the air. It rose into a frenzied screaming. We stared deeply into each other's eyes, unable to avert our gaze, held fascinated by the significance of those piercing screams: a soul in anguish, protesting against the encroaching and inevitable doom.

"That's Buddy," Dan said, a note of awe in his voice. "It's got him—he's blowed his top."

Two months later I called at the hospital to complain of recurrent pain in my lungs. The doctor looked sharply at me, listened through a stethoscope he held to my chest.

"How long are you doing?" he asked.

"Life."

"Murder?"

"No. Robbery and prior conviction."

"Well"—he paused and seemed to be considering some problem—"well—you've got T.B. I'll have you transferred to the other prison, where the climate is less severe. But—" he busied himself with the next patient.

That *but!*

In the open-air court atop the hospital building of the other prison I was seated in a canvas steamer-chair with a book lying open before me. A small, dwarfed thief, whom I have known for years, hobbled up to me—a visit pass in one hand. Looking cautiously about, he whispered: "Say, Dan an' another guy beat the joint up above, yesterday."

Dan free! Good old Dan! Better to be dead than live in that heat, he had said. And he had escaped! . . . Buddy hanged, Red shot to death, myself doing life as an habitual criminal—but Dan—free!

With his words I knew a sudden thrill. At least all four of us had not lost!

The next evening, at count-time, the guard passed down by the row of beds and paused at the foot of mine. Removing a cigar from his lips, he looked at me.

"They got your pal Dan," he said.

"No!" I almost shouted it.

"Yes," he said, "found him stiff about twenty miles from the prison—died of exposure."

He flicked the ash from his cigar and continued on down the ward.

Noir classics from

Bodies Are Dust P. J. Wolfson
"Plenty of hard edged banter, muscular prose and clever riffing on jazz melancholy in this cruel and poignant tale . . . despair that rings so true it hurts."

—Paul Burke, *Crime Time*

I Was a Bandit Eddie Guerin
"Colorful language keeps the pages turning . . . True crime fans will welcome this memoir by a forgotten but once famous criminal."
—*Publishers Weekly*

Round Trip/Criss-Cross Don Tracy
" . . . you won't be disappointed. A tour de force of noir magic."

—Larque Press

Grimhaven Robert Joyce Tasker
"A notable, a keen and intensely moving account of what happens to a man in prison . . ."

—*New York World*

Fully Dressed and in His Right Mind Michael Fessier
"It's one of those books that can affect readers in so many different ways . . . I found it sublimely mysterious and fantastically satisfying."
—J. F. Norris, *Pretty Sinister Books*

How to Commit a Murder Danny Ahearn
" . . . a truly dangerous book . . ."

—*Lansing State Journal*

Room Service Alan Williams
"There's about everything the thrill reader could want…"
—*The Birmingham News*

Fiction and true crime from the Jazz Age—only $12.99 each.

Stark House Press, 1315 H Street, Eureka, CA 95501
Available from your local bookstore, or order direct via our website—
www.starkhousepress.com.

www.ingramcontent.com/pod-product-compliance
Lightning Source LLC
LaVergne TN
LVHW021803060526
838201LV00058B/3214